00

v

3

Collecting

Picture
Postcards

A real-photograph card showing a local sub-post office. Various postcards and packets can be seen in the side window. Local directories show that Miss Susannah Spiers ran this 'Stationers, Post Office and Fancy Repository' in succession to her father in the 1912-14 period.

Collecting
Picture
Postcards

Geoffrey Godden

Phillimore

1996

Published by
PHILLIMORE & CO. LTD.
Shopwyke Manor Barn, Chichester, West Sussex

ISBN 0 85033 928 6

Printed and bound in Great Britain by
BIDDLES LTD.
Guildford, Surrey

Contents

List of Illustrations

Acknowledgements

My first acknowledgement should be to my parents or to my upbringing, for I have acquired the valuable practice of enquiring, of asking questions, of seeking information, of carrying out basic research. Had I not had such an enquiring mind this book would not have been written and I would have lost much of the interest which I have gained from my postcards.

My next acknowledgement must be directed to the designers and publishers of all the cards in my collection and in particular to the local photographers who took many of the more interesting local-view or event cards. The illustrations used in this book have been drawn from my own collection. I have been at pains to record in the caption the name of such publishers or photographers where they are recorded on the card but unfortunately many earlier cards do not bear such helpful details. I do believe, however, that my use of these owned cards in a reference book on the history and study of old picture postcards is fair and reasonable use of the material. Certainly, most books give far less acknowledgement on the source of the illustrations than I offer. I am deeply conscious of my debt to all the, largely unknown, originators of these social documents, the local-view picture postcard.

I have tried to quote the source of all quotations in the main text. Some are extracted from 19th- or early 20th-century works that may now be difficult to trace. Other brief comments derive from the writings of more available contemporary authorities—such as John Smith of the I.P.M. Again, I believe that the credit will enable the interested reader to check the reference or delve deeper into that source. I, however, gratefully acknowledge the work of all these previous authors, who have added so much to our understanding of this huge subject. This acknowledgement includes the many collectors and dealers who have contributed articles or letters to various magazines, such as *Picture PostCard Monthly*. One reads such periodicals, subconsciously digesting at least some points which may later be regurgitated as our own views! My favourite reference works are listed in the Select Bibliography; again, my gratitude to all previous researchers for publishing their own helpful books from which we all benefit.

On a more personal basis I would like to acknowledge the help given to me by the following persons: Jonathan Godden, Derek Loader, John E.O. Hobbs, D. Robert Elleray (of the Worthing Society of Postal Historians), Derek Gardiner, Murray Hayes, Peter Jones, Station Commander M.C. Osborne, Mrs. B. Parker of the Worthing & District Camera Club, Geoffrey Pyle, Lady Mary Teviot and Mrs. J.B. Williamson (the Librarian, the Royal Automobile Club).

Also, of course, the helpful assistants at Worthing Library and the Worthing Reference section, and to the past and present curators of Worthing Museum, John Norwood and now Dr. Sally White. To the staff at the Public Record Office, the British Library (Reference Division), the National Newspaper Library, the Royal Society of Arts, the Guildhall Library, the National Art Library at the Victoria & Albert Museum, and the Brighton Library; also to the Worthing Town Council and West Sussex County Officers and the local fire, police and postal services.

My debt to the West Sussex County Council and its Worthing Public Library is very great. This authority, like no doubt all others, has collected over the years and now makes available to any researcher a mass of local history material. I have shown in my chapters on local history and research how useful such collections of local directories, town council minutes, and local newspapers and journals can be to the serious enquirer. I have in particular made good use of announcements and advertisements which appeared in the *Worthing Gazette* some eighty or more years ago. The source is again credited in the text, but I here acknowledge the extra interest and authority that such contemporary material gives to views of events that happened long before one's birth. Thank you local editors; your successors carry on similar good work which will in turn assist future historians.

Although this credit may be out of place I would like to acknowledge the helpful service which I have received from Messrs. Vera Trinder Ltd. of 38 Bedford Street, off the Strand, London WC2E 9EU. This firm stock all or most books in print on postcard collecting, and have a large assortment of albums.

I also acknowledge the professional help of the local photographers at Messrs. Walter Gardiner of Worthing and also the steadfast uncomplaining assistance of Miss Janet Belton who has so ably interpreted my written script and numerous amendments, producing a neat typescript for presentation to my publishers.

I thank you all plus, of course, all the fellow collectors, postcard dealers and auctioneers who have enabled me to build up my collection and to learn something of the interest and delights of postcard collecting.

GEOFFREY A. GODDEN
Worthing, 1996

Preface

This book is about picture postcards, in particular about local-view postcards.

Why do I and tens of thousands of other folk collect such trifles, most of which were produced in the present century, often by continental manufacturers?

There are very many reasons why local-view postcards are so collectable. Perhaps most of us collect such cards purely from nostalgia: we like to be taken back to see our towns and life in general as it was, and was enjoyed, in the time of our grandparents or in our own childhood.

I and very many others take the cards rather more seriously. We might specialise, to collect and research special facets of local history. There seems no end to individual interests. One can collect and research a local pier (or piers in general), lifeboats, windmills, town halls, churches, public gardens, shops, individual streets, pubs, hotels or railway stations.

There is also the very interesting and important social history angle. Postcards are very wide ranging, almost open-ended. They can embrace dress, public and personal transport, housing, hotel life, beach fashions and amusements, home entertainments and public entertainments, carnivals, outings, food and drink and its packaging or presentation, sports, local industries, local services (the fire brigade, postal services, police, etc.), schools, domestic life and so on.

Picture postcards have also recorded aspects of post-1900 local (and national) history. The town's many changes, visits by royalty or other notables, celebrations, disasters, extremes of weather or merely life as it was before the First World War—typical beach or high street scenes—nostalgia—happy memories.

Even the brief original messages can now be of interest, throwing light on the simple entertainments in fashion before the First World War. Who would write today, as did Hannah in August 1911, on a picture postcard of Steyne Gardens in Worthing:

> We went to these gardens last evening, to see the fireworks which were
> very good. We had a motor ride this morning, are going to a confetti battle
> this evening.

Simple pleasures before the advent of television or before some of our towns became the scene of other more dangerous battles.

All these and many other facets of history are well illustrated in often quite inexpensive picture postcards, social documents that are still reasonably easy to find and can be conveniently displayed in albums. Especially interesting cards can also be enlarged and framed to form splendid wall decoration. Slides can easily be taken from old cards and interesting talks given on your chosen subject of interest.

All this arises from simple pictorial message-carriers selling for a penny or less. What fun, what joy, what potential!

In this book, a case-study using a single town, I illustrate some of the hundreds of different facets of postcard collecting and the way that these small cards can today take us back to former times and illustrate changes in our activities, our lifestyle, in our very lives.

Collecting postcards is uncomplicated; one does not worry about watermarks, errors in printing or trivial details. It is the visual impact that is all-important.

To all postcard collectors—
past, present and future
and of course to all the photographers
who made our collecting possible, rewarding and so interesting

Introduction

Most of us live in a city, a town or village. Such centres may not be ancient but they nevertheless have a history, and they will have changed greatly in appearance over the years. Generally, it is felt that they have lost much, or all, of their old charm or character.

How do we look back to the 'good old days', recapture the appearance of our 'home town' and its inhabitants? Such harking back is natural, and to many professional, or amateur, local historians it adds to life's pleasure; it is our hobby, our delight.

Local booksellers or the public library will no doubt have a selection of well-illustrated books on your county, city, town or village. You will find the Edwardian illustrations fascinating. In nearly every case these illustrations—fifty or sixty perhaps—will be copied from picture postcards. Many books show by their title that they are wholly based on old postcards—*Potteries Picture Postcards: A Portrait of the Six Towns*; *Edwardian Childhood in old Picture Postcards*; *Railway Picture Postcards* and very many similar titles—but even when this fact is not made clear in the title or introduction, the author's main source of old photographs will be postcards. But without too much trouble you can collect hundreds or thousands of such interesting cards, far more than any author can illustrate in his book.

Recently, whilst staying with friends in Lincolnshire, I found by my bedside two well-illustrated books. They happened to be the *Book of the Lincolnshire Seaside* by David Robinson (Barracuda Books, Buckingham, 1981) and *Lost Lincolnshire Houses* by Terence R. Leach and Robert Pacey (Old Chapel Lane Books, Burgh le Marsh, Lincs., 1990). No word of postcards in these titles. Now I have no interest in Lincolnshire whatsoever (well, apart from my friendly hosts), but I found these books fascinating. In the case of that showing the development of the Lincolnshire seaside resorts, I could at once relate these changes, developments and aspects of social history to far away Worthing on the south coast. You could likewise relate to any of our very many seaside resorts, that were established in the Victorian period and enjoyed their heydays in the Edwardian era—the 'Golden Age' of the postcard. This book, of course, was illustrated with old picture postcards—it had to be to tell the story adequately.

The book on *Lost Lincolnshire Country Houses* featured 19 great country houses all lost since 1900—destroyed by fire, neglect, or just demolished to make room for modern blocks. All these old homes, estates or mini-communities were preserved for, and presented to, the reader via picture postcards, which outlived the buildings they illustrated!

These two books, placed quite by chance in my bedroom by Mr. and Mrs. Jim Briggs, served not only to give me pleasure but to illustrate some of the many virtues of postcards—they represent valuable historical source material or, on a lower plain, pure nostalgia. Later in the day we visited a splendidly preserved stately home—Burghley—where we found that the tradition of visitors and tourists buying colourful picture postcards was still continuing. The professionally-taken exterior and interior views, as well as good pictures of the paintings and other furnishings and fittings, were available in postcard form and were either sent to friends or retained as personal souvenirs of a delightful historical visit.

Whilst, as I have explained, there are very many books that use postcards to illustrate interesting aspects of the history of towns and villages, I have here reversed the process. I have used my town to illustrate the history, development, charms and interest of the picture postcards themselves. I also seek to show how the humble and often still inexpensive picture postcard can materially assist local history research and bring former times back to life.

The scope of picture postcards—of local-view or topographical postcards—is truly vast and interesting. I have chosen to describe this, and to show that the former penny postcards are now social history documents, by examining in some detail the cards that were available in my own 'home town'—Worthing.

This book is certainly not intended to be a history of my town; it is rather an outline of popular postcards that were produced for the mass-market in the period 1900-30. My reason for centring my story on one Sussex town is simply that I have some years' experience of collecting Worthing cards, and as a life-long citizen of Worthing I have a knowledge of the locality, its history and development. Consequently I can write from first-hand experience—no bad thing for an author!

The first point to remember about Worthing is that it is a seaside town, a resort. This adds greatly to its importance in postcard terms, for so many mass-produced pictorial picture postcards were made for popular seaside resorts—they were surely the backbone of the trade. Postcards were almost invented for the seaside visitor! In my Worthing collection views of the pier, of the front or promenade and of the beach outnumber all other local views. This will be true of all seaside towns or resorts. The seaside was the attraction. Folk visited Bournemouth, Brighton, Blackpool and all such places to be 'beside the sea'. Here too were congregated most of the souvenir shops, kiosks, cafés and other places that would be displaying local-view postcards to boost their income. These outlets tended to display cards depicting their locality, the main attraction being the beaches, the pier, the bandstand and such traditional aspects of the British seaside.

When we come to the non-pictorial postcards, the amusing, comic or slightly risqué cards by Donald McGill and others, these too almost invariably featured the seaside and the types of adventure that could happen (hopefully) whilst on holiday. Looking back, our resorts, or at least the beaches, were far more crowded in the 1920s and '30s than they are today—for most people took their holidays, as a family unit, in Britain. They did not fly off to foreign beaches.

I believe that this local coverage exemplifies in so many ways the cards produced for, and available in, every town in the land and in many overseas countries, for postcards of the general types in this book enjoyed a worldwide appeal and served a worldwide need. Today they enjoy a truly international interest and popularity.

The brief quotations that you will find at the head and end of each chapter are taken from cards in my own collection, for the object of the postcard was to prompt and deliver a brief message. Today, these mainly inconsequential quotations can be interesting especially when they relate to postcard collecting, to the subject depicted or to the cards themselves.

Glossary of Postcard Terms

It is obviously beneficial before we commence the story to have some knowledge of the postcard terms to be found in books or auction catalogues, and those used by fellow collectors and dealers. The following terms are in general use although other descriptions are self-explanatory.

Standard abbreviations are listed on page xix and a summary of the main postcard periods is printed on page xx.

Advertising or Advert Card
A card produced to advertise a product or other commercial venture. Such cards were often given away or used by a firm for its own correspondence. These cards can be highly interesting from a social history or local research point of view, although they are not always visually attractive. For this reason few were added to collectors' albums. *See* plates 20, 35, 46, 48-51, 116-17 and 202, for typical examples. Some advert cards appear to be standard cards with the advertising matter on the address side, as plates 43-4.

Amateur Photographs
Many amateur-taken photographs or snaps were printed on to postcard blanks. Some of these were sent through the post to friends and they can therefore correctly be classed as postcards. However, most of them (especially when uncaptioned) are of little or no interest outside the family unless a special event or interesting background is included. In this way plate 120 is of some local interest.

Applique
Extra material added to the basic printed card to embellish it, or to form a novelty feature. Such additions contravened post office regulations and such cards should have borne the full, letter, postage stamp.

Art Deco
The style associated with the jazz age or with Odeon-style architecture of the mid-1920s and '30s. Many Art Deco-style cards were designed by leading artists or designers and the best of these examples are in demand, although they are not featured in this specialist book on local views.

Art Nouveau
A style named after the Paris shop *L'Art Nouveau*. This *fin-de-siècle* style with its curved, lively lines dates from *c*.1895 and continued up to about 1910. Art Nouveau-style cards, especially those bearing the reproduced signature of leading artists and designers, are highly regarded and can be very costly. They fall outside the scope of this book.

Artist-drawn
A postcard design based on an individual artist-drawn or artist-painted picture. These designs, like the A.R. Quinton paintings, were mass-produced. This term does not indicate that individual cards are hand decorated.

Back
There is confusion over this description. Officially the address side of a card is the front and the picture side the back! However, we now tend to regard the address and message side as the back.

Booklet or Detachable Cards
From the early years of the century some postcards were sold in booklet form. Typically 12 view cards would be bound together by the extended left-hand edge which was perforated so that individual cards could be torn out and used in the normal way. These booklets were protected by a decorated cover which normally had a window through which one could see the top card.

These perforated-edged detachable cards are not generally favoured, perhaps because the views are standard tripper-market, popular views. However, such booklets offer an inexpensive way to purchase cards and, from a local historian's point of view, a book of pictorial cards provides a linked series of photographs which were probably taken at the same period.

For example, I have just purchased from a local dealer a complete booklet entitled 'Souvenir of Worthing. 12 views detachable for use as Post Cards'. The set was priced at £6.50, rather less than half the price that I would have been asked if the cards were sold individually. In this case the booklet proved very interesting as the top card was a Worthing pier view that was new to me; it showed festoons of flags and tubs of flowers supporting a banner reading, 'Welcome to Worthing's new Pier'. This rebuilt pier was opened on 29 May 1914, indicating that this photograph was taken soon after the opening, in say early June 1914.

This pier view helps to date the other 11 view cards. This booklet also illustrates the point that purchasers of such booklets may well find included some odd cards—this example includes two views of the town of Littlehampton, several miles to the west. Such booklets are surprisingly neglected and are usually inexpensive.

Cartophily hence Cartologist
Names sometimes given to the hobby of postcard collecting and to such collectors. These terms are not favoured by most postcard collectors and seem to have been taken over by cigarette card collectors. *See also* 'Deltiology'.

Chromo or Chromolitho
Abbreviations for Chromolithographic printing, a quality and

relatively expensive form of multicolour printing. Much practised by leading continental publishers, mainly in the early period of picture postcards before about 1905. The best 'Gruss aus'-type cards were printed by this method, which shows depth of solid colour and sharp detail. Such cards command a higher price or are more desirable than the later three-colour printing or screen-printing techniques. Some cards bear a printed credit, such as 'Chromographed in Saxony'.

Circa
An approximate rather than an exact date. 'Circa 1905' or '*c.*1905' means 'approximately 1900-10'.

Commissioned (or sponsored) cards
My term for cards that were obviously specially commissioned by a private person or firm and which were not usually sold commercially. Most studies of individual houses were obviously commissioned by the occupier and were privately used by him or the family. Most hotel, school or other advert cards were similarly commissioned. Many photographers undertook such commissions, showing local sports teams, school groups, etc.

Composite
A card which with others in the set forms a large picture. Individual specimens may be likened to a single jigsaw puzzle piece!

Court-shape or Court-size
The small, rather tubby, standard-size (approx. 3½ x 4½ ins.) British postcard in use from January 1895 to 1898, and often continued into the early 1900s. *See* plates 22-4, 28, 36-39.

Credit
The printed or impressed details of the publisher or manufacturer of a card. Real-photograph cards often bear a credit to the photographer.

Deckle Edge
In postcard terms a decorative, usually wavy, edge to a card, as opposed to a straight edge. These wavy-edged cards came into favour in the 1930s and in general terms deckle-edged is a rather dismissive description, indicating a late, mass-produced postcard.

Deltiology (Deltiologists)
One of several early names given to the hobby of collecting postcards. Rather a mouthful and now seldom used except in North America. The basic English term 'postcard collecting' is surely preferable.

Divided Back
Cards, like standard modern examples, where the address side is divided to permit a message to be written on the non-picture side. The divided-back cards were permitted first in Great Britain in January 1902. Other countries followed this example in later years but some British undivided-back cards remained in circulation for a few years after 1902. The French authorities permitted divided-back cards in 1904, the Germans in 1905 and the United States of America as late as October 1907.

Embossed
Usually early, high-quality postcards issued by leading firms, where part of the design is stamped out to give a raised pattern.

Estimates
Many catalogues add after the basic description of the lot an estimated price, such as '35-45' or '40-50'. This is the price in pounds sterling which a lot might be expected to command. Such pre-sale estimates should be taken as approximate guidance only. Most especially desirable items will exceed the estimate, sometimes by a considerable amount.

Event Card
Usually photographic cards depicting a purely local event. These can be very collectable, especially when well captioned and dated. Event cards were by their nature only sold in the locality and for a relatively short period. Some can consequently be very rare and desirable to specialist collectors. Typical Worthing event cards are shown in plates 24, 83, 118, 127-9, 161-2, 170-2, 177-86.

Faked (or amended) views
Several major firms amended stock views to introduce novelty or faked versions. In this book plate 57 shows a view of Worthing pier and front on a sunny summer day and the faked winter version, where a stormy sea has been painted in. In many other cases, a daylight view has been amended to a night scene with lit windows etc. These faked views were commercially viable for the publisher and sold in large numbers, but they are of no interest to local historians.

Front
Like the back, a confusing term which can indicate either side! The official post office view was that the front was the address side—the side that concerned post office staff. Most modern collectors, however, regard the all-important picture side as the front!

Full out
A design or photograph which entirely fills the picture side of the card.

Full size
This larger size card (approx. 3½ x 5½ ins.) was permitted in Great Britain on 1 November 1899. These superseded the earlier court- and intermediate-size postcards. However, continental cards were usually of this full size before they were permitted in this country, for inland use. These cards are also referred to as 'Postal Union'-size.

Glitter
Metallic addition sprinkled on some cards in the approximate period 1900-10 to give a novelty effect. Much of the original glitter has now worn off or tarnished; such additions tend to spoil a card.

Golden Age
The 'Golden Age' of postcards is regarded as being between 1902 and 1914, when the collecting hobby was at its height. Cards of this period, as well as being well produced (in most cases!), gave a special interest and charm, although by no means all Golden-Age cards are valuable. Some books use this term in their title—*Picture Postcards of the Golden Age, a Collector's Guide* by Tonie and Valmai Holt.

Gruss aus
German for 'Greetings from'. This term was much used on

German cards depicting an individual place which were intended to be sold to visitors within that town. These cards tend to predate 1910 and may be regarded as the earliest general type of local-view card. Their widespread use and attractive and interesting nature did much to popularise picture postcards and the collecting hobby. Typical examples are plates 25-7.

Hand-coloured

Many pre-1914 cards were hand-coloured. The labour was cheap and the cost of hand-colouring very low. Hand-coloured cards are not necessarily more desirable than good colour-printed examples.

Heraldic

Cards comprising or incorporating in a larger design the heraldic arms of a city or town. Many continental 'Gruss aus'-type cards incorporated such arms, as did many British local-view cards (see plates 29 and 88). Several British publishers issued heraldic sets incorporating only the town's arms. Such cards were obviously on sale in the places featured, which tended to be the larger popular tourist centres.

Hold to Light or 'H.T.L'

Cards which, when held to a light, appear to change slightly, either because of a ghost-like object appearing or the buildings etc. appearing to be lit from inside, due to a series of small cut-out portions allowing light to penetrate.

Intermediate size

A British postcard size approximately midway between the early court-size card and the full- (or standard-) size card. The intermediate cards measure approximately 3 x 5 ins. and were in use in the approximate period 1894-1900.

Lever-action

Mechanical-type cards where the picture is changed or activated by means of a small lever. A typical 1907 example is shown in plate 155.

Lévy

The name of a leading and popular Paris-based form of mass-produced local-view cards based on photographs of continental and southern English towns, etc. See Chapter V.

LL. or LLs.

The standard abbreviation for the French-produced Lévy postcards.

Local Photographer

A photographic card entirely produced by a local photographer, not by a national firm. The Worthing cards produced by and bearing the credit to E. Edwards (& Son) are typical examples of this interesting class, see plates 1, 161-2, 167, 169-70 and 190.

Local Publisher or Retailer

A card bearing the credit to a local firm or retail outlet. These cards were not necessarily produced locally but were usually produced in bulk by national or international firms.

Localised cards

Mass-produced, usually humorous seaside-type, cards of a type made especially saleable by the addition of the name of individual towns. Localised Worthing cards are shown in plates 146-8.

Mail Novelties

A general term embracing several novelty cards, but especially those cards incorporating a string of miniature local views within a pocket. Typical examples are shown in plates 150-4.

McGill

The name of Donald McGill (see Chapter VII) is associated with a vast array of cheeky, comic seaside-type cards, but by no means all such cards were originated by Donald McGill. Typical signed McGills are featured in plates 137-9.

Monochrome

A card printed in shades of one colour.

Multiple Views

Mainly local-view cards which include more than one small-size view. Such cards are plentiful and not usually regarded with favour. Typical examples are shown in plates 60-6.

Novelty cards

These non-standard cards occur in great variety. Most had additional material or elements which made them due for the full postage rate. The unusual feature(s) or novelty made them all the more saleable to some buyers, but some novelty cards are not easy to mount in an album. Nevertheless selected novelty cards can be great fun.

Official Cards

Those issued by a government or postal authority for general use. These originally bore a printed postage stamp and were not pictorial. The first printed postcards were Officials, printed and sold by the government. The first such British cards were placed on sale shortly before the first day of use, 1 October 1870. They were simply standard-size message carriers that could be posted. Some later Official cards were semi-pictorial, in that the design might relate to a special occasion or event. A plain postal stationery card could be printed with advertising or other matter by the purchaser but the cards would bear pre-printed stamps.

Oilette

A trade name introduced by Messrs. Raphael Tuck in 1903 to distinguish a class of mock oil-painting effect incorporating embossed brush strokes. Later the term came into more general use for any facsimile of a hand-painted design. The cards were mass-produced, but the effect of the early Tuck Oilettes can be very realistic.

Oversize or Giant Cards

Cards which are larger than the standard approved size. Such novelty cards can be very large. One Worthing view series measures 11¾ x 9 ins. It is headed 'Book Post', but the printed notes explain that the card could be sent for a halfpenny provided only the name and address, plus the sender's name appeared. Otherwise the full postage (one penny) was required. Oversize cards present problems of mounting in an album but they can be of interest to a local history student. They are very prone to damage.

P.H.Q.

These initials relate to cards issued by the British Post Office from July 1973 onwards. They comprise enlargements of new issue postage stamps. The initials stand for Postal Headquarters. They have become very collectable and many folk subscribe to them, receiving each new issue on publication. They are, however, collected rather like stamps and most are retained in a mint state. Some of the early issues are quite scarce and relatively valuable, as their popularity took time to become established and the early print runs were small in comparison with later orders.

Printing Processes

The various printing processes and techniques are outside the scope of this book and hardly concern the collector of local views or social history subjects, where the subject is all important. However, some processes are more expensive and give better results than others. Anthony Byatt's *Picture Postcards and their Publishers* gives information on the processes and the publishers who used the various named techniques. *See* his index, under 'printing processes'.

Postal Union

The Universal Postal Union (Union Postale Universelle) was formed in the 1870s to regularise and standardise international rates and so avoid the confusion caused by each country having its own regulations and postal rates. But even with the new Union there were two different rates for countries within class A or class B! Cards intended for overseas often bore Postal Union wording. British postcards printed before July 1875 should not have been sent abroad.

Postal Union Size

The official Postal Union approved postcards were larger than the tubby shape British court cards. The Postal Union cards measured 3½ x 5½ ins., that is, approximately the size of the standard continental cards. This size was approved by the British postal authorities for home use from November 1899.

Publisher

The person or firm who places the card on the market, paying for its production and receiving the initial financial rewards. The publisher will commission the design from an in-house or independent artist or designer. Except with early cards, the name of the publisher, such as Raphael Tuck & Sons, usually appears on the product. This may well be different from the name of the artist; the name of the retailer may also occur.

Real Photograph

Postcards bearing a glossy real (untouched) photographic image. This class is huge, ranging upwards from amateur snaps printed on postcard blanks to highly detailed and interesting professional studies. Real-photograph cards are superior to mass-produced commercially printed cards. Some, mainly local-event, cards were published in small quantities. They can be highly interesting from a social history or local history point of view.

Shop-fronts

A self-explanatory term for photographic cards depicting shop-fronts, usually with the staff posed in front. These were specially commissioned publicity (or vanity) cards and were extremely popular with many tradespeople. Such cards are very popular with local historians and collectors and can be real social history documents. A few Worthing shop-front cards are in plates 71, 122-3 and 202.

Smiler Cards

My term for slightly humorous cards that would make the would-be buyer smile and purchase. These are not as humorous or comic as the real McGill-type, slightly vulgar or cheeky cards. Typical 'Smiler'-type cards are illustrated in plates 131-3.

Sponsored Cards

As with commissioned cards, those that were especially ordered for use by an individual or firm, mainly for their own use. Many sponsored cards are of a publicity nature.

Stamp Box

The printed outline in the top right-hand corner of the address side of the postcard. Useful postal-rate and other information can be printed within the box outline. If the halfpenny postcard postal rate is quoted the card will have been printed before 3 June 1918, *see* page 34. The publisher's name, trade name or initials can also occur in this space.

Stationers' Hall

A small number of pre-1912 postcards bear copyright protection such as 'Entered (or Ent.) Stationers' Hall'. This shows that the design had been registered at Stationers' Hall in London. The records are now deposited at the Public Record Office at Kew and show when the design was first registered and by whom. However, the Acts basically applied to 'literary matter' and the available records include few relating to postcards. The fee-paying registration of such material at Stationers' Hall ceased on 30 June 1912.

Stereoscopic or Stereo Cards

Photographic cards comprising two images of the same object or scene taken from a slightly different view point. When seen through a special viewer these images give a realistic three-dimensional effect. The much more common stereoscopic view (not postcards) is shown in plate 13.

'Sunny Snaps'

My name for the quite common real-photograph cards taken in the 1930s by street photographers seeking custom from passing pedestrians. These photographs were printed on postcard blanks in order to achieve multiple sales, rather than a single print. The price for individual 'Sunny Snaps. The best all-British Walking Picture postcard', was sixpence. Repeat orders were quoted at three for one shilling, six for two shillings or 12 for three shillings and sixpence.

Usually these are only of interest to the person(s) depicted, but in some cases (plate 121) the costume and the street background can be of wider appeal. There is also the point that such local 'sunny snaps' bear at least the year that they were taken—more than can be said of most photographic cards.

Topographical

Picture postcards depicting landscapes or townscapes or in effect any views of places. There are many possible subdivisions of this large category. With true topographical cards, the object, such as a church, is more prominent than other features.

Trade name

Many publishers used special trade names for their cards, or to indicate special processes or effects. I have mentioned some of the most common trade names in this book, but a long and useful list is given in Anthony Byatt's *Picture Postcards and their Publishers* (Golden Age Postcard Books, 1978) within indexes three and four. Such names are also given in alphabetical sequence in A.W. Coysh's *The Dictionary of Picture Postcards in Britain 1894-1939* (Antique Collectors Club, 1984).

Trimmed
A card that has had its edges trimmed, perhaps to avoid a missing corner or rough edge. It follows that the card will be slightly smaller than normal or will be of incorrect proportion. Such trimming, whilst it may improve the look of the cards, will affect its value from a serious collector's point of view. I much prefer an untrimmed card, with all its faults showing.

Under-size, Miniature or Midget Cards
Many novelty cards are quite small. Some are miniatures of standard cards or views. The Edwardian Rotary 'Midget Post Card' measures under 2¾ x 3½ ins. Others are long and narrow, like a bookmarker, measuring approximately 5½ x 1¾ ins. Apart from their rarity, they are in little demand, being too small for useful study or display.

Undivided Back
Postcards with an undivided address side. This means that any message had to be added to the picture side, which was designed to facilitate this. The standard early postcards were of the undivided-back type before the British postal authorities relented in January 1902, but stocks of the old cards remained in use for some years! *See also* Divided Back.

Vignette
A small view often on early cards, framed in an elaborate surround. Some cards incorporate several vignettes. Such cards can be attractive, but owing to the small size of the picture they are not favoured by local historians—unless no other large-size view of that period exists. Typical early vignetted designs are shown in plates 40, 41 and 45.

'Write away' cards
This term is applied to a variety of usually well-designed, mildly humorous cards of the 1900-10 period where the start of a message is printed and relates to the design. Messrs. Tuck in particular issued some very attractive and amusing 'Write away' cards (*see* plate 135) and many other publishers followed this firm's lead. The Tuck examples in particular are very collectable and not necessarily costly.

Abbreviations

The reader should be aware of the main standard abbreviations as used in most specialist books, magazines and auction-sale catalogues.

a.c.m.
Album corner mark. The impression or other mark found on most cards that have been mounted in an old-type postcard album for a number of years. These, or any other markings, can affect the value of a card but in this case, not to a great extent, especially when the card or subject is important.

a.m.r.
Adhesion marks to reverse. Such marks will occur when a postcard or photograph has been stuck down in an album or scrapbook. In some extreme cases the old glue or backing will completely spoil the address side of a postcard and greatly affect its commercial value.

However, if you are collecting picture postcards purely for their local or social history content, such damage might well be overlooked, as it occurs on the uninteresting side.

B.P.
Buyer's premium. The additional percentage charged to the buyer by most auctioneers, on the final bid. This can appreciably lift the final price especially as V.A.T. is added to the buyer's premium!

When buying at an auction it is important to read the various conditions of sale as printed in the catalogue.

c.
Circa. Printed before a date, period or number-count, meaning that dating or number is approximate only.

C.S.
Continental size, meaning a large card of the early period when the British cards were of the court-size and shape. In the case of court cards this word is normally spelt in full.

D.B.
Divided back. Cards printed to permit the inclusion of a message on the address side. Permitted in Great Britain from January 1902.

EX.
Excellent condition. Like other condition gradings, much used by auctioneers.

FR.
Fair, a general condition grading, one with little real meaning.

G.
Good, a general condition grading. Often means medium condition!

H.T.L.
Hold to light. Edwardian novelty cards with cut-out section, so that windows, the moon etc. appear to light up when the card is held to a light source.

LL.
Louis Lévy. Photographic-based cards printed by the Lévy firm in Paris. *See* Chapter V.

MT.
Mint. This condition grading should, as for stamps, be reserved for unused cards in the same brilliant, unblemished state that they would have left the publishers. Few cards remain in a truly mint state.

P.
Poor, a general condition covering many types of defect. Unless highly important from a local history (or other specialist) point of view, cards rated as poor should be left well alone.

Pc.
Postcard, a standard abbreviation.

P.H.Q.
Postal Headquarters. British cards issued from July 1973 in the form of enlarged special-issue postage stamps. Mostly collected for their philatelic interest.

P.U.
Postally-used. A card that has been sent through the post. Such cards should still have the stamps in place and should bear a clear, readable posting date.

R.P.
Real photograph. A glossy-surfaced real photograph printed on a postcard back. Some real-photograph cards are very rare, often being commissioned subjects purchased in small quantities, but many R.P. cards were standard mass-produced products.

UD. or UDB.
Undivided backs. Usually pre-1902 (or occasionally later) cards of the early type where only the name and address could be written on the non-picture side.

V.G.
Very good, a condition grading which should mean a bright card with no obvious defects.

VR.
Varying condition, an abbreviation and description used by auctioneers when a lot contains several or many cards which are in varying condition. One might expect some to be good, others poor. Usually most are in a less than good state!

W.A.F.
With all faults. A very important abbreviation to note. These initials should appear pencilled on a card or price label when the card has faults that affect the price or desirability. Such faults can include tears, missing corners, various unsightly markings or repairs. Indeed, it is an all-embracing term covering 'all faults'!

Postcard Periods

For convenience, the period of production of postcards is divided in the following manner:

1869-1900	Period 1
1900-1914	Period 2
1914-1918	Period 3
1918-1939	Period 4
1939-1945	Period 5
1945-1969	Period 6
1969-onwards	Period 7

It will be seen that there is a slight overlap; a 1900 card could be classed as Period 1 or Period 2 and a 1914 example as Period 2 or 3. The tendency is, of course, to group it in the earlier classification for, all other elements being equal, the earlier the card, the more desirable it is felt to be.

I prefer to relate my cards to British royalty:

Cards datable to 1901 or before being Victorian
Cards datable to 1901-10 being Edwardian
Cards datable to 1911-36 being George V
Cards datable to 1936-52 being George VI
Those from 1952 onwards being Elizabethan.

This system may only be meaningful to British collectors and admittedly the later periods cover rather long periods.

The true collector, like the local historian, will not be too worried about the period classification—it is the card and its picture that is the main attraction.

Illustrations

Unless otherwise stated the illustrations are of standard-size postcards. Unless stated they are in an unused state and do not bear the name of the photographer, retailer or publisher. Quoted postal dates indicate only that the card was used at that period; the date of the photographic original and the date of publication of the card may be somewhat earlier.

Chapter I

Home Town:
An Introduction

'It's so lovely here and very bracing—feel much better already'

'We are staying here in Worthing. Seaside place and having a very jolly time ...'

My wife and I, and both sets of our parents, had the good fortune to be born and brought up in Worthing, a seaside resort in West Sussex. We therefore have a natural interest in our home town, its past history and its many later developments and changes.

Our view of late Victorian and Edwardian Worthing, and of Worthing into the late 1930s can be greatly influenced by picture postcards. Our—and your—home town, its inhabitants and their dress and recreations, their thoroughfares, and shops, their very lives are depicted in tens of thousands of postcards originally sold for a penny or so. Cards that may have been colour-printed in Germany when it was still divided into states, as Saxony, Prussia, etc., or by British publishers in London or Scotland, or by local firms or by the photographer just around the corner. All their skills help us to look back on our town as it appeared less than a hundred years ago.

These inexpensive humble cards are a vital source of British social history.

I am naturally particularly interested in postcards relating to my town of Worthing. However, most of the points that I will be making relate equally to most other towns, certainly to our many popular seaside resorts, the starting-point for millions of typical 'picture postcards'.

Firstly, let me give you a very brief outline of my town, so that you can compare it with yours or any other municipality. You will no doubt find many points of similarity. Also we all share a common history; our towns expanded as the population grew and house-ownership became more general. We shared the same sovereigns, the same governments, the same laws. We, or our loved ones, went off to fight the same wars, we suffered or rejoiced over similar events, wherever we lived. Much the same types of postcard sold equally on the south coast as they did at Blackpool on the west coast, or at Great Yarmouth on the east, or in Scotland.

We were united by our postcards.

Like most popular Edwardian seaside resorts, Worthing grew rapidly in the 19th century, in our case from a quite modest fishing village. The popularity of sea bathing and the medical benefits of sea air had been recognised at Brighton (or Brighthelmston as it was originally called), and the royal visits to that and other towns set a fashion. Worthing and similar towns had their 'Seasons'; hotels were built and houses were erected to be let during 'The Season' to the folk that enjoyed the innocent pleasures of the seaside.

The flood of visitors was assisted by the spread of a good railway network. The rail service between London and Worthing was probably as quick and more reliable 50 years ago than it is now. More folk would have travelled by rail (mainly in the long-discontinued 'third class'), perhaps on the old 'London, Brighton and South Coast' line, than is the case today when so many families have their own cars.

More visitors, more hotels and more houses meant more shops. Resorts spread rapidly—even into the sea, for every resort worth the name boasted one or more piers. Coastal vessels and pleasure paddle-steamers plied their way along the coast, stopping off at the resorts en route.

The 1851 *Post Office Directory*, published when there were still punishment stocks outside our Town Hall, linked Worthing with the then separate parish of Heene and the ancient village of Broadwater (only a mile away from the centre of Worthing), and stated:

> Worthing is a fishing and market town, and watering-place on the English channel, in the parish of Broadwater ... 56 miles from London and twelve west from Brighton. The population, in 1841, was 4,702; assessed in 1842 as £24,907. From an inconsiderable fishing village it has risen to become a bathing town of importance ... it has on the seaside a long range of

smooth sands, extending three miles to the east and seven to the west, on
which races are held in September, and also a kind of pleasure fair. The
town is well laid out, and has some good streets ...

The baths are very good; besides the machines on the beach, there
are two bathing establishments, for warm, cold and medicated vapour
baths ... There are libraries and a theatre ... Assembly rooms are attached
to the new Steyne hotel. There is a Literary Institution, a Dispensary and
national schools ...

Later population figures are provided by census returns. These show the
growth of the town, from under five thousand in 1841 to just over eight thousand
in the 1860s. Later figures are:

1881	11,816
1891	16,606
1901	22,567 (my grandfather was included)
1911	30,305 (my father was included)
1921	37,050
1931	46,224 (my turn to be counted)
1941	no wartime figures available—restricted area
1951	69,431
1971	86,610
1981	92,100
1991	98,960

These figures, however, tell only part of the story, for the census, taken at
10-year periods, was carried out in the spring and as such mainly relates to the
inhabitants, not to the influx of visitors attracted to all popular resorts during the
summer 'Season'.

In July, August or September the actual population of any seaside resort
might well double or treble, especially on Bank Holidays. The visitors or 'trippers'
would descend by train, charabanc or coach, or from the 1920s and '30s in their
own transport—car, motor cycle and side-car, or bicycle. These holiday-makers
were great purchasers of picture postcards, depicting the sea-front, the pier, the
parks and other popular spots.

It was for this largely seasonal trade that the great national firms of picture
postcard firms catered, producing black and white or colour-printed cards to sell
for a penny or two. Their output was enormous, the visitors' demand huge.

Towns and resorts tend to cater for different classes. For example, where
Brighton has always welcomed day-trippers with open arms and catered for them
all along its commercially orientated sea-front, Worthing has always prided itself
on being a cut above. As early as 1823 Pigot & Co.'s directory commenced its
résumé of my town:

Worthing is a bathing place of considerable importance, increasing in
celebrity every season as a fashionable retreat for those persons who prefer
a situation more retired than that of Brighton.

Historically, the Town Council, if not the tradespeople, have tried to sell
Worthing as a healthy, rather select, residential town—a pleasing and convenient,
hill-free, place in which to retire. They have not sought to attract the trippers or
short-term holiday-makers, as might the ruling bodies at Brighton, Blackpool or
Yarmouth. In Worthing we have endeavoured to attract new residents who
would contribute rates into the town coffers, enabling various improvements to
be made in the town for the benefit of all.

These differing town policies, with an emphasis on trade and trippers or otherwise, have repercussions on the postcard trade, and on the types of card sold in any town. But even in Worthing the residential policy never completely kept out the holiday-maker or the day-tripper, on whom so many local shopkeepers and hoteliers depended for their livelihood. Yet, we were not seeking to compete with Blackpool or with nearby Brighton.

Also, Worthing in the summer of 1893 (three years after having been created a borough) suffered dreadful national publicity when there was a serious outbreak of typhoid in the town. In an effort to overcome this real setback to our prosperity, the Corporation set about publicising the town as it had never been publicised before. On 15 June 1894 the *Sussex Coast Mercury* reported:

> ... Worthing, emerging from a terrible trial is seeking, with renewed vigour, to establish itself once again in public favour as a healthful and pleasant seaside resort ...
>
> The Advertising Committee has been engaged in drawing up an advertisement which it is proposed shall be inserted in the leading London and provincial newspapers ... and it has in view the free distribution of an illustrated guide to the town and neighbourhood ...

The brief newspaper advertisements inserted in London and provincial papers featured the attributes thought attractive to visitors in the 1890s. They included:

> WORTHING - Splendid Sea Front and Promenade, safe bathing, firm and extensive sands, charming drives, equable climate, delightful scenery, handsome Pier and Pavilion, with Concerts daily.

> WORTHING. Golf, Cricket, Lawn Tennis, Boating, &c., daily. Trains and Brakes to charming resorts - Arundel Castle, Bramber Castle, Highdown Hill, Cissbury and Chanctonbury, Goring Woods, West Tarring, with renowned Fig garden, Palace of Thomas a Becket, &c.

> WORTHING. Comfortable Hotels, well appointed Boarding establishments and apartments, at moderate charges.*

Rather better results might have been achieved had the 'Advertising Committee' given each visitor to the town a dozen picture postcards showing the local delights and bearing the basic message 'Greetings from Sunny Worthing', the equivalent of the very popular German 'Gruss aus' cards. But in June 1894 the continental-type picture or view postcard was not officially available in the British Isles.

This is surprising to us today for, by 1894, the use of the plain (non-pictorial) official postcard had been firmly established; tradesmen used them to invite or acknowledge orders, or to notify that a representative would call at such a time, etc. Many local photographers were also practising their craft. Photographs of British and foreign places of interest were being advertised in this same local paper by 'The Continental Photograph Agency' which claimed to hold the 'largest stock in the world'; lists and samples were available for sixpence. Worthing and other towns published guide books; G. Kirshaw advertised both *The Worthing Directory and Almanack* and his separate *Visitors' Guide and Handbook to Worthing*, with map and photographs at one shilling. What had not occurred in this country— or was still in its infancy—was the combination of the blank postcard with the photographer's skill or the scenic-engraver's art.

Yet a mere 10 years later, by 1904, all these Worthing attributes were being extensively featured on hundreds of different picture postcards on sale at numerous places at a penny or tuppence a time. They were doing far more good for Worthing (and for every resort) than all the old-fashioned verbal blurbs in

* The local delights or attractions also featured in this 1894 newspaper included fine old Irish or Scotch whisky at 3s. 6d. a pint and a half bottle; gin at 2s. 6d.; wedding rings were available at 5s.; shops were available at a pound a week. Good houses were available to rent at little over 10s. a week: 'A very nice double fronted Villa, Braemore Lodge, Gratwick Road a good central position, rent £30. Close to the sea, four bedrooms, two sitting rooms, kitchen, scullery, 2 W.C.s. Price of freehold £500.'
This house is now divided into two, having changed ownership or occupancy three times between 1891 and 1895 but still remains, outwardly at least, much as it did in the 1890s—which is more than can be said of its value!

newspapers. The postcards cost the town nothing and provided profit to many traders and local photographers.

Indeed, in 1904 the 'Borough Association' had the enterprise to send out 'attractive postcards ... and the sunshine statistics of the town were printed upon it; the card being sent in large numbers to members of the medical profession and otherwise distributed'. Later in the year the Yarmouth Corporation was reported to have sent 'thousands of picture postcards to leading hotels in all the large towns for distribution'.

Worthing and Great Yarmouth may not have been the first or the only towns to have used picture postcards to advertise at low cost the attractions of their towns. (I have not yet come across a 1904 Sunny Worthing 'Borough Association' card printed with our superb sunshine records.)

Nearly every facet of the changing scene in Worthing can be reconstructed from the old postcards that have been preserved, and this is equally true of every town and many villages in the kingdom. Edwardian and later postcards enable us to look back on the changing townscapes of our grandparents. The scope for such research is endless; I can only hope that my example will stimulate you to seek out and preserve these little pictorial documents and to enquire further into the history of your town.

In considering postcards, one must remember that, just as the population of any town was divided between long-term residents and visitors, so the postcards on sale were likewise divided into different basic types. However, I am dealing specifically with local-view or 'topographical' cards; but you must always bear in mind that the majority of cards were mass-produced; it was very big business.

The great printing firms were interested in popular local views, of the sea-front, of the pier, the main streets or popular parks—scenes of places where holiday-makers would congregate and where there were several places for the cards to be on display. With minimal profits of a fraction of a penny a card, they were after the mass-market. Their sea-front scenes had to sell over a long period; consequently they were not too concerned if their 'real photographs' happened to be out of date, or had been 'doctored' (see plate 57).

In general terms, holiday-makers required only a general pretty picture—atmosphere rather than accuracy. They were, after all, merely going to add a very brief message, of the 'Having a wonderful time', inconsequential type. In the late 1890s and very early 1900s the novelty of the inexpensive picture postcard prompted its sale. Cards were being used for their true purpose—as convenient and brief message-carriers. They were not intended as source material for later social historians or for those that, fifty or sixty years later, would use them to re-establish the face and character of the town in 1900, 1910 or 1920.

The present-day historian must bear in mind, however, that pictorial cards printed or published by the large non-local firms enjoyed a long sale spread over years. For example, cards showing views of Worthing pier as it was in 1910 or 1912 were still on sale in the summer of 1913, by which time the pier had been destroyed in a great gale. These same cards were most probably still on sale in 1915 after the replacement pier had been built and opened!

Both these purely local events—the destruction of the pier (during the night of 23 March 1913) and the reopening of the new one on 29 May 1914—are very well represented on other 'real-photograph' cards, but these were mainly issued by enterprising local photographers, not by the giants of the trade. These locally produced cards are the subject of Chapter VI, and a selection of pier-event cards is shown in plates 1-3.

The fortunes, or rather the misfortunes, of the pier and nearly every town event from the early 1900s to at least the 1930s were depicted on local-view

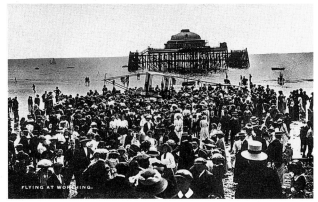

postcards. Chapter IV gives information on the many general types that were produced for this and every other town—the scope is amazingly large and interesting, the pleasures to be enjoyed great, the financial outlay quite small.

It must not be thought that, for the local historian, postcards are the sole or the earliest source of information. This is far from the truth; the modern photographic postcard came relatively late, in the 1890s, and most date from 1900 onwards. Various printed material predates the postcard age. Visitors to resorts have always sought mementoes, handbooks and such like for their own amusement and education, to give as a gift, or to retain as a keepsake. Local shops and private libraries would have kept a good stock of such material for tourists.

From the beginning of the 19th century various books and guides were published in Worthing. For example, John Evans' two-volume work *Picture of Worthing to which is added an account of the adjacent villages and of the rides and excursions in its vicinity* (William Phillips, 1814). These now very scarce and costly books were available at two local libraries, Spooner's and Stafford's, and also in London! Other local or county guides also featured Worthing and local sights.

John Evans' 1814 publication claims to be the first attempt to describe Worthing and the vicinity, and was inspired by this London author's visit to the town in July 1804. It is a charming book that could well be republished today or compared with the experience of a present-day visitor! The first 35 pages give

1 *(far left top)*
Storm-wrecked Worthing pier, 22 March 1913. An Edwards & Sons real-photograph card. It was used postally three days later with related message. Many cards depicting this event were issued, and most are still not rare.

2 *(far left bottom)*
A Ramsden Brothers real-photograph card of crowds around an early aeroplane which has landed on the sands by the wrecked pier. The event is datable to 29 July 1913. Eric Pashley was based at Shoreham Aerodrome and often took passengers on flights from Worthing beach.

3 *(left)*
Unsigned real-photograph card entitled 'Reconstructing the Pier, Worthing. Feb 27th, 1914'. A rare card.

4 *(right)*
A colour-printed standard seaside-view postcard which sold in thousands. Postally-used in March 1907 and obviously taken before that 'Season', but the beach was more used than the bathing machines.

an account of the eight-hour journey from London—'presenting to the eye - the charms of a well-cultivated country'. Worthing was singled out: 'of all the watering places in Great Britain WORTHING is, on account of the recency of its origin, entitled to special attention'. The town may be modern but within five miles there are the remains of Neolithic settlements and even industry—the mining of flint and the shaping of arrowheads and basic tools. Many Roman remains have also been found in the centre of the town. Perhaps the greatest difference between John Evans' view of the relatively new resort in 1814 and today concerns the beach and bathing:

> To the conveniences at WORTHING must be added, that of Bathing in the sea, at almost every part of the day; when proper persons attend, who are to be recommended for their civility.
> The price of Bathing is one shilling for each individual, and sixpence for children under seven years of age. The machines are used apart from each other for both sexes, therefore every proper attention is paid to decency.

Bathing then consisted of dressing up merely to be dipped in the sea by an adult helper. To partake of this pleasure you paid to clamber into a bathing machine (plate 4) and to change into a regulation all-embracing garb supplied by the attendant. The machine was then drawn into the sea so that the front steps permitted the bather to descend or be dipped into three or four feet of water. These machines were situated at special bathing stations and were let out by the Corporation as a franchise.

A well-known local resident and tradesman, the late Jack Watts, has written an interesting account of his childhood in Worthing in or soon after 1906. Of this period he relates:

> For the better off, bathing machines, like a garden shed on four wheels, could be hired, which were then drawn out into a sufficient depth of water by a horse to enable one to splash around. For the ladies, extra security could be had by lowering a sort of canvas tent that came down to the water level, thus ensuring that no prying eyes overlooked this ritual ...

A 1908 local directory gives the official regulations relating to bathing from the foreshore. How times change—these Edwardian ideas seem almost prehistoric these days. Let me quote briefly:

> There are stands for 106 bathing machines along Marine Parade; 57 of these for gentlemen and the remainder for ladies ... for adults, over twelve, the charge is 9d for a time not exceeding half an hour ... for adult females requiring the services of an attendant, the charge is 1/-. ... Open bathing is permitted at East Worthing beyond the confines of the Parade. Boys and girls under eight may bathe together. Mixed bathing under certain conditions is permitted.

No details are given of such 'certain conditions'—perhaps after dark!

In fact, relatively few visitors to the town would have been able to swim, but paddling was fun. Few postcards before the 1920s depict swimmers in the sea; bathing machines and segregated beaches remained in fashion until after the First World War.* Some mixed bathing took place on unregulated beaches where the bathing machines were not in operation, and even in 1913 one Ethel was moved to write on a Worthing beach-scene postcard: 'This is where the mixed bathing is going on'. Such goings on!

By the middle of the last century various handbooks and directories were published, several of which contained advertisements which give us at least a flavour of life some hundred and fifty years ago. Many of these advertisements make interesting reading today. Let me quote a sample from John Phillips' *Worthing Directory*:

Miss Guy's

Establishment for a limited number of young ladies. The system of this Establishment is conducted upon a plan suited to the present extended views of Society, and combines all that is desirable and essential to a highly finished education.

Professors of eminence are in attendance and a resident Parisian Lady.

Many local establishments also catered for would-be young gentlemen. In the interests of equality I quote part of the 1849 advertisement for the Wortley House Academy, then conducted by Mr. B. Brown:

Young Gentlemen

are received as Boarders, and instructed in an efficient course of Education, comprising Religious and moral instruction—Latin and Greek classics; French and English languages; History, Geography, Mathematics, Arithmetic, and such other branches of Knowledge as it may be advantageous to introduce.

The boys did not apparently have the services of 'a resident Parisian Lady'; at least she is not mentioned!

Most of the traders' advertisements were very brief, but they show that the townsfolk were well provided for, even by the numerous smaller shops:

E. PURSER
Fruiterer & Greengrocer.
8 High Street

Fruit and Vegetables may be had fresh from his Garden at any hour of the day.

The largest modern superstore cannot emulate this service.

*   Many beach scenes of the 1920s and '30s show a later development of the wooden bathing machine. The new version was a squarish tent in which to change in or out of one's bathing costume. Many local families had purchased their own, while others rented them by the day or the week. The intermediary stage between these tents and the old bathing machines was a canvas-type tent which was mounted on wheels, so that it could still be taken into the sea. This type is shown in plate 92; all the varying classes of bathing machines are recorded on seaside picture postcards.

W.HARDHAM
Pastry Cook & Confectioner.
French & English Bread & Biscuit Baker.
Soups, Ices, and Jellies, Ginger Beer, Schweppe's [sic] soda water and Lemonade.
Free access to Hardham's Pump, of excellent Water.

This mid-19th-century advertisement serves to remind us that our towns did not enjoy the basic services we expect today. Water had to be raised by pump. Municipal electricity did not come to the town until 1901 and even then its popularity spread slowly—by the end of that year, there were only eight consumers.

John Phillips, the publisher of the 1849 *Handbook and Directory*, treated himself to a full-page advertisement, listing some of his stock, which as 'Bookseller, Binder, Stationer, News & Toyman' he kept for inhabitants and visitors alike. The list is long, and to me well worth reproduction today.

A well-selected stock of the following Articles always on Sale:-
English, French and German Baskets - Writing Desks and Work Boxes in rosewood, mahogany, maple and leather. - Vases, china, glass and Wedgwood. - Toilet and Smelling Bottles. - Best match Cricket, Bats, Balls, and Stumps, made by *Duke, Cobbett, Clapshaw* and *Dark*. - Walking Sticks in great variety. - Water Colours, Drawing Pencils, Papers, Boards, from the most approved manufacturers. - Berlin Wools, Canvas Patterns, Purse Twist, Slides, Tassels, gilt and steel. - Eau-de-Cologne, Perfumery, Soaps, Bear's Grease, &c. - Brushes and Combs in every variety. - Writing Papers of every size and quality; Envelopes, &c. - Ledgers, Day Books, Diaries, Metallic Memoranda, &c., &c., - Quills, and quill, steel, and gold Pens, from the most approved manufacturers.
A very large and choice selection of Modern Works for Young People, and a well selected Stock of Theological Historical Writers, &c., new and second-hand. - Tunbridge Ware, German, English, and French Toys, too numerous to particularize.
A Splendid Collection of Stones-Moss, Calcedony, Petrified Wood, Sponge, &c. found on the Sussex Coast. Stones cut and polished to order.
Periodicals, Newspapers and every description of Publications supplied at London prices.

The only illustration in this one shilling 1849 *Directory* appeared by courtesy of John Fowler. It formed part of his advertisement for the newly titled *'Royal' Sea House Hotel* where 'Families may be accommodated with any number of Rooms, on moderate terms. Commercial Gentlemen also will meet with the greatest attention'. It is also interesting to read that 'Families [are] provided with Dinners from the Hotel at their own Residences'.

The neat engraving of the centrally placed hotel (plate 5), opposite the pier, serves to show how engravers were permitted, or encouraged, to use artistic licence to enhance the subject. In this version the hotel is made to stand on a promontory with the sea on two sides, not merely in front. This is an 'improved' view of an earlier engraving. The postcards issued later by or for hotels also tended to show off, to enlarge the premises or to glorify the surroundings, as do present-day travel brochures.

Many charming but generally small-scale engravings of local views, residences, etc., were used from quite early in the century as headings to writing paper, or in booklets. These engravings occur both neatly hand-coloured and in the one-colour 'penny-plain' state. One Worthing example of both types is included in plates 6 and 7, but very many others were published, on two basic sizes of folded writing paper. Frank Staff, in his classic book *The Picture Postcard & its Origins* (Butterworth Press, London, 1966), chose also to illustrate a writing paper coloured-

Royal Sea House Hotel Worthing

Warwick Street, Worthing

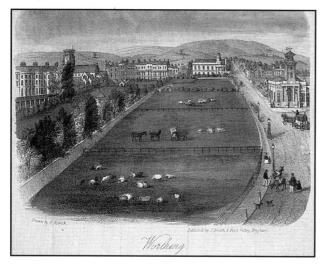

Worthing

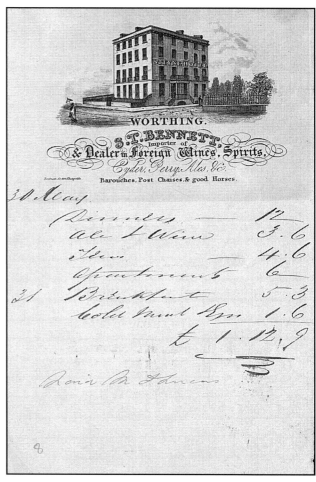

5 *(top left)*
An 1849 *Directory* engraving of the premier Worthing hotel, centrally situated on the sea-front.

6 *(middle left)*
A mid-Victorian letterhead engraved in London but published by C.H. Knight, the Worthing bookseller and stationer, whose premises are shown on the right.

7 *(bottom left)*
A mid-Victorian engraved and hand-coloured letterhead showing the centre of Worthing, with open fields to the west of the Town Hall. Such letterheads displayed local scenes well before the full development of photography or the introduction of postcards.

8 *(above)*
Another source of pre-postcard home-town views is printed billheads used by various traders. In this case, a hotelier's account for dinner and drinks, *c*.1860.

engraving captioned 'South View of Worthing taken at Sea', dated 1832. Almost every town in the kingdom would have featured on such special notepaper. Even Queen Victoria's paper was headed with engravings of the royal residences. I have a sheet with the coloured Royal Arms and an engraving of Osborne House on the Isle of Wight. Such engraved paper is most attractive and typical of its period, but complete sheets are now scarce, as many views were long since cut off and stuck in Victorian scrapbooks.

With regard to the 1835-45 view of the now pedestrianised Warwick Street (plate 6), we can usefully note that the Worthing engraving bears two credits. One is to the local publisher, 'C.H. Knight, Bookseller &c. Worthing', whose premises are prominently featured in the engraving! The other credit is to the engraving firm 'Newman & Co., 40 Watling Street, London'. Here is the same situation as was to obtain later with scenic postcards, where a large London firm of designers or printers supplied local firms with a series of special subjects to include the name of the local retailer. Some early picture postcards were remarkably similar to the scenic notepaper of the 1830s and '40s. Similar engraved and often coloured views were in books of the period and were also widely available as individual prints.

One of the foremost suppliers of engraved letterheads was Rock Brothers of London. This firm's name and address will be found as a credit under many of these local engravings. At the 1851 Great Exhibition, Rock Brothers & Payne exhibited not only 'fancy note and other papers', but also three scrapbooks 'containing nearly two thousand lithographed views in England'. Some forty-five years later Rock Brothers reused some of these old engravings on their local-view postcards!

Similar small engravings, though usually of single premises, can also be found on the billheads of local tradesmen (*see* plate 8), but such material is now difficult to find. Examples may, however, be preserved in your local library, museum or record office.

Other representations of Worthing and similar resorts were also available well before Queen Victoria acceded in June 1837. Several leading porcelain manufacturers produced ornamental objects, such as baskets, trays and vases, very well painted with local scenes or views of major residences. The Rockingham factory in Yorkshire in particular produced some splendid pieces depicting south-coast resorts. These were presumably on sale in these towns, but were costly articles and would only have been available in the better-class shops. A selection of local-view Rockingham porcelain is in the Worthing Museum collection. The Spode factory in Stoke-on-Trent and the Coalport factory in Shropshire likewise catered for the Worthing, Brighton and Hastings trade. (*See* plates 9 & 10.)

Most of these fine paintings on porcelain were probably copied from published prints or from illustrated books of the period. In the days before photography, a mini-industry flourished in painting local views, many of which were especially commissioned by engravers, print-sellers and publishers. Most local museums, libraries or county record offices have a representative collection of such engravings, many of which were published in London but were mainly sold in the locality of the subject. Many were tastefully tinted by hand whilst others were sold in the cheaper, uncoloured, state—as would be the case much later with many postcards.

On a rather lower plane, the South Staffordshire manufacturers of small enamelled copper-based boxes (usually termed patch-boxes) produced an assortment of goods catering for most British towns, cities and even villages. Plate 11 shows a selection of such Worthing boxes, which presumably were originally sold for a shilling or less as visitors' mementoes, in the approximate period 1800-20, quite early in the history of seaside resorts. These small enamel boxes are usually associated with Bilston in Staffordshire; most certainly they were not produced at

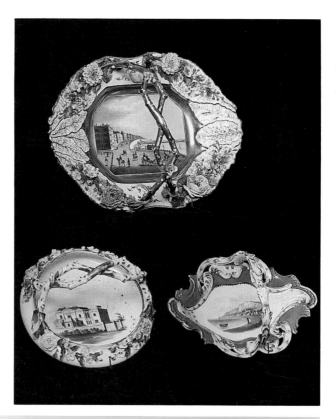

9
A selection of early 19th-century porcelain baskets hand painted with Sussex views for sale locally. Top basket from the Rockingham factory in Yorkshire, *c.*1835.

10
A Rockingham porcelain tray, embellished with a painted view of the Suspension Bridge at Shoreham, 10 x 7½ins., *c.*1835.

the much earlier and highly regarded enamel manufactory at Battersea. Some of these 'Bilston'-type boxes have attractive if rather naively engraved local views, and are very collectable objects today.

At this point I should briefly mention the town's industries. These were few and they may not be everybody's idea of industry, for they were silent. They comprised fishing—that is inshore fishing from small boats that were kept on the

11
Four 'Bilston'-type south Staffordshire enamelled small boxes, suitably inscribed for local sale to visitors.

beaches and appear in numerous post-1900 postcards. Next in chronological order was market gardening; large areas of Worthing were under glass. My present centrally positioned premises are on the site of an old nursery. Gradually, as land has become more and more valuable for building, the nurserymen have moved outwards.

An 1897 Queen Victoria Jubilee publication on the town includes the following paragraph:

A NEW INDUSTRY. - CULTURE OF FRUIT AND FLOWERS

Facility of transmission to the London and other markets has brought into active and extensive operation an industry of which no one seemed to have any thought twenty-five years ago. In the cultivation of grapes, tomatoes, cucumbers and flowers, a large number of persons are employed, and the glass houses in which the produce is reared and brought to perfection are estimated to extend, if placed end to end, fully fourteen miles. Tons of fruit are sent daily to Covent Garden and to the markets of Birmingham, Manchester, and even Glasgow and Edinburgh. The fertility of the soil and the salubrity of the climate are proved by the fact that fruit can be ripened three weeks earlier in Worthing than in the neighbourhood of London. The industry is one in which the inhabitants of the borough may justly feel pride, inasmuch as it has done, and is doing, a great deal in furtherance of the prosperity of the town.

Our harvest was large and commercially important. Worthing tomatoes were household words from the 1880s until modern times; likewise grapes, cucumbers, strawberries, etc., were sent from Worthing to Covent Garden every day. My wife's father, a well-known grower, supplied Worthing strawberries to the royal family. 'Worthing grown' meant much. Experiments were even undertaken in 1913 to grow tobacco as a commercial crop, under Mr. Pullen-Burry's newly invented travelling glasshouses or 'Tranverse Travelling Houses'. Worthing was one of the centres of the British fruit and flower growing industry.

Strangely, this aspect of the town is little represented on postcards. It was tucked away from the sea and proceeded silently, but to redress the balance I include a family photograph of my father-(or grandfather-)in-law's cucumber crop (*see* plate 12).

The other local industry was the tourist industry, catering for holiday-makers. This was big business. It is well represented on postcards to be featured later. The town's delights, the hotels, the shops, the entertainments, all these and more will be seen on post-1900 picture postcards.

By the 1870s and 1880s photography was coming into its own. The town supported several professional photographers—mainly engaged in portrait and general photography as well as selling cameras and photographic equipment. In the summer season these photographers would also sell prints of local views, available in various sizes and mounted and framed in different ways.

One of the earliest and most interesting aspects of Victorian photographic technology is represented by the rare stereoscopic cards—two side-by-side views which, seen through a special viewer, present a realistic three-dimensional scene. These cards were extremely popular in Victorian homes; a wonderful range was available, encompassing foreign lands, exhibitions, scenes, interiors—almost any subject. Plate 13 gives examples from a set of Worthing-view cards. These pre-date picture postcards by thirty or more years. The photographs are credited to H.W. Freeland of nearby Angmering and were published and sold by Charles Knight, the Worthing book and print seller, already mentioned above. Such

12
A family photograph of a Worthing glasshouse containing a good crop of cucumbers. The growing industry was hardly represented in local postcards.

13
Three scarce stereoscopic photograph cards showing Worthing views before the days of picture postcards, *c.*1870.

14
An interesting mounted photographic view of Brighton beach. Such local-view photographs were sold by photographers before the advent of the smaller picture postcards. Taken by E. Hawkins & Co. of Brighton, *c*.1890.

splendid stereoscopic-view cards are now rare, but are very important for a local historian and well worth seeking.

Of course, local photographers did not only produce these small stereo prints. The majority of their prints were much larger and mounted on thick card or other types of backing. Plate 14 shows a very detailed (but not pretty) mounted photographic print of Brighton beach. The reverse of the mount carries a printed label including the Prince of Wales' crest and mottoes. We also learn that the photographer, E. Hawkins (& Co.), had succeeded the earlier partnership of Hennah & Kent in Preston Street and in Kings Road. The new company was grandly described as 'Artist Photographers, Miniature & Portrait painters'. Photographic portraits could be 'enlarged up to life size and painted in oil or watercolour to order'. Apart from portraits, photographs of landscapes and animals were undertaken and carbon enlargements were supplied.

Photographic views of the size of *cartes de visite* were very popular and were probably also inexpensive. *Carte de visite* portrait cards were advertised by a local photographer, T. Green, at 7s. 6d. a dozen. This price, however, included the cost of the initial sitting in the photographer's studio. Outside views would not have incurred this cost and any expense would have been spread over the sale of a hundred or more view cards. Plate 15 shows the unusual and relatively early photographic view of the *Royal Sea House Hotel* on the sea-front opposite the pier, previously illustrated on page 10 in a pre-1850 engraving.

The reverse of this photographic card bears the name of the photographers, A. & E. Seeley, and of the Worthing retailer C.H. Loveday, stationer of 22 South Street, near the hotel, the pier and the sea-front. Loveday was in business here from at least the late 1860s until 1878. It is interesting that this small photographic local-view card was sold by a stationer, not by the photographer. This also applied when picture postcards later came into fashion.

Photography and printing took vast strides in a comparatively short time. Kelly's 1851-2 *Post Office Directory of the Six Home Counties* does not include any photographers, nor a photography section in its 'Classification of Trades' and traders.

Within a short time, however, the new photographic *cartes de visite* (introduced in 1854) were very much in fashion. Photographs on thin, stiff card

15
A small mounted photograph of the *Royal Sea House Hotel*, *see* plate 5. Taken by A. & E. Seeley and retailed by Loveday, bookseller and stationer of South Street, Worthing. These pre-postcard photographs are now scarce as they were issued in much smaller numbers than the later picture postcards.

cut to visiting-card size were produced by local photographers, who soon added views to their repertoire. The photographic *cartes de visite* were sometimes sent by post, perhaps with a brief message, and such cards could be considered very early picture postcards, except that most were enclosed in envelopes so did not qualify for reduced postal charges—this was still in the distance. There were many special *cartes de visite* albums that were avidly purchased and filled, as were the later postcard albums. Before the days of Worthing postcards, Mr. Kirshaw's Library in Warwick Street held 'the largest stock of *cartes de visite* and photographic albums'. The Victorian *cartes de visite* were quite small, about half the size of a later postcard.

Many local amateur photographers were practising their skills by producing prints and often glass-mounted slides for their own amusement. Worthing (West Sussex County Council) Reference Library is lucky to possess the Watts collection of local-view slides, which has been well used in local publications and talks. Mr. N.L. Watts was a founder member of the Worthing Camera Club and his grandson Jack Watts added greatly to the collection, while ensuring that it was safely housed in the local library for the benefit of future generations. No doubt many other towns have similar collections.

By at least the mid-1880s local commercial photographers were supplying prints ready mounted in special booklets. In some ways these slim local-view booklets or albums are related to the later postcards. Some were issued by well-known postcard publishers such as Valentine & Sons of Dundee, and most were printed in Germany. The famous Liverpool postcard publishers, Messrs. Brown & Rawcliffe Ltd., issued their *Album of Views of Worthing* in the 1890s. It was specially bound in red and gold for the local South Street firm of Walter Bros. (the 'publisher' of so many post-1900 postcards) and many of the scenes inside were based on photographs taken by Walter Gardiner—a celebrated Worthing photographer (and pioneer British postcard designer) who was to supply prints to many internationally known postcard publishers. His family business, 'Walter Gardiner, Photography', is still in existence and has materially helped to illustrate this and other Godden books—Walter Bros.' own advertisement has been affixed to the back cover. In fancy typefaces it informs the buyer that this 'Drapery

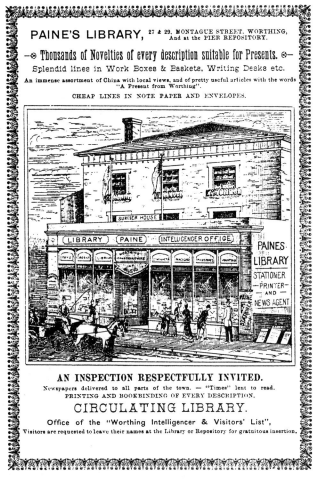

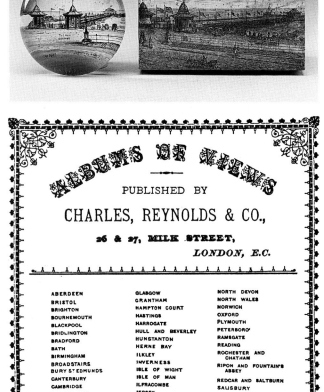

16 *(above)*
The publisher's advertisement from *Paine's New Album of Worthing Views*. Many such publications were issued before the postcard age.

17 *(above right)*
Inexpensive local-view trinkets of the type widely available in local private libraries, bazaars and tourist shops. The wooden 'Worthing Pier' box was made in Germany, as were many of the early postcards

18 *(above)*
A page from Charles Reynolds & Co.'s *Album of Worthing Views*. It shows other towns covered by similar pictorial publications, before the arrival of the picture postcard.

Bazaar ... contains the largest, cheapest and Best Variety of Novelties in Worthing. View Books. Mounted and Unmounted views. Photo Frames, Albums, Bags and Baskets'. By at least 1907 Walter Bros. were including in their local advertisements the claim that 'We hold the largest and best variety of Foreign Fancy Goods in Worthing and an Immense stock of Picture Post Cards'.

A similar slim German volume is entitled *Paine's New Album of Worthing Views*. It does not bear a publisher's credit, although the main centre spread is inscribed 'Eyre & Spottiswoode, London'—a firm well known to postcard collectors. The endpaper advertised the local and long-established Paine's Library. This is worthy of reproduction (plate 16), for it shows the type of goods stocked at popular private libraries, which were social meeting places—in the way that London coffee-houses were in the 18th century. The libraries stocked and also lent the London papers and displayed 'Visitors Lists'. Similar establishments, after the turn of the century, would have carried large, varied stocks of picture postcards.

ST. BOTOLPH'S CHURCH, HEENE, NEAR WORTHING.

THE NEW INFIRMARY, WORTHING.

THE VILLAGE OF HEENE, NEAR WORTHING.

THE VILLAGE OF TARRING, NEAR WORTHING.

19
A group of small, rather basic, engravings of local views reproduced from Charles, Reynolds & Co.'s *Album* (*see* plate 18). The later photographic picture postcards offered better views at a nominal cost and fulfilled a useful postal purpose.

Mr. Kirshaw's 1882 *Worthing Directory & Almanack* carried his advertisement which underlines the pre-postcard interest in local-view goods. Under the heading, 'Novelties in Stationery. Local Views', he listed:

Royal Cabinet Album of Worthing, 1/-*
Twenty views, original, of Worthing, 1/-
Worthing views, a book for the Boudoir, 1/-
Views of Worthing on note paper, per quire, 2/-

It is surprising that the early Victorian scenic headed notepaper was still advertised in the 1880s, indeed it was being issued into the 1890s.

Local libraries and other shops stocked and advertised 'China with local views and of pretty useful articles with the words "A Present from Worthing" '. These were inexpensive trinkets and consequently very popular as presents and mementoes. Like later picture postcards, most of this seaside china of the 1880-1914 period was made in Germany, and was often inscribed to this effect.

Apart from local-view china, many other trinkets or mementoes were available for visitors to every resort or popular town. Plate 17 shows a popular, inexpensive glass paper-weight, the base bearing a hand-coloured engraving (photographs were used later) of a local view which was magnified by the curved glass. The other object is a small light wooden box bearing an engraving of the ever-popular pier. This, like many others stocked by British shops, was made in Germany; it is stamped 'Made in Saxony'.

Many local-view albums were issued by Charles, Reynolds & Co. of London. They list 86 localities covered by the 1890s, alphabetically ranging between Aberdeen and York. The Sussex towns represented were Brighton, Chichester,

* Comprising engraved not photographic views.

Eastbourne, Hastings and Worthing. All were later well catered for by the postcard publishers and all, except Chichester, were seaside resorts. This and other late Victorian albums include many small saleable postcard-like photographs or engravings of popular local sights (*see* plate 19).

What was to come and to take off to an amazing degree was the marriage of photographs and colour printed scenes to the thin (then plain) official postcards. It was a marriage of convenience, a happy uniting that gave rise to a great new industry. It led to the preservation of images of our town and life, and became a 'collecting mania'.

Before discussing these local-view and other types of postcard, the next chapter describes the origins and subsequent history, or landmarks in the history, and development of the postcard—that little slip of card that we all now take for granted. It should be noted that in W.T. Pike & Co.'s *A Descriptive Account of Worthing Illustrated* which was published in 1895, there is not one mention of postcards. This is a fascinating publicity exercise giving details of various traders and their stocks, including stationers, newsagents and photographers. There is an article on Mr. and Mrs. Walter Gardiner, who I suggest were pioneers in the story of Worthing-view postcards, but this aspect of trade had not yet materialised, although Mr. Gardiner had taken most of the illustrations that grace this 1895 publication. None of the views is to be found on postcards. If that book had been published five years later, it would, I fancy, have been very different—postcards would have been to the fore.

In closing this initial chapter dealing with illustrations and mementoes relating to your locality I would appeal to those who find themselves in the unenviable position of clearing up perhaps a family home to spare a thought for future generations who might well wish to carry out research. Do not throw out old local-view photographs, guide books or directories, your library or museum will no doubt be pleased to preserve them under good conditions and make them available to interested students, or a local dealer may well know of a local collector or researcher who would welcome such material with open arms, even with open wallet!

Here is a pretty picture—Lovely place, lovely sea, lovely band in fact every thing is lovely—people included—weather is just right for holidays

Joyful message on an Edwardian Worthing view, Tucks 'Oilette'
postcard, posted in July 1910.

Chapter II

The Introduction and Evolution of Picture Postcards

'Many thanks for your pretty card from Sheffield. This is the latest of Weiman.'

'Arrived just in time for tea, will send you another card later on.'

Even the most casual of postcard collectors will benefit from a basic knowledge of the evolution of the picture postcard as we know it today. It will also help to be acquainted with the dates when fundamental changes in format came into general use. An understanding of the reasonably simple history of the postcard will also increase your enjoyment of the subject.

Whilst it is generally accepted that the modern postcard was 'invented' on the continent, a form of private 'Postal Card' had been introduced in the United States of America early in 1861. This was devised by John Charlton but his copyright was soon assigned to H.L. Lipman of Philadelphia and issued under the name 'Lipman Postal Card'. Only four such original Lipman cards are known today, none of which were ever posted.

It is not, however, generally appreciated that in the first half of the 19th century England, not Germany or the United States of America, led the field in simple 'message cards', which were introduced in the 1820s by W. Creswick. These message cards possibly differ from the later postcards in that they were intended to be posted with an envelope. However, we cannot be sure about this, as separate envelopes were not then in use, and letters were folded and sealed. These early message cards would not have borne a stamp (the early examples, of course, predate the introduction of the first adhesive prepaid postage stamps in 1840) and were not 'official' post office publications. Some of these Creswick message cards may, however, have been overprinted with trade publicity or with engraved views of the letterhead or billhead type. I have not yet seen a Creswick message card but they were produced and apparently widely copied for they represented a bright new idea in the 1820s.

We are here mainly interested in European and British picture postcards and with the introduction of official State-issued postal cards. Dr. Heinrich von Stephen, attending the Austro-German Postal Conference at Karlsruhe in 1865, outlined his ideas for an *Offenes Postblatt* or open post-sheet. After setting out at length the drawbacks of using a letter and envelope for a brief message, he expressed the view that there should be sold at post offices, and by postmen, forms for open communication. The size was to be that of an ordinary envelope and to be of stiff paper. On the front of this card could appear the name of the district with an appropriate device. The reverse side would contain the written message. The charge was to be as low as possible; indeed there was to be no charge for the cards other than the postal payment.

The doctor predicted that such open post-sheets would present no difficulty to the post office staff as money order cards or *Post Anweisung* were already in use and had proved popular. The size would be uniform, the position of the address constant and cards were pre-stamped so that the postage was paid at time of purchase. Surprisingly the idea was not adopted. Yet the seeds had been sown and were soon to germinate into an industry that must have consumed countless large forests!

The idea was again aired in January 1869, this time by Dr. Emanuel Herrmann of Vienna, a professor of economics. The timing was right and on 1 October 1869 the Austrian post office issued what we now regard as the world's first official postcard. Called the *Correspondenz-Karte*, it bore a printed stamp depicting Franz Joseph I and was remarkably similar to the 1865 design visualised by Dr. Heinrich von Stephen. The first postcard was therefore designed for sale within the great Austro-Hungarian Empire. Its form remained constant for many years, and its basic format was adopted by most postal authorities.

The scheme both met a need and caught the public's fancy, for it is recorded that more than two and a quarter million such *Correspondenz-Karten* were sold in the first three months.

On 26 May 1870 the British Postmaster-General recommended that the United Kingdom should issue 'correspondence cards' based on the German pattern. It is believed that an article in *The Scotsman* of 17 September 1869 prompted this official British action. Our first postcards were issued on 1 October 1870, and were printed by the great printing firm of De La Rue under an exclusive contract. Halfpenny stamps were introduced on the same day.

The new postal stationery cards bore the official new British name 'Post Card' but otherwise displayed little similarity to the later picture postcard. There was, however, nothing to stop the plain card being variously overprinted with advertising or other material. These cards were originally issued in two sizes but the larger was discontinued as soon as the initial supplies were used up. The cards were printed in purple and bore a narrow border design, plus the Royal Arms. The card was of a buff colour and bore a printed prepaid halfpenny stamp showing Queen Victoria's head. The stamped side (officially the front) was reserved for the address while the reverse side was intended for the message. They were sold at no more than the postage rate of a halfpenny each, prior to 1 April 1872.

The cost to the post office of producing these postcards in quantity was extremely small. In 1870 the post office ordered no less than a hundred million at a cost of four shillings a thousand. This is under five old pence per hundred or ten for just under a halfpenny. The profit margin was in the modest postal charges. The very low cost, the charge to the public being merely the halfpenny postage, ensured the new mode of message carrier its popularity. It may not have been so much the actual card that proved so popular for similar cards could have been sent previously at the full postage rate. However, from October 1870 onwards the cards were readily available and the postage had been slashed in half! They sold in very large numbers; by the end of the first day 675,000 had been sold. Reputedly some seventy-five million were sold in the first year. Much the same giant leap in demand had happened 30 years previously when the standard penny postage was introduced for inland letters. The low cost of the early plain postcard assured success from the start. The habit had been formed and could later be increased with the attractive developments in picture postcard production.

Do note, by the way, that the card's description was originally rendered as two words—Post Card—giving rise to the abbreviation P.C. But the modern usage is postcard—the form I will be using except when quoting original statements.

A breakthrough in the advance of postcard design came in June 1872 when private firms, other that is than De La Rue, were permitted to print their own cards provided that they were sent to be officially printed with a prepaid stamp design. On 1 February 1875 a thicker-gauge or 'stout' card was introduced and sold at eightpence per dozen. This was rather more expensive than the original issue as now the cards were charged at twopence a dozen, not the mere cost of the pre-printed halfpenny stamp.

Many of the privately printed postcards bore printed advertising matter. Many business-type cards were produced and proved exceedingly popular because of their low cost. These non-pictorial cards could be used for seeking orders (plate 20) or perhaps for expressing regret that an order could not be met. Others gave notice that a salesman would call in a day or two. One advertisement card seemingly printed on an official post office card featured an illustration by Gustave Doré. It was issued in March 1872 and included views of St Paul's Cathedral, London Bridge, The Tower of London and The Monument. This 1872 card was most probably the earliest British topographical view postcard.

Most importantly, the establishment of the 'Postal Union' was brought about at Bern in 1874. Now international postal rates and conditions could be agreed, at least for those countries within the Union, and postcards could be sent abroad to most European countries at known rates. The British postal authorities in 1875 introduced the slightly larger 'Foreign Post Card' bearing a one-and-a-quarter pence printed stamp, representing half the overseas letter rate.

In May 1890 an official card was introduced to commemorate the Jubilee of the Penny Post, linked to the exhibition at the Guildhall. This card bore the arms of the City of London. Although an official card, it was slightly over the then permitted size and therefore needed the full letter rate of one penny! We were yet again being suffocated by red tape! A very few special commemorative cards were officially printed in the 1890s, including the 1891 Eddystone Lighthouse card sold at the Royal Naval Exhibition held at Chelsea Hospital (see plate 21). It bears a special cancellation indicating that it was franked at the small post office atop the replica lighthouse. The novelty of such commemorative cards is underlined by the fact that they were sold at a shilling each—a large sum in those days. As with later examples, the special related July 1891 postmark adds interest and value. Indeed, they became early collector's items. The editor of *The Picture Postcard* wrote of these in 1901 as the most 'interesting and valuable in my collection'. An example was privately advertised for sale in the December 1901 issue—'great rarity, what offers'.

After years of campaigning, chiefly by John Henniker-Heaton, Member of Parliament for Canterbury, the British post office permitted printed postcards to be issued without the printed prepaid stamp. The good news was communicated to the trade in the 30 August 1894 issue of the *Stationery Trades Journal*, where it was recorded under the heading:

THE "WILTSHIRE TIMES" COMPANY
(LIMITED).

39, Market Place, Devizes, *Nov 10th* 1877

Sir,

I beg respectfully to solicit your order for the insertion of your Advertisement *John Moore decd*

in the "Wiltshire Times," which has attained so high a position among all Classes as to justify the assertion that it is without a rival as a County Organ. It incorporated the "Wiltshire Independent," established in 1836, and has met with a success almost unparalleled in the history of the provincial press.

It circulates among the Nobility, Clergy, Gentry Professional, Trading, and Agricultural Classes in Wiltshire, and to a large extent among the same classes in the neighbouring counties of Somersetshire, Gloucestershire, Hampshire, Dorsetshire, Berkshire, and the Western and South Western counties generally. Few provincial newspapers have a richer or wider circle of readers, so that advertisers appealing to the monied classes of the Western counties, and those wishing to bring their announcements before the best families of those districts, have in its columns one of the most effective mediums of publicity that can be found.

Your obedient Servant,

HENRY BARRASS,

Editor and Manager.

20
A 1877 pre-printed advertisement card, used by the editor of the *Wiltshire Times*.

The New Post Card Scheme

It has now been arranged that from 1st of September next the public will have the privilege of sending through the Inland post, as post cards, private cards bearing halfpenny adhesive stamps. The following are the regulations:
The cards must be composed of ordinary cardboard, not thicker than the materials used for the official post card. The maximum size must correspond as nearly as may be to the size of the ordinary post card now in use. The minimum size must be not less than 3¼ x 2¼ and the card must not be folded ...
Now that the size has been definitely decided, stationers can go ahead in producing suitable cards, and as a good field is offered, no doubt some very excellent goods will shortly be on the market.

Worthing had available a set of local-view cards within five weeks of the concession being granted. Some three months after the date when the public were given the 'privilege' of sending private postcards through the post, the regulations were further eased, for from 21 January 1895, the 'court-shape' postal stationery cards could be used. These rather 'chunky' correspondence cards had previously been used within an envelope but now they could be used as postcards attracting half the standard letter postage rate. They may have been so used from September 1894.

21
The special printed view card issued at the 1891 Royal Naval Exhibition. This bears a special elaborate Eddystone Lighthouse cancellation and was aimed at the collector.

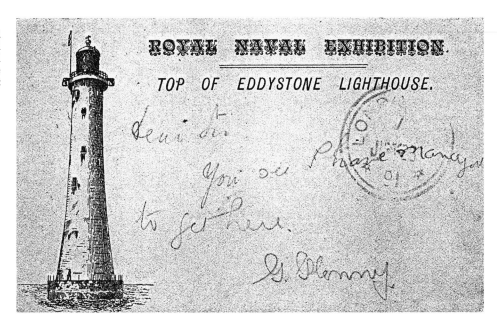

These court cards were squarer than the narrow official cards, measuring 3½ x 4½ ins. As such they were smaller than most continental postcards, but the court cards remained the standard British format until a larger size was introduced in November 1899. Typical British court-size cards are shown in plates 22-4, 28 and 36-41.

There remains some debate as to which firm first issued pictorial-view postcards to be sold locally at tourist resorts as a form of greeting card, similar to the earlier popular continental colourful 'Gruss aus' cards. Currently, in the mid-1990s, the honour is being given to Messrs. E.T.W. Dennis of Scarborough, based on recent researches by Mr. George Webber, a specialist collector of early British postcards. His findings were first published in *Picture PostCard Monthly* of October 1992 and, after correspondence published in the same magazine, Mr. Webber's views were restated in the centenary issue of September 1994 under the title, 'It all started here ...'. Mr. Webber's findings, based on the earliest postally-used local-view postcards known to present-day collectors, are now generally accepted.

The first-known Dennis of Scarborough picture postcards were, naturally enough, two coastal scenes of Scarborough, showing artist-drawn (not photographic-based) printed views of Scarborough's North Bay with castle, and one of the South Bay. Other local-view cards may have been issued to make up a linked set of six, but as yet no other 1894 Scarborough cards have been reported. One postally-used Scarborough card in Mr. Webber's collection is dated 15 September 1894 and was sent to Miss Queenie Cooke in Willesden. The message on this historic first-recorded British resort card reads simply:

Dear Queenie,
      Hope everything is alright. We are. We have walked about all morning. Love to all.
      Your loving
      L L

Yes, just the sort of inconsequential message that would be sent to millions of other folk from seaside resorts all around the kingdom from that day onwards. Keeping in touch with family or loved ones, showing they were not forgotten but that the sender was lucky enough to have afforded a seaside holiday. Messages that could mean so much but which cost a trifle.

These first greetings postcards were rather drab, being printed from original pen and ink drawings without added colour, but they were well designed, leaving room for the message to be added to the picture side. The design also incorporated the wording 'Greetings from Scarborough', and small, almost hidden, initials of the publishers, 'EWD'. In all but colour they closely emulated the earlier continental 'Gruss aus' postcards. They also slightly predated the court-shape British card which was permitted from January 1895. These early Dennis cards were slightly longer and narrower than the tubby court cards. As research and interest in early postcards increase we may well discover other 1894 or 1895 Dennis postcards; already Mr. Webber has found an 1895 card of Whitby, and others may be around. Such early examples predate the collecting of such trifles, so that few, if any, were preserved in albums, but were discarded after a few days of life!

In George Webber's September 1994 *Picture PostCard Monthly* article he makes the interesting claim that Messrs. Dennis are the longest-established surviving postcard publisher in Britain, if not the world! It all started with two black and white seaside greetings cards back in 1894. The firm is certainly still very active in the postcard business today and, to mark the centenary in 1994 of the first British picture cards, the present firm of Dennis Print & Publishing issued an interesting set of Scarborough cards, including a copy of Mr. Webber's 1894 card to Queenie. Alas, the old cards had to be borrowed from collectors, for the Scarborough works were destroyed by enemy action in March 1941 when all the records and samples were destroyed—the fate of many London-based publishers also.

The information given on these early Dennis local-view cards is recent and results from the research of one interested collector. Two standard reference books, however, both suggest that this firm first issued postcards in or 'about 1901'. You too can research local postcard publishers and perhaps uncover interesting new facts.

Prior to Mr. Webber's 1992 article it was generally considered that the first British pictorial postcard was issued in summer 1894, when Messrs. George Stewart & Co. of Edinburgh introduced cards bearing a small printed view of that Scottish city which were soon accepted by the postal authorities as being legally entitled to the reduced postal rate of one halfpenny. Apart from George Stewart, other firms including Messrs. Corketts of Leicester later claimed the honour of producing the first British postcard, in or about 1894, but the earliest British cards seldom bore a credit, making present-day research very difficult.

In an interview given to *The Picture Postcard* magazine in September 1900 Mr. J.G. Bowerbank, the manager of George Stewart's London agency, stated:

> The idea of publishing pictorial post cards occurred to us after having issued note paper bearing views and this idea was put into execution immediately after the postal authorities allowed post cards to be made by private firms ... and during September 1894 we published a set of views of Edinburgh by process blocks and we followed this up with view cards of towns in Scotland by lithography. We have customers' invoices dated September 1894, proving that our cards were on sale in the shops during that month ...

They would now be a rare and most desirable find.

It would appear that Worthing too was in the vanguard of postcard design. Walter Gardiner, a local photographer, was a pioneer in the introduction of continental-style photographic-based local-view cards in Great Britain. He designed a set of at least eleven related local-view postcards, featuring at least forty small vignetted photographic local views (*see* Chapter VI). This set had been produced by the first week in October 1894, only five weeks after privately published cards

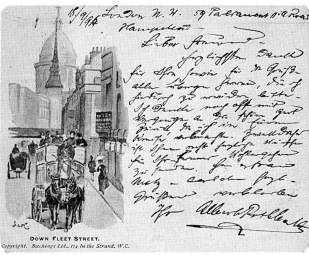

22
Two early British court-size London-view cards issued by Beechings Ltd. in 1895.

were first permitted by the British post office. A start had obviously been made in this great trade yet the issues of the aptly named *Stationery Trades Journal* only contain references and advertisements relating to plain (non-pictorial) postcards up to the issue of May 1895. But then we find a rather belated first reference to British pictorial cards:

'Every Day' Post Cards

Messrs. Beechings Ltd., 174 Strand, London W.C., have just brought out a novel idea in post cards. The cards are in Court 8VO shape and have the usual printing on the address side, while the reverse has different designs printed in colour. These designs consist of 'clean your Boots, Sir' with a portion of the London Pavilion; a policeman on his beat; a view of Oxford Circus, with flower girls; Fleet Street; and sandwich men parading. The cards, which we may also say are of good material, are certainly interesting to Londoners, and should sell well. Supplied in packets of six to retail at 3d. each.

Although the trade announcement stated that these 1895 cards were printed in colour, compared with most continental examples they were very drab. There is only one colour in addition to the main print. I believe that the price of threepence refers to the packet of six cards, but some authorities have stated that each card cost threepence.

Plate 22 shows two slightly different Beeching 'Every Day' London-view cards of this type, both of which were postally-used in 1896.

In the *Stationery Trades Journal* for June 1895, we find a further reference to new picture cards:

View Post Cards

We have received a sample packet of Messrs. Langley & Sons cards—and they are of a high class well finished character. The set sent is devoted to London, and is the first of the 'steel-plate' series. The cards are of good quality, double thick, with a 'fine surface' and give views in varying forms of St Pauls, the Tower, Royal Exchange, &c, worked in a pleasing steel-grey tint. Ten cards in a well displayed wrapper selling at 2d.

Plate 23 is an interesting, early English local-view or rather 'event card'. It is captioned 'The Pier and Prince Consort Gardens, Weston-Super-Mare on Lifeboat Saturday, August 13th 1898'. It was postally-used at Weston on 1 October of that year. It is quite unusual (but not unique) for its period in that a single picture is shown, not several small vignettes. The scene, too, is obviously taken

The Pier and Prince Consort Gardens, Weston-super-Mare,
on Lifeboat Saturday, August 13th, 1898.

23
An early English special-event
card relating to Lifeboat
Saturday at Weston-super-Mare
in August 1898. The address
and stamp have been incorrectly
added to the pictorial side.

from a photograph, not an engraving. I may have introduced a new postcard
category, the 'event card', a term which aptly describes local cards that depict a
special, precisely datable 'happening'.

Reports and advertisements in the *Stationery Trades Journal* are most important,
affording us today a contemporary account of the gradual development of the
postcard industry in this century. I therefore make no apology for including a
selection of extracts from this prime source.

The following from the September 1896 issue, refers to photographic views
especially angled at visitors to the Isle of Wight:

PICTORIAL POST CARDS

Messrs. Rock Bros. Ltd. of 69 Paul Street, Finsbury, EC are producing a
series of cards with views of different localities that are very attractive in
get up, and will doubtless be widely used both by visitors and residents of
the place to which they refer. The latest is devoted to the Isle of Wight,
and each card bears miniature photographs in half-tone, the subjects being
Osborne House, the Needles, and Carisbrooke Castle. These are let-in
upon a graceful floral design which forms a head and side border of a quite
ornamental character. The Pictorial cards are supplied in packets of a
dozen to sell at 3d. and fresh places are being steadily added to the list.

Rock Brothers were, you will recall, one of the leading manufacturers of ornamental
writing papers earlier in the century. These sheets were engraved with various
local views (*see* plates 6 and 7).

Two pictorial cards of the then current small 'court'-size are shown in
plate 24. It will be readily observed that these 19th-century English resort cards
are quite dull, and they certainly compare badly with the more colourful and
larger continental postcards, but the German publishers in particular had an early
lead, as they had not been hidebound by the restrictions imposed for so long by
the British postal authorities.

A series of reports published in the *Stationery Trades Journal* in the 1897-8
period, gives an interesting insight into the development of the postcard trade in
Germany at a time when we in the British Isles had yet to follow the continental
lead, although some dull English cards were being produced. These articles from
the magazine's Berlin correspondent may well have led English publishers and
retailers to join the rush to cash in on the new craze—it was little less than this,
as I explain in the following chapter.

The first 'Berlin letter' to mention very belatedly the continental fashion for
postcards is dated Berlin, 27 April 1897, and appeared in the May issue of the
Stationery Trades Journal:

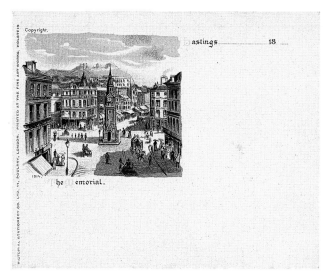
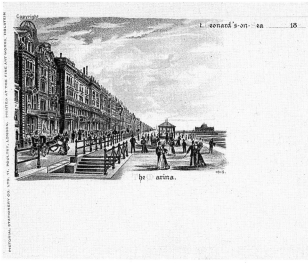

24
Two Pictorial Stationery Company local-view cards with 19th-century year numerals. These court-size cards were printed in Germany for the London publishers.

What could be more prolific than fashion! ... A new craze, for which an appropriate name will of course have to be invented in England should it spread there is now raving wildly in the Fatherland. It consists of the collecting of post cards. These cards chiefly contain views of the places at which they are being sold, and being generally most artistically executed, a collection consisting of specimens from all parts of the world must be very interesting. Special albums can now be bought in which to fix the cards, and they sell largely. Surprise has frequently been expressed to me that English pictorial cards have not yet made their appearance abroad, and I think it is a pity that this new stationery article has not been taken up to any extent by your stationers, as it has proved very profitable for their German colleagues ...

Our writer returns to the subject in the September 1897 issue:

... Pictorial post cards are the only article for which there is now a larger sale than ever, and it is only surprising that the English public has not yet caught on to the line. British tourists on the Continent are using them largely for their correspondence with friends at home, and seem to be especially pleased with those showing artistically executed views in coloured print, a snapshot with figures is then reproduced in photgravure and by similar excellent processes ...

Plates 25-7 show a few colourful continental 'Greetings from ...' or 'Gruss aus' cards of the 1890s. We must not assume that Germany was alone in favouring picture postcards. Indeed the same British trade journal published in its October issue a letter from a French correspondent:

Paris September 30 1897

... Photographic reproductions of views of the principal sites in Paris adorn note paper and post cards and enjoy sale amongst English visitors as I have reason to know, for nearly every acquaintance who comes over from the Mother country is sure to ask me where he can get post cards with views of Paris

Our correspondent returns to the subject of postcards in his letter of 31 May 1898 which reviews the Pictorial Post Card Exhibition then being held.

... The Pictorial post card exhibition is an international one, and it contains more than 10,000 exhibits, but so far as I could ascertain ... not a single English firm is represented, although even Japanese firms were to be found.

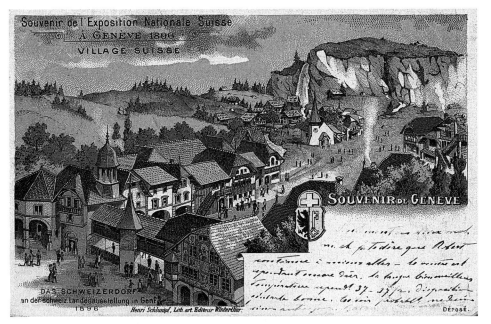

25
A colourful Swiss *carte postale*, a souvenir of the 1896 Swiss National Exhibition at Geneva. Note the very small clear area for the message.

English firms did not, perhaps, see what benefit they could derive from participating, as it is very likely not known to them that collecting such post cards has become quite a craze on the Continent. I have repeatedly been asked by collectors to procure English picture cards for them, and people in the trade here assure me that if the craze were to die out suddenly, the array of the unemployed would at once be swelled by tens of thousands.

The subjects chosen for the embellishment of the cards are chiefly views from town and country, as well as typical figures in national dress representing the different countries ...

In August 1898 the British Consul-General at Frankfurt, Sir Charles Oppenheimer, had reported that the number of postcards posted from 'spots frequented by visitors is enormous'. The Berlin correspondent of the *Stationery Trades Journal*, in a letter from Berlin dated 26 July 1898, gives further information on the spread of the habit:

It is very quiet in Berlin just now ... the only Stationery trade article with which the summer heat and holiday season cannot interfere are the pictorial post cards, which I am afraid have not yet caught on in England.

The illustrated post card craze is no longer confined to Germany and the German speaking nations, but has got hold also of France, Spain, Italy and other countries. German manufacturers, always ready to make hay while the sun shines are therefore now printing such cards suitable for the different nationalities, bearing words of greeting, dedications, or what ever may be in the respective languages. From a price list I have just received, I learn that some enterprising manufacturers, for instance, supply a certain kind of illustrated card with words in twelve different tongues.

In a letter dated 31 October 1898, the Berlin correspondent of the *Stationery Trades Journal* felt that at last his work had borne fruit and that the picture postcard had caught on in the British Isles:

The news that the pictorial post card has, after all, gained a foothold in England, seems to have filled the hearts of many of our manufacturers with the hope that this, new field has been opened for their wares. I have of

26
Two good quality German 'Gruss aus' cards. The top example is die-stamped in relief, *c.*1899.

late repeatedly been consulted as to the most suitable subjects for the embellishment of such cards destined for the English market. It is, however, not easy to give advice in the matter as people here will not understand at present that a great deal of the gaudy, silly and inartistic rubbish in picture post cards which is sold to the German public would never find buyers in London ...

He may have been wrong on this last count! But the postcard craze most certainly spread to these islands; but was it caused by the arrival on British doorsteps of these novel and decorative continental cards, by the business drive of the continental manufacturers and their agents here, or did these 'Berlin letters' supply the impetus?

27
An unstamped German 'Gruss aus' card, bearing only a name and year and as such no doubt purchased and sent with a letter as a gift to a postcard collector.

The German 'Gruss aus' pictorial cards (plates 25-7) were all the rage on the continent. All the cards produced on the continent for that (non-British) trade are full size, the approximate size of a modern postcard. Here in Great Britain we were still restricted until 1898 when an intermediate size was introduced, which measured about 3 x 5 ins. An early intermediate-size London card is illustrated in plate 28 with a court-size London hotel card for comparison.

By at least November 1898 English postcard publishers were issuing night-time view cards and winter scenes. Novelty was being sought, for the unusual sold. Such cards were advertised by Messrs. Geiger & Co. in the November 1898 issue of the *Stationery Trades Journal* to be 'ready in a few days'. A linked editorial notice read:

NEW PICTORIAL POST CARDS

Messrs. Geiger & Co., of 7 Jeffrey's Square, St Mary Axe, are the latest firm to introduce these goods, and they are offering a copyright series of London views in collotype, of a very superior quality. There are 25 different views giving the most popular places and buildings, together with several views that we have not seen reproduced before. These are daylight scenes with the traffic in full swing, but there is also a series by moonlight and, what will very likely prove unusually saleable by reason of their novelty, a set from negatives taken with snow on the ground ... The price is the usual one penny each—Messrs. Geiger's cards are amongst the best at present to be had.

A most important development came into effect on 1 November 1899, when the British post office at last permitted the sale of a larger continental or 'Postal Union'-size card (3½ x 5½ inches) for inland use which was to become the so-called 'standard' size up to recent times. Messrs. Raphael Tuck were the first to issue the new card, having received advance notification of the intended change. It must be remembered, however, that the stock of the old court-size cards was not destroyed and that many manufacturers continued for some considerable time to print on their existing stock of smaller cards.

The majority of the early British-market cards were printed in the German states, although they were often designed in this country and the views—

28
An unused court-size card shown with a narrower, so-called intermediate-size, pre-November 1899 postcard. Both were printed in Germany for the English market.

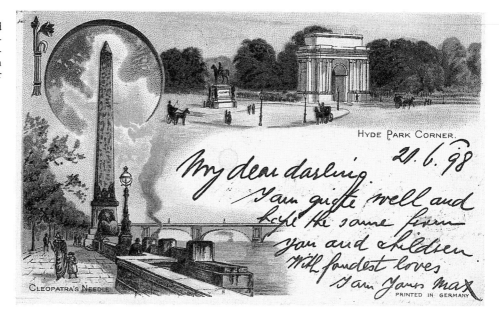

* Mr. Peter Jones, in a most important and interesting article entitled 'How do you define a picture postcard?' published in *Picture PostCard Monthly* of January 1996, has pointed out that from 1897 it was permissible to add a message or small picture to the address side, provided it did not encroach on the stamp area and that the address was clear. However, this fact was seemingly not generally known and the divided-back postcard as we know it today, came into use in the British Isles from January 1902.

photographic, painted or engraved—were supplied from British sources. One therefore often finds double credits such as 'Designed in England. Chromographed in Saxony', which represents a standard early Raphael Tuck form of printed credit.

In one most important respect the British postal authorities led the world for, in January 1902, the prohibition of the addition of any message or other wording on the address side was lifted.* Now the plain address side was divided in two—as it has been ever since—permitting the message and the address to be written there so that the whole of the pictorial side could now be given over to one of tens of thousands of decorative motifs, including splendid views, both British and foreign. It took a little time for cards to be printed and distributed in the new style so that you would be extremely lucky to find a postally-used divided-back card with postmark prior to August 1902. Other countries were somewhat slow to follow our lead; the French authorities in 1904 and the Germans the following year, but the United States of America only awoke to the improvement in October 1907 on the agreement of the Universal Postal Union.

From this point on the postcard remained quite standard in size. However, some of the divided-back printings, from 1902 onwards, may include wording that underlines the novelty of the new position. One example in my collection reads: 'This space, as well as the back, may now be used for Communication, but for inland only'. However, from 1902 the back, or 'view', side seldom had room for any message. As soon as the message could be written on the address side, the newly designed cards made full use of the pictorial side—the old space for the message was taken up with an enlarged illustration.

In September 1915, when Europe was in turmoil and all national and local papers were full of lists of killed and injured servicemen, the Chancellor of the Exchequer, Mr. McKenna, had the temerity to suggest contributing to the costs of war by suspending the halfpenny postal rate for postcards.

This great 'blot on the Budget' aroused public indignation—perhaps more than the threat of Zeppelin raids or of the bombardment of coastal towns. The editor of the *Worthing Mercury* played his part in the outcry. In his issue of Saturday, 25 September 1915, under the heading 'The ½d. Post', he wrote:

> It is becoming increasingly clear that Mr. McKenna has made a bad blunder in proposing to abolish the ½d. post ...
>
> This blunder, if it is put into practice, will not only ruin the post card trade but the Christmas card trade as well, and from these two sources the Government have hitherto derived very considerable revenue.
>
> Printers and Stationers and newspaper proprietors have resolved to place the facts before the Chancellor. Meanwhile, we would urge traders of every class to bombard Mr. McKenna with post cards of protest, so this blot on the budget ... may be removed.

Public outcries regarding budget changes seldom have the desired effect, but in this case the Chancellor did climb down, and in the issue of 16 October the editor returned to the subject:

> A Wise Decision
>
> The proposal to abolish the half-penny postal rates has been dropped—wisely we think –
>
> The announcement made by the Postmaster-General in the House of Commons on Tuesday night (12 October 1915) has been received with great satisfaction in business circles throughout the country.
>
> In view of the disturbance of business arrangement that would be involved by the changes the Government will not proceed with the proposed increases in the post card and half-penny rate ...
>
> Now that the Government have seen the mistake, we must give them credit for yielding gracefully to the wishes of almost the entire nation.

The postcard postage rate remained at a halfpenny; the world was changing daily but the postcard soldiered on, thanks to the support of its allies!

The original halfpenny (a penny for most overseas destinations) postage rate remained constant until June 1918. The basic size remained the norm up to recent times, although most cards are now slightly longer, at about 6 ins., with a greater height of 4 ins. or so. At various times ultra large or very small miniature cards were issued, but these were gimmicks or novelties, which did not effect the mass production of standard-size cards. Soon after 1900 glossy 'real-photographs' views occur, although many were issued with a matt surface. Over the years, of course, the subjects changed, as did the range of available cards. In subsequent chapters I will give details of these developments, and in particular the scope of the ever popular local-view or topographical postcards.

But first, a brief résumé of the key dates, relating to inland use within the British Isles:

Some Helpful Postcard Landmarks

1894 British postcards permitted to be produced without official pre-printed stamps from 1 September. A locally published Scarborough local-view card postmarked 15 September 1894 is at present the earliest known datable specimen.

1895 First British 'court'-shape postcards issued with printed local views. The so-called 'court'-shape or size British cards measured 3½ x 4½ ins. They had been permitted since 1894 but were not in general use before 1895.

November 1899 Larger 'Postal Union'-size postcards permitted by the British postal authorities. These measured 3½ x 5½ ins. and approached in size the standard continental cards.

April 1900 New blue-green Victorian halfpenny stamp replaced the old (1887+) vermillion stamp from 17 April 1900. Therefore cards with the blue-green variety must postdate 17 April 1900. Cards bearing this stamp, lightly postally-used on the day of issue, are of considerable interest from the philatelic point of view.

January 1902 New Edward VII postage stamps issued to replace the former Victorian stamps. Of course, Victorian examples can occur on post-1901 cards whilst stocks lasted, but a card with an Edwardian stamp could not have been published or sold before 1 January 1902.

From January 1902 also the modern form of postcard came into being in the British Isles. The address side was divided in two, providing space on the left for the message which hitherto should have been written on the view side. These new-style 'divided-back' postcards are seldom found before, say, August 1902, as new supplies had to be printed and distributed. Many old-style cards also remained in stock and were used over several years.

Other countries were rather slow to take up the new British divided-back; France followed in 1904, Germany in 1905 and the United States of America in October 1907.

November 1904 The new yellow-green Edward VII halfpenny stamp was issued, replacing the old blue-green version. Examples postmarked on the day of issue, 26 November 1904, command a premium.

June 1911 New issue George V stamps issued on 22 June. The King's hair is darkish.

January 1912 Revised light-hair version of George V halfpenny stamp issued.

June 1918 Old halfpenny postcard postal rate discontinued and rate increased to one penny from 3 June 1918. This remained in force until June 1920 when it was increased to 1½d. It returned, however, to a penny from 29 May to 30 April 1940. From then until 30 September 1957 it was twopence, when the full postage rate was only 2½ old pence; the original half-price concession had, in fact, been discontinued in 1918. Even when a card does not bear a stamp, the printed information in the stamp-box may prove helpful in dating the card.

The regulations relating to the initial half standard letter rate for postcards were quite complicated and were amended from time to time. Basically, nothing could be added to the flat card, other than the design, plus the additional message and address. Some cards, however, carried instructions as to how the card would qualify for the 'printed paper rate' so saving a halfpenny! A typical postcard warning reads:

> If there be any writing beyond sender's name and address and a greeting of five words a penny stamp must be used, otherwise half penny stamp is sufficient, ..

Many types of novelty or souvenir postcard breached the postcard regulations in some way, but in general the application of the full rate—which after all was only a penny—up to 1918 does not seem to have affected sales of popular types of special or novelty cards.

In general, the low value postage stamps on postcards are of no value, although many have been soaked off, presumably by young children starting a (perhaps lifetime) interest in philately. Obviously, some special issues such as the British Empire Exhibition (Wembley 1924 and 1925) have some value but the real rarities may lie in perforation changes or watermark variations. For example the sideways watermarks on the 1929 Postal Union Congress stamps is desirable— I refrain from giving precise values which can vary.

The postmark can also be of interest and value for the postal historian. Postcard collectors worship the postmark as it helps to date the card or view (in fact it only shows the place and date of posting, not of its production) but the postmark can be rare or desirable—a special cancellation perhaps at an exhibition or other event, or it may indicate the first day of issue of the stamp. All these can add greatly to the interest and value of an otherwise ordinary postcard. There is, therefore, a commercial value in large numbers of dross or otherwise unsaleable cards, as they are sold by the trade at so much a thousand to folk who check the stamps and postmarks for desirable variations. I would not, however, advise a non-postal historian or advanced philatelist to purchase postcards for the stamps they bear; it is the postcard that matters!

Chapter III

The Collecting Mania

'Dear Old Girl, I heard you liked post-cards. I am sending you one. I can't get a colour one of Brighton ...'
(Coloured London-view card, posted in Brighton in September 1901)

'I thought you would like a card for your album' (1901)

As these and hundreds of other written postcard messages show, many cards were purchased solely to be added to a collection—for this was an extremely popular hobby. Clearly, those cards bearing this type of message were purchased by one person to be sent to another collector. Except, that is, for a few keen collectors like Anny, who in July 1899 wrote to her Auntie Clara:

> Thank you so much for taking us out. We got home quite safely. <u>Please</u> will you send me back this post card ...

Poor Aunt Clara—the return post, presumably in an envelope, would have cost her a penny, probably more than the cost of the rather dull Arundel view in this early Valentine's postcard.

In the majority of cases, cards purchased for one's own album would be added in an unused state, merely for the pretty or interesting picture. The extent of the craze can be gauged from the large numbers of Edwardian postcards that can be found in this unused state. They were purchased for the postcard album, not to send a postal message. Postcard albums became part of home furnishings, to be brought out and shown off as some folk today inflict their holiday snaps or cine films on unlucky guests!

The Berlin correspondent of the English *Stationery Trades Journal*, who wrote in 1897 that the British had not yet caught on to this continental craze, may not have been wholly correct. An interesting earlier message, reported in the March 1994 issue of *Picture PostCard Monthly*, appeared on a Sandle Bros. 'Greetings from London'-view card with the postmark date: 24 September 1896. It bore the message 'I believe these postcards are some of the first ones out in England I saw them in London the other day ... so I bought them to send over to you as I expect you collect them too'. The modern correspondent doubted whether a September 1896 London-view card could be regarded as amongst the earliest produced, but I find this credible for these Europe-produced Sandle Bros. cards, or for any British view cards. The main interest in this 1896 example is the mention of collecting.

The British picture postcard had certainly very much 'arrived' by at least 1898. By the start of the Edwardian era in 1901 it had been fully accepted and a vast selection was being produced both here and on the continent. They were being sold in extraordinary numbers.

In August 1899, a writer in London's *Standard* newspaper was able to report:

> The illustrated post card craze, like the influenza has spread to these islands from the Continent, where it has been raging with considerable severity. Sporadic cases have occurred in Britain. Young ladies ... have been known to fill albums with missives of this kind received from friends abroad; but now the cards are being sold in this country and it could be like the letting out of waters ...

Very many British cards and their messages bear witness to the fashion for collecting postcards. The attractive and well-produced Raphael Tuck 'Hastings rough-sea' card (plate 29), for example, bears the simple message: 'I thought you would like this for your collection, don't you think it is very pretty'. It was sent in May 1904 simply for someone's (Miss Elsie Wall's) collection, and that is why it is still in existence today.

Why, one may ask, were postcards being collected, when other articles were not? Telegram forms, which also bore a brief message, have never—as far as I am aware—been collected; *cartes de visite*, even when featuring interesting photographic views, held but brief interest; colourful Christmas cards were not mounted in albums; even the delightful Victorian Valentine cards, although admittedly now

29
A typically good quality
Raphael Tuck heraldic and
local-view card of the type
made for most popular resorts.
Produced in Bavaria, it was
postally-used in May 1904
when sent to a young lady
postcard collector.

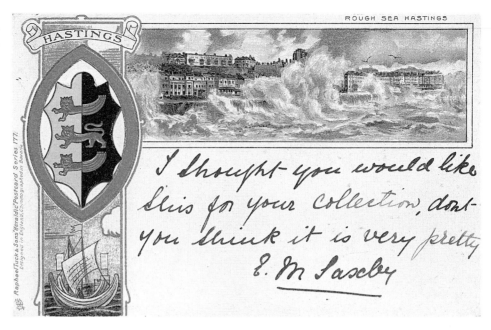

very collectable, did not inspire the lasting or wide interest occasioned by later picture postcards.

Frederick Corkett (of Tuck's), in a lecture delivered to the Royal Society of Arts in April 1906, asked much the same question—why are postcards so collectable? He attributed their popularity to the local views depicted:

> Illustrated postcards have, to a great extent, taken the place of the photographic print trade, for, whereas tourists were accustomed at one time to buy a dozen or two silverprints of each district visited, now the penny postcard takes the place of the view and answers the same purpose, and at a much less cost. Here, therefore, is perhaps the greatest reason for the popularity of the view postcard, and as this section of the postcard trade is its backbone and mainstay, I see reason to think it will always remain so. Valentine cards have come and gone, Christmas cards are still with us and likely to be, but the popularity of the picture postcard will outlast either.

Incidentally, this leading figure in the British postcard trade also noted:

> On my holiday last year 1905 I was really astounded at the length to which the 'craze' had gone. At every station, from Paris to Venice, postcards were on view, and wherever opportunity offered hawkers came along the carriages offering excellent cards, showing, of course, the local views. At the first station after the passing the Mont Cenis Tunnel in the early morning, two earnest-eyed lads were waiting for the train, each laden with postcards for our examination. At the hotel in Venice the first person we saw was addressing postcards as for dear life, and the intimation that the hall porter had a fine selection of postcards was still ringing in our ears while we gazed at that marvellous enchanting sight, St Mark's, a few yards away.

Of Victorian paper-based inventions and passing delights, only the postage stamp was taken seriously as a subject for collecting, and even this might have had financial undertones: the prospect of making a profit from one's investment. Philately was mainly a male preserve. Postcard collecting, or rather 'cartophilia' or 'cartophily' to use early terms for it, was largely a female hobby. The old term for a collector which *has* survived, at least in America, is 'deltiologist', but British collectors tend to shun this mouthful!

There can be no doubt that from soon after 1900 the collecting of postcards swept the country. This fashion undoubtedly spread from Germany or German-speaking nations, where in the 1890s it was hard to walk the streets, sit in a cafe or travel by train without being accosted by postcard sellers. Even postmen sold a selection of postcards from trays whilst carrying their postbag on their back. A drawing in the *Illustrated London News* of 2 October 1909 shows a postman as a 'walking stationer and Letter-box', selling his cards from an 'ice-cream' tray, whilst ladies are sitting around writing brief messages on their newly-purchased cards.

By the late 1890s every developed country was producing decorative postcards of good quality. They became an international industry. The number of picture postcards produced in the early years of the 20th century was quite staggering: in 1904, 734 million postcards were sent (quite apart from those that went straight into collections in a mint state). One wonders how the postal service coped with such a flood of postcards in addition to the normal mail.

Many cards bear only a name and address—no further message nor writing. These were obviously intended for a collector or a collection. Many others are unused, without a written message or address. These were often chosen by the collector, not sent to him or her by a friend. However, as so many unused postcards exist even from early periods, it is possible that many of these unstamped cards were sent to a collector in an envelope, perhaps with a letter explaining that the cards were for 'the collection'. The postcards would be added to the album and the letter discarded. In most collections there is a surprising number of postcards which were not posted, but purchased to be added to the album just as mint stamps were added to a collection. I have purchased complete albums of mint postcards, originally purchased for the family postcard album.

These fashionable albums have turned out to be a mixed blessing, as with old postage stamp albums. They preserved the cards in a flat state and kept the coloured cards away from sunlight. But, just as old stamp mounts or hinges damaged the back of a stamp, so the cut corners in the postcard album over the years have left their mark or slight impression near each corner of the card. Some tinted album pages have also tended slightly to discolour a card, especially if the album has become slightly damp. Still, on balance albums did more good than harm; the corner marks were usually caused when albums were stored flat, perhaps with weighty books or other articles on top. Albums should be stood upright, so that there is no pressure on the contents.

On the continent, in particular, postcard collectors formed clubs. Examples of cards were exchanged. These 'sendings' and 'swops' reached a surprisingly large number of collectors in various countries, and special exhibitions of postcards were held, and advertising postcards were issued. Plate 30 concerns the club day, in May 1899, of the central club of collectors of view postcards.

An international exhibition of picture postcards was held in the rue Bonaparte, Paris, in September 1900. Some 150,000 cards from all parts of the world were on view. One would like to see a recreation of this 1900 display today.

The Victorian period saw the publication of the specialist British magazine *The Picture Postcard* in July 1900. This was edited by E.W. Richardson, who was also to publish *The Post-card Collectors Handbook*. Within a year the monthly magazine was reduced to a penny an issue and was available from railway and other bookstands. It contained articles and notes on postcards from a wide variety of countries and did much to popularise postcard collecting.

Apart from publishers' advertisements and notices of new issues which are now of great interest to specialist collectors, the magazine published lists of private

30
A rare Austrian postcard relating to the local-view postcard collectors club in May 1899. The collecting craze was then all the rage on the Continent but had not as yet spread to the British Isles.

collectors, mostly female, who wished to exchange cards. For example Miss Fox at Littlehampton, Sussex, wished to exchange 'English cards for foreign and colonial, stamped on illustrated side'. Various other swappers also requested that the illustrated side bear the stamp, in the continental fashion. Several stipulated that the cards must bear the postmark of the town depicted, but others required 'cards to be sent under wrapper and not written upon'. Sets of these and other cards from early collections are now scarce and costly, but of great interest to researchers and postal historians.

Yet, for all the help given to the hobby and the promotion of the production of quality British cards it must be admitted that the British postcard market failed to reach the heights that it did on the continent. An American, Julian Ralph, wrote in 1901 of his impressions of the trade in Germany:

> In one celebrated German watering place, where all the shops are upon a single long street, every third window displays these cards for sale, yet I do not remember that any two shops showed similar cards. Only a few displayed cards of a similar class or order ...
> Germany is the land of the souvenir postal card and the Germans and Austrians appear to use these cards almost as freely as the foreign tourists ... I saw them writing on these cards everywhere—in the railway cars and stations, in the beer halls and restaurant-gardens, in the shops and, indeed, in any place where pen or pencil could be had.

This same American observer played down the British card, writing:

> In England one sees pictures of St Pauls, the Tower, the Tower Bridge, Temple Bar and indeed all the noble landmarks, a collection of military types and an especial type seen nowhere else—illuminated cards, that show buildings and streets which when the card is held against the light, appear to be suffused with the glow of many lamps* ... one does not look for such a variety of beautiful, often artistic cards as the German, the French, the Dutch and the Italians produce ...

However, many British cards can be very tasteful and well produced, indeed many were manufactured, colour-printed or relief-impressed by the same firm that

* The cut-out 'hold to light' type cards mentioned by Julian Ralph as seen only in England were in fact introduced and issued by W. Hagelberg of Berlin, under patent 88077. Most relate to London and major cities but some provincial views were issued, including some for Worthing. Others certainly were issued for continental cities and fashionable resorts, such as Wiesbaden. These cut-outs were popular novelties in the early years of the century but most were adapted standard views. One can therefore find normal and pierced 'hold to light' versions of the same card. Most were probably used in the period 1901-5.

printed the best continental examples. The cards produced by or for Messrs. Raphael Tuck are excellent products and the company was rightly awarded a royal warrant. This London-based firm also did much to foster postcard collecting in this country. One of Tuck's successful ideas that helped materially to promote collection was to organise national competitions with very worthwhile prizes. The prizes benefited the winners and Tuck's, who must have sold tens of thousands of their cards as a result. Tuck cards were purchased by thousands of folk seeking to amass the largest collection. Obviously, very few won the prizes, but many collected up to five hundred, a thousand, or more cards—the total sold is incalculable.

The first Tuck £1,000 competition was due to close on 31 December 1901, but was in fact extended until 25 February 1902; the next opened on 1 March. By the 1905 competition, the prizes had been increased to £3,000. Apart from the prizes which Tuck's gave to collectors, this leading firm also made money awards to the trade for their window displays of Tuck postcards. It is quite amazing how many outlets there were in every town and village for postcards. Shops, stores, cafés, hairdressers—everybody seems to have a hand in retailing postcards, which took up little room, were in great demand and were profitable. The ready availability of the cards helped to stimulate demand for them. Many Tuck postcards advertised these competitions for cash prizes for those buying or collecting Tuck's postcards, one of which is shown in plate 31.

Messrs. Raphael Tuck were great publicists; they used to send selections of their new cards to local newspapers and journals with a publicity blurb underlining their leading rôle in the fast-growing industry. Here is as an example of the review published by the *Worthing Gazette* in February 1903:

31
One of many special Tuck postcards advertising this leading firm's postcard competitions and their very worthwhile rewards.

Pictorial Postcards
Successfully meeting Continental Competition

We have received from Messrs. Raphael Tuck & Sons Ltd, a copious assortment of their popular pictorial postcards. It is but a comparative short time ago that these illustrated missives were introduced, yet already the number sold runs into millions, and this one firm alone have more than trebled their output during the last twelve months, and they confidently anticipate the home demand will approach if not exceed, that which prevails for this favourite form of postcard on the Continent.

The artistic merits of the cards produced by Messrs. Tuck have become so well recognised that they are already in a position to successfully compete on the Continent against the home product, and quite recently a Vienna firm placed a first order for half a million cards. In connection with this extensive branch of the business Messrs. Tuck have originated a £2,000 prize competition for collectors of their postcards, particulars of which are furnished with the packets ...

These samples obviously fell on fertile ground and resulted in the desired publicity. Perhaps, however, the free publicity is not so surprising, as the retail shop run by the publishers of the *Worthing Gazette* stocked and sold Tuck's postcards!

Worthing was most certainly not the only town to receive a selection of Tuck postcards for reviews or publicity in the local press. The firm's 1903 price-list devotes its back page to a wide selection of brief quotations from various papers, including *The Scotsman*, *The Irish Times* and *The Times*. Journals that responded include *Woman's Life*, *The Field* and *The Gentlewoman*. These were stated to be a few extracts from 'upwards of 3,000 Notices on Raphael Tuck & Sons' Picture Post-Cards'. Not a bad publicity harvest.

The Tuck hand-outs on occasion were open to question. The notice published in April 1905, for example, incorrectly claimed that the firm were 'pioneers' in the trade:

MESSRS. TUCK'S MOST RECENT POSTCARDS

The latest illustration afforded by Messrs. Raphael Tuck & Sons Ltd., of successful design and execution in pictorial postcards is to be found in what is termed the 'Wide Wide World' series. The numerous sets in the series are reproduced in the firm's famous 'Oilette' process direct from either an original oil painting or water colour drawing, and reach a high level of excellence as is to be expected from such a source ...

The firm, who are the pioneers in this really marvellous industry, are now conducting their huge competition, the generosity of their operations being indicated in the fact that the prize list has this time been increased to £3,000.

The educational value of postcards now receives the fullest recognition.

All good free publicity for Tuck's and for the sale of postcards in general. But, by 1906 the editor was, one fancies, getting a little tired of publishing reviews of Tuck's new issues:

More of Tuck's Postcards

Such fertility of resource is exhibited by Messrs. Raphael Tuck & Sons Ltd, in the production of their world-renowned pictorial postcards, and so high a standard of excellence is attained, that it is difficult to find fresh phrases to express one's appreciation—'Perfection' seems to be the most apt expression to apply to the latest specimens that have reached us.

They are veritable artistic gems, and readily command the unequivocal delight of all who devote themselves to the increasingly popular cult of the collection of postcards.

It is not necessary to enumerate the several sets comprised in the latest productions of Raphael House, but mention must necessarily be made of six exquisitely coloured heads, after Asti, from the Paris Salon ...

The famous Oilette postcards of the firm, which enjoy a really phenomenal popularity in every part of the world, are represented by a number of new and interesting series, among which 'The Rise of our Empire Beyond the Seas' and 'British Battles' have a special claim to historical value. We have the educational use of postcards illustrated in a series like 'British Birds and their Eggs', whilst it may be noted that the popular 'Wide Wide World' series has been appreciably enriched, the most recent additions comprising views and subjects extended from the Continent of Europe to the far-off British Colonies.

Messrs. Tuck & Sons are simply unapproachable in their own particular line ...

The Tuck or Tuck-related publicity blurbs often emphasised the collector's interest at the expense of the postcards' basic practical use. For example, the editor's comments on Tuck's new series of 'Oilette' Pageant postcards, featured in the *Worthing Gazette* of 26 June 1907,

> These cards, whilst they cannot but enhance the already high reputation of Tucks, will prove interesting to collectors as illustrating a popular phase of social doings.

The large firms, such as Tuck's and Stanley Gibbons, also produced (or had produced in Germany) series of decorative postcard albums. The variety in size, capacity, shape and design of these albums is quite extraordinary. The market was there and collectors were being catered for.

For collectors there were also magazines to give advice on collecting, to give notice of new issues, of competitions, and in general to help to spread and foster the hobby. They may not have continued for many years (*see* Bibliography) but in the early 1900s they were popular publications. These British postcard collectors' magazines also carried advertisements and requests for contacts with fellow collectors. My 1900 card of the officers' quarters, Whittington Barracks, was seemingly sent in response to such a request. The message is: 'I should like to exchange post cards with you. Hilda Franklyn'.

The vast majority of early postcard collectors were true amateurs. They sought out and preserved their cards for pleasure, rather than for profit. Some collectors with several full albums probably had not purchased any of the cards themselves. In a few instances it was suggested that a profit could be gained from the purchase of some cards, but this was probably to boost the demand. Most cards were initially purchased singly or in packets of six or a dozen, yet by at least 1903 it was possible to purchase bulk lots or even whole collections from well-known dealers.

Messrs. Stanley Gibbons, the internationally respected stamp dealers with premises in the Strand in London and on Broadway in New York, took a costly full-page advertisement in the leading collectors' magazine *The Connoisseur* of March 1903. In this they advertised unique collections of stamps (priced up to 5,500 guineas) as well as packets of stamps 'for young people': 1,000 varieties for £1; 2,000 for £10 10s. 0d. and so on. This firm of stamp dealers also offered unused, mint, postcards, for example: '392 Postcards of Great Britain and the Colonies, all different, £4. 1005 Postcards of Foreign Countries, all different, £8 10s. 0d.'.

We have no way of telling what type of postcard was offered at less than two and a half old pence each in 1903, but probably the postcards offered better, long-term profit than the packets of 'young people' stamps at a fraction of that price. (Incidentally, Messrs. Stanley Gibbons temporarily returned to the postcard market in the 1970s and '80s and published annual postcard catalogues under their name.)

The original craze coincided with the Edwardian era (1901-10), and was helped along by many amusing cards gently poking fun at postcard collectors. I think the 'postcard collecting' card sent to Miss Maggie Parry in May 1905 is great fun. The desolate-looking young postcard collector is saying 'Only a wretched cheque and Uncle promised to send a Pictorial P.C.' The written message states only 'Dear Maggie. I hope this will fill a corner in your album. Kind Regards'. This card is not rare, it was a popular subject sent as a mild joke to many young female collectors.

Postcard collecting was respectable. I have owned several albums which were given as prizes to star pupils at Sunday schools. Normally such institutions might give bibles, volumes of Shakespeare or some other accepted classic; in the 1900s postcard albums joined the list of other accepted and acceptable small rewards for good work or behaviour. I even have an album given by the Borough

32
Two typically decorative mock oil-paintings by A.R. Quinton (signed with the initials 'A.R.Q.'), reproduced and published by J. Salmon of Sevenoaks, c.1915-25. Standard popular views are not costly.

of Worthing Education Committee to a young lady attending my own 'elementary' school in 1909. She won this award for 'Perfect attendance and Good conduct during the year ending 31st March 1909'. Young Clarice made very good use of that album, too. It contained some very interesting local-subject cards; several of which are featured in this book. Think what we might have missed should she have blotted her copy-book!

In the early 1900s many folk, more often than not girls or young ladies, were introduced to postcard collecting at quite a young age and the hobby remained with them for several years. Many probably gave up when the novelty wore off, or when an album was full, or when postcards generally became less interesting.

How were these albums compiled? There is no simple answer; each is unique. No two albums will contain the same selection of cards. Most 'collections'

THE BROADWAY, WORTHING

33
Two further very decorative Salmon postcards, mass-produced from original oil-paintings by A.R. Quinton and signed with his initials.

SALVINGTON MILL Nr WORTHING

were random gatherings of miscellaneous picture postcards sent by family or friends. Today, for convenience, we divide all cards into various types, categories or classifications. Catalogues use these divisions, and many collectors now specialise in one category or subdivision of that class. When the average original collection was being built up, however, few worried about classification. A postcard was a pretty object to be slipped into the album—few would have been discarded as being without interest or not worthy of inclusion in the collection.

An album started in 1905 or 1910 would therefore contain a very varied selection. I have been thumbing through several old postcard albums that I purchased direct from the original family, which consequently are probably in their original state. As one would expect, most of the cards are views: picture postcards of seaside resorts, of popular country views or of London tourist sites. These cards are mass-produced. They are highly interesting historical pictures but do not demonstrate variety.

34
A locally produced picture postcard showing the village of Rustington as it was in 1860, 50 years before this card was purchased in 1910. This scene is found in matt and glossy finish. Nostalgic but rather unwanted in collecting terms.

The old mixed album would also contain photographic cards of once well-known and popular actors and actresses; a few theatrical subjects or even cards advertising individual plays; many art reproductions, that is, photographic copies of famous paintings or sculpture. Royalty, British and foreign, were very popular subjects with postcard manufacturers and were saleable over a long period.

More fun are the very many subjects including children and animals; these can be charming. Many cards are floral (again not in general demand today); or reproductions of oil-paintings or water-colours painted especially for the postcard publishers. These are usually very picturesque (if not accurate representations of the scene), for only the most saleable would have been chosen for reproduction. Most of this type bear the signature or initials of the artist, some of whom, like A.R. Quinton (plates 32-3), were extremely prolific.

A.R. Quinton (1853-1934) covered an amazing amount of ground, it is believed, painting well over 2,000 views especially for the postcard market, at a fee of five pounds per view. Most were published as postcards by Messrs. J. Salmon of Sevenoaks in Kent. The full credit appears on the address side, with the artist's name or initials 'A.R.Q.' on the front. Several other firms, including Tuck's, reproduced long series of water-colours or oil-paintings, often enhanced with mock brush-strokes. They can be very decorative and inexpensive.

Many cards, especially those in a child's collection, will be of the greetings type. Floral cards with birthday wishes, cards celebrating Christmas or, more rarely, New Year and Easter—all were sent in large numbers and many were proudly mounted in an album.

Certain popular cards, however, do not often appear in a child's album. Most comic, seaside-humour or cheeky cards were sent to adults who would better understand the point. Likewise, cards showing semi- or complete nudity were not included in family albums that might be passed round the drawing or living room. Such cards might now be classified as 'glamour' or 'art studies' and are popular with many collectors.

In general, the average collector seeking to fill her album would not bother with the many novelty cards (*see* Chapter VI) issued by publishers to attract buyers for such fancies. These (often thick) novelty cards with extra units affixed were not really suited to being slipped into an album. Likewise the larger than average card and the small mini-cards would not fit the standard-size cut-corner mounting. The casual collector sought attractive colourful standard-size pictorial cards. This usually meant mass-produced local-view cards, penny cards posted for a mere halfpenny.

Although postcard collecting swept the country, we must remember that not all cards were preserved. The basic object of a postcard was always to relay a message; most cards were purchased for this purpose and were discarded when they were received. Most cards that remain with us today were 'collected' or otherwise preserved.

The postcards in my collection or in yours, which illustrate this or any other book, owe their survival to various factors. They may have been especially meaningful to somebody, depicting the collectors or friends, their home or road. They may remind them of a happy holiday, an interesting tour or journey. They may just have been interesting for no known reason. They may well have lain neglected in an album since before the First World War. How fortunate are local or social historians that this craze spread from Europe to engulf our own kingdom, so preserving such evidence of our parents' or grandparents' times.

We collect old cards mainly for such nostalgic views of the past. This is not by any means new—many cards of the early 1900s depict engravings, drawings or paintings of scenes that were old or quaint to Edwardian buyers. One such postcard of nearby Rustington as it was in 1860 is plate 34. It is natural to look back to the 'good old days', even if they were in some respects rather primitive.

'I am enclosing you this P.C. for your collection. I hope you have not got it already'
(Hastings beach scene, April 1902)

'Ow many Post Cards 'ave you now in yr halbum'
(Russian card, sent to England in 1900)

Chapter IV

The Popular Local-View Card

'I am sending you a PC of Worthing to let you know that I haven't forgotten you.'

'I don't think I've sent you this one before, but it's a job to get views except what I've sent you, especially as the season for views hasn't started yet.'

I have already told you a little of my south coast home town—Sunny Worthing. We can now examine the postcard scene in this medium-size seaside town. We are concerned primarily with local-view or topographical cards, the main class of card sold locally but by no means the only type (*see* Chapter VI). In fact, tradespeople and others sending only a commercial message or request would use inexpensive plain or blank postcards available from post offices or stationers. Some leading tradespeople may well have printed their own cards with publicity material. Such cards, as shown in plate 35, can be very interesting but they are not pictorial and were not usually added to a postcard album. They are, consequently, now quite scarce.

One must remember that postcards were very low-priced commodities, selling retail at a penny or less. The producers, publishers, or wholesalers (often different people or firms) had to sell very large quantities in order to recoup their costs and gain a profit. Consequently, London and other large cities or very popular tourist centres were covered by the picture postcard manufacturers before they spread to the smaller towns or less popular centres. Some ninety per cent of early British cards were concerned with local views.

Two typical London-view court-size cards are shown in plate 36. Both were posted in 1897. Both characteristically bear small views or vignettes, were colour-printed in Saxony and were published by the London firm of Sandle Brothers. That showing views of the Tower of London and the 'New Tower Bridge' is rather unusual as it includes the printed 'Gruss aus'-type wording, 'Greeting from London'. This card is also interesting because, although a London card, it was written and posted in Cambridge in November 1897. One might suggest that at this relatively early date for British postcards Sandle Brothers and other publishers had not yet covered such university towns as Oxford or Cambridge.

Indeed, part of that card's message to Miss Anna Chaderton reads: 'I have got a local stationer to invest in a stock of Cambridge postcards, when they come out you shall have one'. Whether the writer, J.W. Iliffe, was really instrumental in spreading view cards to Cambridge in November 1897, we shall probably never know. But undoubtedly this message on an early London vignetted postcard adds great interest.

The London publisher Sandle Brothers was founded by two brothers from East Anglia in 1893. They were wholesale stationers, but were amongst the pioneering English publishers of view postcards. Their name normally occurs on cards which were printed in Saxony. The example shown in plate 36 and postally-used in September 1897 bears the printed reference number 614, which may refer to the printer's records rather than those of Sandle Brothers. Information on the cost of later Sandle Brothers' cards is given on page 52.

By 1897 London-view cards were becoming quite plentiful—the market was well established. The postcard catalogues list similar cards being postally-used in 1895 and 1896, priced at a now considerable premium. Any pictorial card postally-used between September 1894 (the first officially permitted period) and 31 December 1894 is catalogued at over two hundred pounds—rarities indeed—if such 1894 examples still exist!

I would also draw attention to the fact that the vignetted card dated 22 September 1897 (plate 36) is written in French and was sent to a French address—being sent overseas it correctly bears a one penny stamp. It is perhaps surprising how many of these early cards were sent abroad.

1897 is not a particularly early date for London-view cards but it is very early for provincial examples, and certainly for south coast resort cards. The earliest datable nationally produced Worthing card that I had traced up to 1996 is shown in plate 37. (I have since learned that a locally produced set of photograph-based

35 *(right)*
A 1900 business postcard used by a leading local baker. Such cards were rarely preserved in collections or albums and are consequently rare. Nevertheless they have only limited appeal.

36 *(below)*
A continental-styled (and produced) court-shape London-view card published by Sandle Brothers of London. Postally-used in 1897. Written in Cambridge, the card includes a note regarding Cambridge-view cards.

37 *(below right)*
My earliest Worthing local-view card posted on 15 August 1898. Part of a set published by the Pictorial Stationery Co. Ltd. of London and printed at the 'Fine Art Works, Holstein'. View number 1144.

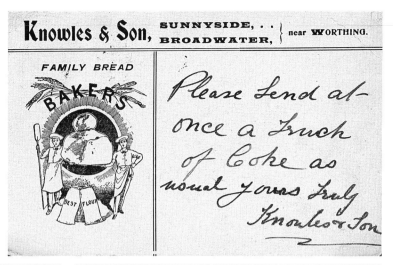

Worthing cards was issued in 1894, *see* Chapter VI.) The card shown in plate 37 is dated 15 August 1898, but was written and posted in Lowestoft so was on sale in Worthing before the date on which it was posted to Munich in Germany. The printed credit along the side of this attractive Worthing-view card reads: 'Pictorial Stationery Co. Ltd. Poultry, London. Printed at the Fine Art Works, Holstein.'. It also bears the reference number 1144 and 'Copyright'. This example has the printed part-date '18', leaving the sender to fill in the full date, in this case 'Aug 15 98'. I have just purchased a slightly later variation, posted from Worthing on 13 December 1901 and received in Brooklyn, New York on 21st. This card does not include the printed number '18'—this feature is replaced by the general caption 'Worthing'. It would seem that this post-1899 change of format was common to all town sets issued by this large and early firm of postcard suppliers.

This London-based company was one of the earliest to produce view post-cards, and was incorporated by John Davis and Walter Keep in June 1897. The company was formed especially to produce 'novel and artistic postcards and stationery'. It quickly succeeded and produced a large number of scenic cards which were printed in Germany. I show another Worthing Pictorial Stationery Company card and a Hastings example in plate 38. They are rather fun.

Plate 39 shows the printed envelope issued by this company to enclose one of their sets of London-view cards. I have a similar envelope of eight Oxford-

view cards. These and similar publicity covers or
envelopes are interesting: we see that the retail price
was sixpence (under three new pence) for eight cards,
i.e. under a penny each. The different views were
claimed to be reproduced from water-colour drawings,
not from photographs. The cards themselves included
the printed part-date '18', indicating that they were
prepared and sold in the 1890s, not in, or after,
1900. The cards are also of the tubby British court
size and shape. The Oxford views bear individual
design reference numbers ranging from 1117 to 1124.
The London views bear earlier numbers, 1017 to
1024.

The reverse of the printed envelopes gives a list
of 93 towns then covered by this firm, and others
were 'in course of preparation'. The Sussex towns

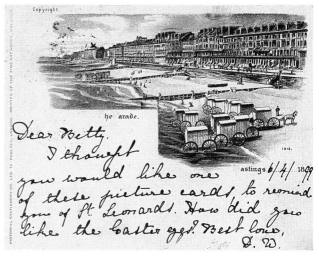

38
A further Worthing-view
Pictorial Stationery Co. Ltd. card
used in 1903. The message relates
to the attractiveness of the
postcards.

included in this pre-1900 list were—Bexhill, Bognor, Brighton, Eastbourne,
Hastings, Herstmonceux, Littlehampton, Pevensey Castle and Worthing. My
Hastings examples bear reference numbers 1013 to 1015, my sole Brighton
example is number 1060 and my two Worthing examples (including that
written in August 1898) are numbered 1144 and 1145. These Pictorial Stationery
Company court-size cards are now very scarce, because of their early pre-1900
date, and it would be nearly impossible to form a complete set of those issued
for the 93 (or more) towns covered by this firm, each town having at least one
set of eight cards. Rare and attractive as these cards undoubtedly are, they are
not highly valued by local historians. They are pretty, but they are engraved
from water-colour drawings that may well have been amended to suit the card
and its attractiveness. They do not necessarily represent an exact or accurate
record of Worthing or the other towns in the 1890s.

Sandle Brothers and the Pictorial Stationery Company were by no means
the only firms to cater for the growing trade in local-view cards for the popular
resorts.

From the local historian's point of view, the much duller black and white
or monochrome cards may well be more interesting, in that they incorporate
photographic views. At first, these views were reduced because of the size of the
court or intermediate cards, and the need to leave room for the written message
on the view side.

I show in plates 40-1 a few early Sussex photographic-view cards of the
1899-1902 period. The quality of the photographic reproduction can be extremely
good but the size of the image can be very small. The September 1899 view
of the West Pier at Brighton (plate 41 right), for example, bears no message at
all, yet it was sent to a young lady in Paris—presumably for inclusion in her
collection.

Many of the early British-market postcards were rather fussy in the
continental fashion. This was the accepted style, so that when some more
restrained cards were issued they initially came in for criticism. For example, a
writer in the August 1898 issue of the *Stationery Trades Journal*
commented:

PICTORIAL POST CARDS

Messrs. Biggs & Sons of Salisbury Court, E.C. have sent us samples of a
series they are publishing, which will cover many hundreds of views in
Great Britain. The views are in half-tone from photographs, printed in

39
A group of Pictorial Stationery Co. Ltd. cards shown with the original printed envelope in which they were displayed and sold. The set of eight was sold for 6d., *c.*1898-9.

blue ink on a white card, but we are sorry that we cannot say they come up to our idea of tasteful or artistic productions. The blocks area all rectangular with a straight border line, and are therefore hard and stiff in appearance and the arrangement of margins is not all perfect, while the lettering on the address side is poor. They are intended to sell at 6d. per dozen ... and as the views available are unusually large in number, may meet a certain market, but English manufacturers must aim at something more than ordinary if they wish to retain any of this business when the boom does arrive here. Surely the first step is to see exactly what is already done abroad.

Perhaps the blue-printed Worthing-view cards shown in plate 42 were produced by Biggs & Sons. Similar blue cards will be found featuring Brighton and other south coast towns. These cards may lack the colour and the Art Nouveau scroll-work found on most continental cards—thereby attracting criticism in the *Trade Journal*—but the photographic views are very sharp and, for their

40 *(above)*
A rather dull Worthing quadruple-view court-shape Valentine's card of *c.*1899, and a 1902 larger view card showing a standard view of Worthing pier. Both are of reasonably inexpensive type.

period, they are of a large size. Straight borders they may have, but from the local historian's point of view they score highly. The photographs also show Victorian, rather than Edwardian, Worthing.

Two of the major manufacturers, or rather publishers and wholesalers, of British-market postcards were Stengel & Co. and E. Wrench; I will discuss these firms below. There were, however, hundreds of others—far more than I can list or discuss in this book. Indeed my collection of Worthing-view postcards, according to the printed credits, was produced by over sixty national or non-Sussex firms. In addition, I can trace the names of some forty local publishers or retailers.

Messrs. Stengel & Co. of Dresden and Berlin employed O. Flammager of Bishopsgate Street, London, as their British wholesale agent. The retail outlet traded as Collectors' Publishing Company of Fleet Street. By the latter part of 1901 Stengel & Co. advertised in *The Picture Postcard* that they held the

> Finest and largest selection of picture postcards of London, suburbs and surroundings, also best known seaside and inland places. Phototype and

41
A messageless posted Brighton-view card presumably sent to a collector, and an early (1899) Valentine's Arundel-view card which the sender requested to be returned! This Valentine design was adapted to cover many different towns.

Worthing from the West Parade.

42
Two photographic-view cards printed in blue. Cards of this general type were produced in sets for most resort towns. These were postally-used in 1902, but earlier examples do occur.

Worthing from the Pier.

hand-coloured. Ten thousand Continental views—Egypt, Palestine, Japan, Australia &c., Famous paintings and sculptures.

Quite a range of subjects. The extent of the collector's market is perhaps underlined by the range of foreign views available in this country—not all such view cards were sent from the places depicted.

By 1901 Stengel & Co. were employing approximately 250 people and were producing some thirty million cards a year—a vast number, two and a half million a month. These were mainly view cards, and were produced by various standard mass-production printing techniques—collotype, or chromolithography in colour (some were hand-coloured) or monochrome.

Stengel's British agent O. Flammager had his initials 'O.F.' added to the Stengel name on credited cards—'O.F. (Stengel & Co. Ltd.) Post Card Publ., London E.C.'. Plate 43 shows two typical Edwardian Stengel local-view cards. The coloured Ealing card is of especial interest as the address side carries advertising matter. It was used as a traveller's trade card by G. Martin of Brixton, and is reproduced in plate 44. Do note that even this great firm, with its German print run in the millions, also specialised in 'The Reproduction of Customer's Photographic Views on Cards bearing their own imprint, etc.'. Many of the Worthing views bearing the name of local traders could well have been produced by Stengel & Co. in Saxony and supplied via O. Flammager, their London agent.

The second of the great postcard publishers in the early part of the century was E. Wrench of Haymarket, London. The editorial in *The Picture Postcard* of

44
The reverse of the Ealing view card shown in plate 43. O. Flammager was Stengel & Co.'s London agent.

January 1902 mentions: 'High-class collotype views of Great Britain, including seaside resorts, inland watering places, public school, naval and military types, national scenes and types, famous pictures, animals &c'.

John Evelyn Wrench later wrote of his early days in the postcard trade. His book was entitled *Uphill, The First Stage in a Strenuous Life* (Nicholson & Watson, 1934). His major involvement in the trade commenced whilst he was on holiday in Germany where he observed the great sale there of postcards and the very low cost at which they could be produced in bulk. As a young man of only 17 he found that he could purchase 25,000 cards for under fifteen shillings. On his return to London he sent local views to the German printers and soon had a stock that only needed to be sold! In the winter of 1900 this was indeed an 'uphill' struggle, but he perservered and had soon founded one of the largest and most important English postcard firms; by the time he was 21 Wrench was employing 100 hands, and 12 travellers were selling his cards to retailers all over the country. The stock included over ten thousand different subjects and ran into millions of cards. Too many, in fact, for this difficult and highly competitive trade. By 1904 he was in financial difficulty and the newly constructed firm of Wrench Postcards Ltd. ceased trading in 1906.

The Wrench trade mark comprises a small printed oval containing a wrench (the tool) and the name. Anthony Byatt gives a good, brief account of the Wrench output in his book, *Picture Postcards and their Publishers* (Golden Age Postcard Books, 1978). His local church cards were seemingly very popular— much less so today! I have a Wrench church card, printed in Saxony, which bears two high reference numbers. The address side records 'The Wrench series, no. 13842' with the Wrench trade mark. The front bears a much higher reference 73842. Much painstaking research could (and should) be carried out on these reference numbers. Here, '13842' would relate to Wrench's own catalogue or list, whilst '73,000' may well relate to the German printer's number. By amassing a long list of postally-used or otherwise dated postcards one might be able to reconstruct an approximate date for such numbers, both for the British publishers and for the main printing firms in Germany. I have sown the seed and will have to leave the cultivating and harvesting to others.

Most other cards printed in the approximate period 1900-2, before the introduction of the new-style divided-back, were rather unimaginative but they were a penny or even less to buy. Two typical, uncredited vignetted view cards are shown in plate 45. They show local scenes and interests, the 'Peoples' Park', the beach and sands; the bandstand and parade and, in the case of the second card, the probable place of purchase—Walter Brothers' 'Drapery Bazaar'.

A surprisingly large number of Worthing shops sold postcards, but Walter Brothers were one of the major outlets.* Several series bear their name and address as the local publisher but probably all the cards were supplied by one of the major national firms. In this case the extent of the order permitted the firm's own well-positioned premises to be featured on postcards.

This photographic-view postcard, featuring (in part) one of Walter Brothers' shops, was written in October 1907. The firm's advertisement in the *Worthing Gazette*, less than two months earlier, shows the variety of wares for tourists then stocked in this shop:

* As a lad in my mid-teens I earned a little pocket money selling wooden toy model tanks to Sydney Walter of this firm for, I believe, a shilling each. The early 1940s was a time of great shortages—certainly no metal toys were available and, in a modest way, I was replacing the pre-war German-made toys.

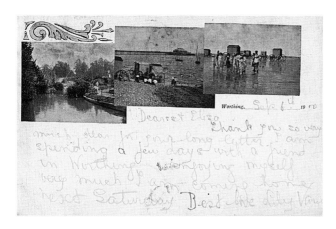

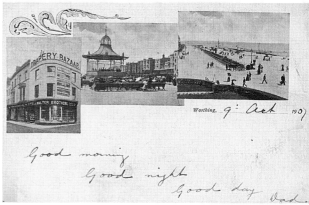

WALTER BROTHERS.
THE NOTED HOUSE FOR PRESENTS.
POSTCARDS IN ENDLESS VARIETY.
View goods, View-Books and Souvenirs of every description.
Savoy and Carlton Arms China.
We hold the largest and cheapest stock of
Fancy Goods in Town.

45
Two rather dull Worthing triple-view cards of the same series, but posted seven years apart in 1900 and 1907. The latter shows the retailer's shop—Walter Brothers' Bazaar, near the pier.

Walter Brothers were certainly not the only commercial enterprise to feature themselves on picture postcards. The lead was almost certainly taken by hotel managements; from the early 1900s into the 1920s most local hotels were featured on postcards. An early Worthing example is shown in plate 46. The *Marine Hotel*, then owned by Mrs. Heuland, was well situated facing the sea, opposite the pier, a good-looking noble building that alas has been replaced by a modern block.

For comparison in plate 47, a glossy real-photograph postcard of the same hotel as it appeared in the mid-1920s when the proprietor, according to this card, was Alfred Cotton. The sun-blinds hide the attractive columns and the front hedge has been replaced by railings. The sender in July 1926 was enjoying her stay at the *Marine Hotel*—'We are having a nice time of it, no meals to get ready, this is what we call a real holiday'. This and other hotels were playing their part in keeping visitors happy. I cannot resist including two other local hotel cards showing the elegant *Stanhoe Hotel* on the sea-front (plates 48-9).

Worthing's third royal visitor, Princess Augusta, the sister of George IV, stayed here in 1829, when it was called *Trafalgar House*. After this helpful royal publicity for the town, it was named *Augusta House* (alongside the renamed Augusta Road) and is so depicted on a Rockingham porcelain basket in the Worthing Museum. It remained a private house until about 1890, when the Misses Burton turned it into a boarding-house. By May 1893 it had been taken over by Mrs. Thimm who made extensive alterations and redecorated the house which she reopened as *Stanhoe Hall*. The tastefully furnished first-floor lounge opened on to a veranda overlooking the sea, a new Erarad grand piano was installed, and also a billiard room for the gentlemen. A 'High Class Boarding Establishment' indeed where life was, we read, 'at all times pleasant and agreeable'.

Stanhoe Hall was later retitled the *Stanhoe Hall Hotel*, as is shown on the 1901 postcard (plate 48). The 'Hall' designation was soon dropped in favour of the name *Stanhoe Hotel*, seen on the card shown in plate 49. This fine building was demolished in 1948 but the site remains an unused grass area, part of a multi-storey car park—one of our most unlovely postwar developments. These *Stanhoe Hotel* postcards recapture some of the former glories of our sea-front.

46
An early Worthing hotel view card of the type that would have been available to guests. This hotel was centrally situated opposite the pier. Dated 1903.

47
A clear photographic-view card of the *Marine Hotel* as it appeared in about 1920. The proprietor's name is given, suggesting that this was only available at the hotel. Surrounding buildings have been blanked out.

The lamented *Stanhoe Hotel* was, like most local hotels, adapted from one or more private houses or complete terraces of houses with, in the case of the present-day *Beach Hotel*, a refaced, pre-war façade. Indeed, the only purpose-built Worthing hotel was reputedly the *West Worthing Hotel*, later renamed the *Burlington Hotel*. Plate 50 shows a Burlington postcard with an interesting assortment of *c.*1910 cars parked outside. Today few if any visitors to these adapted hotels would know that they started life as quite modest family homes, until some enterprising entrepreneur came to play real-life monopoly—turning rows of houses into hotels!

Some Worthing hotels published a series of cards showing various interior and exterior views. One Worthing example I will return to later but first, to avoid too much local bias, I include a splendidly-designed Eastbourne hotel card (plate 51). This is obviously very much in the style of the grand continental hotel cards, although it lacks the colour of German examples. These hotel—and the related

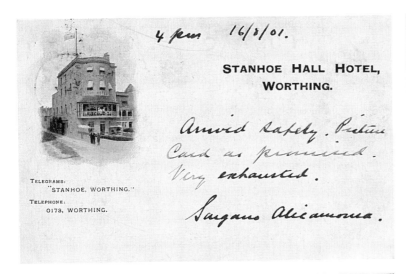

4 pm 16/8/01.

STANHOE HALL HOTEL,
WORTHING.

Arrived safely. Picture
Card as promised.
Very exhausted.

Sargano Alicamonia.

TELEGRAMS:
"STANHOE, WORTHING."
TELEPHONE:
0178, WORTHING.

STANHOE HOTEL,
WORTHING.

The
Burlington
Hotel,
Worthing.

ENTIRELY
RENOVATED
AND MOST
UP-TO-DATE.
FINEST POSI-
TION. :: ::
FACING SEA.

Telephones :
80 & 81 Worthing.

Telegrams :
"Burlington,
Worthing."

H. M. CAVESTRI,
Proprietor.

48 *(top left)*
A 1901 hotel view advertising card, sent to a
collector—'... Picture Card as promised'. An early
example of its type but the view is of small interest
to a collector.

49 *(above)*
A later (1906) local-view hotel card, one that is
more interesting to the local historian in view of
the larger size of the picture of this historic building.

50 *(middle left)*
An interesting hotel advertising card showing the
only purpose-built hotel in the town. A good
gathering of cars is shown outside, c.1910-15.

51 *(bottom left)*
A 1907 Eastbourne advertisement card in the
continental style, written by a young girl. An old-
style card still being used when the whole view
side could be used for the picture.

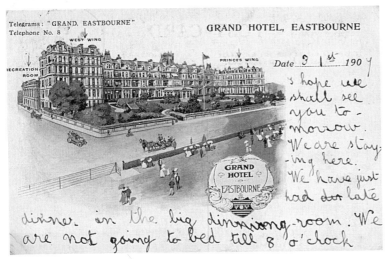

Telegrams : "GRAND, EASTBOURNE"
Telephone No. 8

WEST WING

RECREATION
ROOM

PRINCES WING

GRAND HOTEL, EASTBOURNE

Date 3 1st 1907

I hope we
shall see
you to-
morrow.
We are stay-
ing here.
We have just
had our late
dinner in the big dining-room. We
are not going to bed till 8 o'clock

GRAND
HOTEL
EASTBOURNE

private hotel and boarding-house—view cards were only available for sale in those establishments so they are
relatively rare. They were not usually published by the large national or multi-national firms.

The large national and international manufacturers and publishers of postcards produced cards that would
sell in very large quantities, particularly to visitors or trippers. These trippers early in the 20th century would

52
An early but not rare Worthing pier picture postcard printed in black.

53
A Valentine colour-printed standard view of Worthing pier. This is a 1902-onwards divided-back card which enabled the whole reverse to be used for the view or other design.

patronise our own resorts, very much more than they do today. In Worthing and in most seaside towns, postcards reproduced views of the pier, the sea-front, the beach or parks. I could fill this book with different postcard views of Worthing pier alone.

Each design would differ slightly, but each would be attractive—it had to be, to sell in competition with other manufacturers' cards. Each would be interesting, showing gradual developments and improvements in the structure and the buildings on it. Some cards would feature amusements or concert parties catering for visitors. Plates 52-5 show just a very few of the hundreds of available Worthing pier cards. Likewise views of promenades and beaches—north, east, west and south—it matters not, all were produced by German printers from British photographs. In general terms these popular tourist views, which sold over a long period, are not now in demand by collectors—the views are too common and too

54
A good quality Valentine card showing the Worthing pier with folk listening to a concert.

55 *(left)*
A single photograph of Worthing pier, treated in two of many different ways by Messrs. Valentine. The middle one is a coloured version, framed by a fancy surround. The black and white version below shows the basic scene. Both cards carry the same reference number 15427.

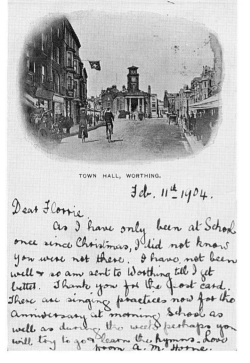

56
On the left is a rather dull 1904 local-view card showing a reduced photograph of the Town Hall. On the right is the same print used on a larger scale in a 'Souvenir Letter Card'.

standard. Consequently they are still relatively inexpensive, usually priced at under a pound.

Some, however, are of interest as they show how large publishers adapted their stock photographs to cater for different tastes and different price-ranges. The obvious, simple trick was to use the same photograph in an inexpensive black and white form and then perhaps in a two-penny, coloured version.

With more ambition the same picture could be framed in all sorts of ornate or novelty border designs. One can have great fun tracing the various treatments given to a simple stock photograph. Just one example is presented in plate 55; the effect from the same photographic image is quite different. It might well be possible to find a dozen or more framings of any popular local-view card—not only of Worthing but of any other town. Some publishers did not trouble to devise a novel frame for an existing photograph; they merely reduced the size or cut down the image. The two cards shown in plate 56 use exactly the same shot of Worthing's South Street looking towards the Town Hall—the focal point of so many celebrations.

What do you make of the two cards in plate 57, the calm and storm scenes? They are actually the same photograph taken on the same sunny afternoon or early evening (note the long shadows) with the tide halfway out and well down the pier supports. In the stormy version the publisher has gone mad with a brush; the calm sea has risen and great waves are breaking over the pier. The sky has darkened, but the sun's shadows remain. Some figures and the paddle steamer have been painted out, as have the two sun-shades in the foreground, but most of the original summer strollers have been left, enabling us positively to identify the print. Curiously enough, no figures are watching the sea break over the pier—one would expect crowds to witness such a scene. Nevertheless this faked rendering appears as an illustration to a recent book on Worthing. The much respected local historian's caption reads 'Worthing Pier lashed by ferociously powerful waves'. Lashed by the artist's brush, more likely, for postcard pictures can be made to lie or at least to fib.

57
A Valentine summer view of Worthing pier (taken within a few moments of those in plate 55 and with the same reference number) and, below, a doctored winter view using the same print with rough sea added and other minor amendments to produce a novel view.

Interesting additions to a standard view can be made in the publisher's office or printer's workshop. Aeroplanes or balloons were fair game. The trick is generally exposed by the lack of interest shown by the crowds. No one is looking at the new-fangled flying machine, no excited hands are pointing upwards, even in the pre-1914 period when such a sight was a real novelty. The novelty of the added flying machines was precisely why they were painted in! Nevertheless, several genuine photographic cards, locally produced, depict early machines which often landed on the sands. Postcards can be important in bringing to our attention early flying machines, their crashes and daring aviators. Worthing was a centre for early aviators as Shoreham Aerodrome, one of the first from which commercial air cargo was flown, is only a few miles to the east. The problem in landing on Worthing beach was the density of the crowds that flocked to see the new contraptions!

58
Two Shoesmith & Etheridge 'Norman' glossy photographic cards of the 1930s. The upper card is the standard daytime view. The lower version has merely been doctored to show a make-believe night scene. The figures and tide remain the same.

Pier Pavilion. Worthing. 2

Pier Music Pavilion By Night, Worthing. 23

Further and later examples of faking include the two 'Norman' real-photograph cards (shown in plate 58), published by Shoesmith & Etheridge Ltd. of Hastings in the late 1920s, which are basically the same daytime view of the Pier Pavilion at Worthing. The night-time version is, however, not real but doctored. The whole image has been darkened, a cloudy semi-moonlit sky has been added (whilst most of the sun's shadows remain!) and various lights have been added to complete the illusion. Such publishers' tricks date back to the earliest period of postcards and examples can be found relating to most towns. No harm was done; an existing, cost-free, negative was pressed into service to produce a new version that would sell to casual buyers, the trippers who merely wished to send home a novel card.

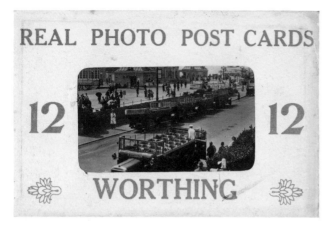

Although we may associate the seaside with sunny and warm summer days, stormy scenes were extremely popular. Large firms like Tuck's issued many stormy sea studies and apparently, by 1906, over five hundred 'rough sea' cards had been published. Many of them had the advantage that they were neutral cards that could be sold at any seaside town. There was no special local association until the sender added his local message, such as 'Fought my way along the Worthing front yesterday'. In the 1990s these studies have decidedly lost their popularity with collectors but 80 years ago they were very much part of the postcard scene.

Many national publishers also catered for the casual trippers' market by issuing cards made up of a montage of small views. Again these were convenient to produce, the illustrations would have been available and most such pictures also exist as full-size pictorial cards.

Although these multiple-view cards were always available singly, it would seem that many of the packages of a dozen or so local-view cards included one multi-view card bearing miniature editions of cards already in the pack. Two complete packs of Worthing views of the 1925-30 period, *see* plate 59, each included in the pack a multi-view card, one of which I show in plate 60. This one is rather good, although the publisher neglected to add his name to any of the cards. Yet some of the same photographs appear in my collection with the 'Norman' trade name used by Shoesmith & Etheridge Ltd. of Hastings.

A double-view card which was postally-used in May 1911 is quite fun. Apart from the two local views, it carries a signed poem relating to Worthing:

> Beneath the famous Sussex downs
> The town of Worthing stands
> A lovely beauty spot is she
> With a stretch of golden sands ...

Such sentiment, such nostalgia, is not to be despised.

Likewise, the outline map of the south east, adapted to house three views of Worthing is amusing (*see* plate 61). The basic idea could, of course, be amended to show views of any other town in the district, or the map could be changed to feature the south west or any other part of the kingdom, with appropriate views.

These multiple-view cards can be charming, but from the postcard collector's point of view they are undesirable and consequently very reasonably priced. Plates

59 *(top)*
Two sets of packaged local-view cards published by the same firm. The selection on the left is composed of glossy surfaced real photographs with sharp details. The photogravure examples on the right are printed in a lighter tone and have been slightly tinted. They are more colourful but not so sharply defined. Most retail outlets would have held stocks of such standard popular views.

60 *(above)*
A 'joker' or multi-view card. Each packet (plate 59) would have contained at least one such card, containing miniature versions of the full-size views. These were also sold separately.

61
A Jackson & Son 'Jay em Jay' novelty card, comprising miniature views of Worthing on a map of the south east. This format would have been used for other localities.

62
An A. & G. Taylor glossy photographic multi-view card. This, produced by a national firm, was superior to local products..

63
An attractive glossy multi-view Worthing tripper-type card, postally-used in 1909.

64
Two Sergeant Bros. heraldic and double-view cards which made use of existing standard photographic views in a new way, *c.*1912.

65
Two further popular tripper-type cards. The heraldic example is a Valentine production for the local retailers, Walter Bros. (*see* plate 45), 1909.

66
A glossy monochrome postwar multi-view card, not really competing in attractiveness or value with some interwar cards of similar type, *c.*1946-50.

67
A dressed-up local-view card using an existing standard view in a novelty setting. These were originally very popular with trippers and holiday-makers but are not so popular now among collectors.

60-6 show more representations of the hundreds of multiple-view Worthing cards that were issued. They were popular with the original users, from the 1890s to the present day. Over the years, whilst on holiday, I have often purchased this type of card. A collection of such cards today might be fun, and should not be very costly.

Other small or reduced views were often attractively arranged in fancy settings. These cards were angled at the holiday-maker or tripper and commanded good sales. However, today collectors neglect this type of pretty, pretty card; examples are available nationwide for less than the price of a pint of beer. The card shown in plate 67 was probably published in the 1925-35 period, and many more similar examples both in colour and monochrome would have been readily available in the town.

Many single-view cards were overprinted with seasonal greetings for sale at Christmas or Easter. In most cases these were standard stock cards with the appropriate wording added at the back or on the picture side (as plate 68). In some rarer cases, however, special mounts were produced, as in plate 69. Such special, seasonal cards must be much rarer than cards that were saleable over a longer period, but as yet they do not seem to be especially desirable or costly.

Many popular novelty cards also incorporate strips or 'Pull-outs' of very small photographic-based prints of local views. These are usually reduced stock postcard prints brought down almost to postage stamp size. For this reason they are not popular today with those seeking to build up a historic photographic image of a town, but the cards are often decorative and amusing. They were certainly popular in the 1910-20 period,

68
A colourful F.C. Morgan & Co. card of the 1910 period, overprinted in gold with 'A Happy Christmas and a Bright New Year', turning a standard postcard into a Christmas and New Year card.

69
A standard local summer view presented in a special Christmas surround to meet a new market, *c*.1920.

even when they carried full postage or were sent at the printed paper-rate without an added message. This type of card is discussed in Chapter VI.

Let us consider where all these postcards were on sale. Up to about 1900, or even a little later, there were probably very few outlets. As far as Worthing is concerned, local directories up to and including 1901 do not mention postcards or retailers making a special line in these cards. This is not to say, however, that postcards were not on sale—not every firm advertised and those that did could not mention every stock line. I doubt if any advertiser has ever mentioned that, for example, he sold boxes of matches. Certain things are taken for granted, or do not repay the cost of an advertisement.

At first, pictorial postcards were sold at stationers' shops—hence all the advertisements and editorial comments in that trade's journal—or at fashionable private libraries that also sold souvenirs and such like. They would have been available mainly at the type of shop that stocked at appropriate periods the better

70
A detail from a French Lévy card showing Tarring village post office with its board proclaiming that 'Pictorial Postcards' were sold. A picturesque street much favoured by postcard photographers, *c.*1910.

quality Christmas or Valentine cards. Often the publishers of such colourful cards also turned to producing postcards. The same commercial travellers would sell and distribute the new postcards.

We have evidence that at least by August 1900 a postcard-dispensing machine was set up at Worthing railway station, for a purchaser saw fit to complain in the local paper:

> Sir,
>
> I put a penny in the slot at Worthing railway station expecting to receive a picture postcard of Worthing, but instead got one of Littlehampton. What a capital way of advertising your town ...

As a result we know that by this quite early date in British postcard history special machines were being manufactured or imported from the continent. By this period they must have been well distributed—the Worthing example (or examples) is unlikely to have been the first; staff were employed to fill (incorrectly in this case!) the machines with cards and to collect the pennies.

An obvious place to sell picture postcards was at the sub-post office in every town or village. They were often the hub of the small community, with a constant stream of people purchasing stamps or other everyday objects. At least one Worthing card shows a sub-post office (that in the ancient village of Tarring, now swallowed up into the enlarged town). You can see in plate 70 part of the board outside: 'Pictorial Post Cards, a good variety of ...'. The post box is next door and the cards and stamps are available inside. In the Edwardian period Worthing had many small general shops-cum-sub-post offices which usually sold picture postcards.

The postcard trade was gaining momentum; it was worthwhile for various traders to carry stock of such inexpensive novelties. It is possible that some travellers or publishers offered postcards on a sale or return basis. The retailer had nothing to lose in taking a stock of the popular postcards.

As demand increased, as it undoubtedly did in the 1900-5 period, so more and more retailers commenced to stock these cards. The new outlets were newsagents, tobacconists and similar establishments. All shops, bazaars and kiosks which sold holiday trinkets and souvenirs would also have stocked seaside-type postcards. They would have carried examples of different makes and price-ranges of cards. One bazaar advertisement in a Worthing directory of 1910 illustrates the variety of goods on offer in such general stores. In this case, postcards are included in the list, although sub-post offices were also selling such articles in the same street:

T.W. WOOD
Broadway
Brighton Road, Worthing
TOY BAZAAR
Household Stores
Speciality -
All kinds of Dolls

73
A real-photograph Brighton (Deane, Wiles & Millar) card showing a local café and its staff. Note the rows of local-view and other popular cards displayed in the window. Postally-used in April 1935. Torn and creased condition.

71 *(far left)*
A small corner shop—grocer's and general stores—formerly at the corner of Ambrose Place. Even this establishment had the door adorned with a display of picture postcards. A sponsored card with written inscription 'Compliments of the Season. Xmas 1914'. The shop was still in business during the Second World War but it is now a private residence.

72 *(left)*
A further interesting shop-front card showing Mr. Green in his doorway, the window crammed with picture postcards and newspapers. Postally-used 'London E', 26 October 1906. These shop-front cards were produced for, and were really only used by, the owner and his family.

skilfully repaired
on the premises.
Dolls dressed to order.
Large assortment of Dolls, Toys, Games,
Prams, Horses, Barrows, Post Cards,
Leather Goods, etc.
Glass, China and Earthenware, Tin &
Enamel Goods, Brushes and all
household requisites.

It might have been thought that the upmarket, superior Tuck cards were only available at better-class establishments, but one finds the famous Tuck name and publicity featured in the windows of many lesser shops.

Plates 71-3 illustrate some 'shop-front' cards showing view cards prominently displayed in general stores, newsagents or refreshment-type shops. Each inland town, as well as the resorts, would have supported several such shops, some in quite modest situations. Perhaps the cards helped to bring folk into the shop to spend more than a penny or two. These sponsored shop-front cards serve to show the type of modest establishments where large selections of cards were on display. They are very desirable, both from the local and social historian's point of view.

Various shop-front postcards show quite small post offices which displayed and sold postcards, along with the required postage stamps. Various tearooms and cafés also sold picture cards of the locality. On the Downs just to the north of Worthing there is the much-photographed Salvington Mill. It still stands and has in recent years been lovingly restored; there was also a popular tearoom on the site. There are apparently well over a hundred different cards featuring Salvington Mill. One of my examples carries the written message:

> Bought the card at a lovely mill tea place, where we had tea when we visited Salvington on Tuesday.

Yes, you could buy picture postcards almost anywhere. Salvington was then largely an undeveloped area on the South Downs, overlooking Worthing and the coastal plain.

Local directories are a rich source for the serious postcard collector or local historian. The changing ownership of shops can be traced and the period of any one occupier checked to within a year or so. The advertisements in these directories can also be enlightening, but it should be remembered that relatively few retailers went to the trouble and expense of advertising. The main postcard era, the Edwardian period, was one of many small shops. Many towns were relatively compact with the shopkeepers and the population living in the centre of the town. Small newsagents and corner shops catered well for the needs of their locality—they did not need to seek other folk's customers.

Nevertheless, some enterprising traders from time to time advertised their specialities. The 1902 *Kelly's Directory* of Worthing (prepared in 1901) for example carried an advertisement for S.E. Lawson of the 'West End Library' at 132 Montague Street, Worthing. (This up-market name referred to the fact that the shop was at the western end of that main road!) This library advertised 'All the latest photographs of neighbourhood and surroundings in view books, picture postcards etc.'. Mr. Lawson was one of several local retailers whose name can be found printed or stamped on cards which he sold.

Another retailer whose name can be found on cards is Henry A. Foyster, Bookseller and Stationer of 10 South Street, Worthing—a good central position near the pier and sea. *Kelly's Directory* of 1906 included Foyster's advertisement for his 'Royal Library (in connection with Mudie's) with Reading Room ... all

74
Two colour-printed Max
Ettlinger 'Royal Series' cards
bearing the imprint of the local
retailer, H.A. Foyster,
c.1910-12.

the newest books, terms and catalogues on application'. Private 'circulating' libraries
were still very popular. The public library was not generally used by middle-class
or better-off inhabitants. The charge at the private libraries was usually 2d. per
book per week at this period. Smith's and Boots and some other subscription
libraries survived in most towns until after the 1939-45 war.

Mr. Foyster was also the publisher of 'Picturesque Worthing' at one shilling.
He also sold postcards, including 'The noted Royal series of black and white at
4½d per packet of 12', less than an old halfpenny each, and the Royal nature-
coloured series at 6 cards for 4½d., or twice the price of the black and white
cards, but still under a penny each.

The 'noted Royal series' was most probably issued by the large firm of
M. Ettlinger & Co. Ltd. Max came to London from Germany in 1902, to exploit
his experience and contacts in the German postcard trade. The firm was well

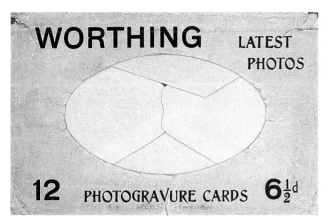

75
A rather tatty envelope relating to photographic local-view cards being sold at 6½d. for twelve. These were obviously mass-produced standard products for the holiday-makers.

known for its novelty cards and reputedly over 100,000 cards were sold within a few months of the establishment of the London office. The Ettlinger trade mark comprises an elaborate cursive monogram of the initials M.E. & Co. with 'The Royal Series' on a scroll or ribbon below. Two local cards bearing the Foyster retail imprint are at plate 74.

The *Worthing Mercury Directory* of 1908 included advertisements for well-known local retailers, such as Walter Brothers' 'Drapery Bazaar'. This firm claimed to 'hold the largest and best variety of foreign fancy goods in Worthing and an immense stock of picture post cards'. This might be expected of a bazaar; it is unexpected, however, to find the full-page advertisement for Lockwood's Haircutting, Singeing, Shampooing & Shaving Saloons featuring not only toilet goods but also postcard albums and postcards. Perhaps one could choose postcards whilst waiting to take the chair.

The publishers of the *Worthing Mercury* for 1908 took a page to advertise their 'New Series of Picture Post Cards'. These were described as 'Genuine Silver Print Photographs of the Town', priced at twopence each. At this price they must have been quite superior 'real-photograph' productions. The *Mercury* offices in Warwick Street also stocked much cheaper and perhaps more colourful examples which on the same page were described as

7 Coloured assorted views of Worthing with arms of the Borough 6d
12 assorted views of Worthing 6d

These less-than-a-penny and halfpenny cards were sold in packets or simple envelopes (*see* plate 75) which kept the cards clean and enabled a sixpenny sale, avoiding the trouble of selling individual cards at a penny or halfpenny a time.

The publishers of the *Mercury* in 1909-10 used their centrally positioned premises at 7 Warwick Street to very good effect. It was advertised as 'The Post Card House' stocking the 'Finest selection of Comic, Pictorial and Local View Post Cards in Worthing'. A possibly unique feature was described as a 'Special Department for Addressing Post Cards'. Were the offices equipped with writing tables or desks, with pen and ink; were postage stamps sold? We will probably never know now; it is unlikely that anyone who used these facilities is still living, as Worthing Post Card House seemingly only existed for a short period around 1910. My grandfather's shop (or one of them) was at that period right next door, at no.5, Warwick Street—'Arthur Godden, Fine Art Dealer'. I wonder if he ever browsed around this 'Post Card House' or what he could have told me of it and of the town in general had I thought to ask whilst he was alive.

I am not sure if the *Mercury* offices sold other items apart from postcards. I am also not sure if we had any shop that sold only postcards—probably not. However, the town was featured in the popular *Punch* magazine in July 1912. An engraving by Charles Pears depicted a group of fashionable ladies partaking of tea, one lady as part of the usual long (unfunny) caption stated '... and she with two kiddies—poor thing, is running a picture post card shop in Worthing'. I hope it kept the two children well fed.

In addition to the *Mercury*'s postcards, its longer-established rival the *Worthing Gazette* also sold postcards. A front-page advertisement in the issue of 10 September 1913 reads:

When you are out see the
Worthing Gazette
window
we have on show a fine selection
of
TUCK'S BEAUTIFUL POSTCARDS
of which we hold the largest stock
in the town

The *Worthing Gazette* had been stocking and advertising its 'Tuck' Christmas and Easter cards since at least 1901 and had long commercial ties with this leading firm of greeting-card publishers.

In June 1914 the *Worthing Gazette* management again advertised its display:

Postcards! Postcards!
Postcards!
The largest and most Beautiful
selection in Worthing
Worthing Gazette Company
Stationers
35 Chapel Road
Don't fail to see the Display
in the Windows this week.

Within three months, however, Britain and much of the world was at war. Tuck's and other publishers were quick to bring out patriotic subject cards and, of course, the import of German-printed cards ceased.

In the issue of 23 September 1914 the *Gazette* management was selling new Tuck cards, advertised as follows:

At the Gazette Co's Stationery Stores, 35 Chapel Rd
Today's issue
of
Beautiful new Patriotic Postcards:-
We'll keep the Flag Flying
Wake up, England (dedicated to Earl Roberts)
The Iron Walls of England
Magnificent illustration of England's greatest
Field-Marshal Earl Kitchener
A splendid new portrait
Admiral Sir John Jellicoe
The French Army
Types of the Allied Armies
President Poincarè
Englishmen of note
The Battleships of England
One Penny Each.
All produced in England by the celebrated firm of Raphael Tuck & Sons

Most of these patriotic cards were probably purchased to be added to albums rather than for everyday messages, although the great days of postcard collecting were fast fading—if they had not already largely ceased. I am not sure how one would help the national war effort by buying these cards. The benefit would appear to be confined to the *Worthing Gazette* management and to Messrs. Tuck! Nevertheless this advertisement in a provincial newspaper does show how the country was affected, even at this early date, by the outbreak of the war. It is also interesting to read that such Tuck cards were being retailed at a penny.

76
A poorly-printed sepia monochrome Worthing local-view card bearing the imprint of the *Worthing Mercury*, a local paper that ran a 'Post Card House' in the centre of the town, *c.*1914.

THE PIER KIOSK, WORTHING.

Of course, the *Worthing Gazette* Company and the proprietors of the *Worthing Mercury* could advertise their penny lines as they did not directly have to pay for the advertisement—they owned the paper and could use such publicity material as space-fillers. Very few retailers of postcards could afford to pay for advertisements; the cards had to proclaim themselves. They were therefore displayed in windows or on special revolving stands just inside, or outside, shop premises.

What types or makes of local-view topographical cards might the *Mercury*'s 'Post Card House' have stocked? From examination of my present collection of several hundred late Edwardian cards—the more popular inexpensive mass-produced cards—the range of publishers will have been much the same for any town or for any large retailer of picture postcards.

Unfortunately, my research into the type of card stocked at this grand-sounding establishment is mainly guesswork, for very few cards bear a credit: I have only one card inscribed *'The Worthing Mercury'*. This is a nondescript sepia-printed view of 'The Pier Kiosk, Worthing' (*see* plate 76). It is at least 'British throughout', perhaps suggesting a wartime product but it would have been of better quality had it been printed in pre-war Germany. We are left with the assumption, however, that most of the stock in the *Mercury*'s Post Card House would have comprised cards produced by the main postcard publishers, bearing only their names. They would have been of similar type to those being sold elsewhere in the country. The *Mercury*, like the *Gazette* and other outlets, undoubtedly also stocked Tuck cards, for they were the market-leaders in this country.

Most of the cards on display at this special gallery would have featured views of the town or neighbourhood. Some might have been overprinted on the front or on the address side with Christmas, New Year or Easter greetings. Other cards would have been designed to send birthday greetings, or to act as Valentine cards. These could be attractive as well as inexpensive, and could be sent with only a halfpenny stamp. The young ladies in the post offices were continually asked for halfpenny stamps—thousands of them. By the way, local papers requested payment for classified advertisements or announcements in the form of halfpenny stamps!

In an attempt to suggest what types or makes of 'Pictorial and Local View Post Cards' were available at this 'Post Card House' in the Edwardian era I will

52844   LIFEBOAT LAUNCH, WORTHING

77
A Valentine monochrome card, one of hundreds produced depicting local lifeboats and related subjects. These were very popular and practice launches always attracted the crowds. Postally-used August 1909.

examine a few of my Worthing cards. The resulting selection, typical of what was available in most other towns, is arranged in chronological order of the cards as they occur in my collection.

Queen Victoria had died on 22 January 1901, when we were engaged in the Boer War. Both these events were very widely represented on postcards. Locally, the polished granite South African War (1899-1902) memorial, erected by public subscription, still stands prominently at the southern end of Steyne Gardens, and is featured on many a local-view card.

King Edward VII acceded to the British throne when his mother, Queen Victoria, died. His coronation was postponed from 26 June 1902 just 48 hours before, due to his illness. This is recorded on Henry Stead's 'Current Event Post Card', which were overprinted on 24 June 1902 with the following note, and were still put on sale that day:

> The world was gravely shocked today when it was announced about noon that His Majesty the King had undergone an operation for perityphlitis this morning. In consequence the Coronation has been postponed, and all arrangements in connection therewith have been upset including our own.

The coronation took place on 9 August 1902. It was well recorded on postcards and with great celebrations in Worthing and all other British towns. The new Edward VII postage stamps were issued on 1 January 1902.

Unfortunately, most early Worthing cards do not bear a credit to the publisher or printer. There are, however, many helpful firms that did print their name or trade mark on the card. An attractive photographic view of the Broadwater district of Worthing, less than two hundred yards from my home, is postmarked 30 August 1902. This card bears the credit on the view side, 'Printed by Valentine Ltd. Dundee'. Anthony Byatt, in his book on publishers, devotes nearly five pages to this firm which he describes as 'One of the most prominent and prolific publishers of postcards from the early days of the court-sized card until the 1960s'. This 1902 example is credited in full, although most have the initials J.V. Later cards often bear only initials 'V & S.D.' or 'V & S. Series', if the standard description 'Valentine Series' was not printed at the head of the address side. This Scottish firm produced millions of local-view cards covering the whole country.

78
A poorly produced Gottschalk, Dreyfus & Davis 'Printed in Bavaria' local-view card of inexpensive mass-produced type. Not all continental cards were of high quality, *c.*1905.

Rare or not, most pictorial or real-photograph cards are very interesting contemporary records. The 'National Buildings Record', collected and maintained by the Royal Commission on the Historical Monuments of England at Fortress House, 23 Saville Row, London W1X 2JQ, has a wonderful collection of very many old postcards. These are invaluable records of our great buildings and monuments. In postcard collectors' terms, most of them are of little interest or value, but gathered together and indexed they become a National Archive.

Plate 77 shows a Valentine lifeboat scene. The boat has returned to the beach just to the east of the pier, after either a rescue or one of the required quarterly practice launches. This same picture occurs in both monochrome and coloured versions, as did so many standard views. These Valentine examples both bear the same high reference number 52844, and the initials 'J.V.' within a circle. The same reference number applied when the same print was used with different border designs.

Very many resort cards depict lifeboats. They were very popular both with the large postcard manufacturers and with local photographers. They were on sale at all types of postcard retail outlets and also at the lifeboat stations—which were usually open to the public, who would, it was hoped, contribute to the collecting boxes. The long and valiant history of the voluntary lifeboat service in Worthing has been very well told in a specialist book (*Edwardian Worthing, Eventful Era in a Lifeboat Town* by Rob Blann, privately published, Worthing, 1991). It is a fascinating story probably mirrored in most other seaside towns.

A rather poor, naively engraved view of the pier and promenade can be seen in plate 78 (part of a series of twelve or more different views). It bears the monogram initials 'G.D. & D.' within a star outline, the G being larger than the Ds as here shown. These initials belong to Gottschalk, Dreyfus & Davis, who had a London office from about 1904, but this example appears to be rather earlier in style. Its primitive appearance indicates economy, as it was probably sold for a halfpenny. A slightly later version of the same view with the spaced-out initials 'G.D. & D.L.' suggests a post-1904 date. These cards were printed in Germany. Various changes in the trade marks were made later, one of which features a child reaching to post a card in a letter-box. The firm's 'Star' series sold over a long period, until Dreyfus left the partnership in 1914.

Better quality photographic-view cards of Worthing bear the trade name 'Victoria Series' arranged around a portrait of the elderly Queen Victoria, with the additional credit 'Published at 11 Poultry, London E.C. Works Wandsbek' at the side of the card. My earliest example is postmarked 20 August 1902, with the view reference number 669.

The 'Victoria Series' was produced over a long period by John Davis of 24 Queen Victoria Street, London E.C. His name and address were sometimes printed in full within the postage stamp box. John Davis is an important figure in the history of British pictorial postcards, for he was one of the two partners in the pioneering firm—the Pictorial Stationery Company. He, however, left the partnership in 1902, and set up his own firm, issuing cards under the name 'Victoria Series', perhaps because of his address in Queen Victoria Street, or because he started to produce postcards in the Victorian period. As with many other publishers, the credits and the design of the address side were amended on many occasions. Close study of the work of such firms will enable the interested collector to pinpoint the dates when these changes were made. Another 'Victoria Series' Worthing-view card (no.955) features 'Worthing. West Parade'. This card is dated '14. 9. 04' in the message and on the postmark, but it could well have been printed in 1903.

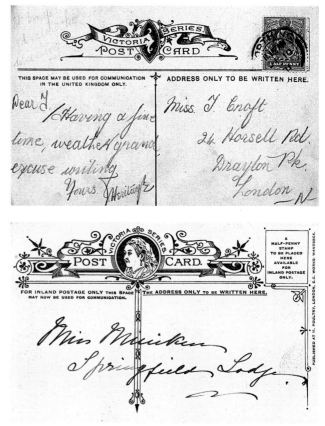

79
The address side of two J. Davis 'Victoria Series' well-produced monochrome local-view cards. The first example had inscribed over the park view on its reverse, 'In memory of this sacred park' and was obviously sent in an envelope. Many very personal cards or those intended for collection were thus protected.

The 'Victoria Series' trade mark now lacks the image of Queen Victoria and the printed credit at the side is fuller than that on the August 1902 card (no.669); another German printing works was apparently used. The credit reads 'J Davis, 24 Queen Victoria St., E.C., Printed at the works, Hamburg'. Two 'Victoria Series' Worthing cards in the 1871-2099 number range are shown in plate 80. By at least August 1908 the printed credit to J. Davis had been dropped from the 'Victoria Series' cards and the view reference numbers had climbed to no.2556, which is a coloured view of Worthing pier. At least one Davis 'Victoria Series' card of the 1904-5 period was reissued locally (image reversed!) in the mid-1980s and is still selling in the 1990s!

An attractive photographic, black and white, card shows the entrance to the Offington estate, Worthing. It is postmarked 10 April 1903 and bears the heart-and-man trade mark used by Frederick Hartmann of London, who is credited with having introduced in 1902 the British divided-back postcard for use within the British Isles. Hartmann was an agent for several German firms and he issued or sold wholesale very many interesting types of card under his name up to 1909, at about which time he went out of business. These Hartmann view cards were printed in monochrome and also in full colour versions. My monochrome examples are numbered 1289, 1290 and 1292—being part of the same Worthing set, but the coloured card is numbered 10822, indicating a later introduction. This firm was one of the largest producers of English picture postcards in the early years of the century. One of my Hartmann cards postally-used in September 1906 is from the 'Miniature Series', in which the picture side is made up of many small views, in this case 14 miniature views of Worthing. This type of multi-view card was discussed earlier in this chapter.

80
Two well-produced Davies 'Victoria Series' monochrome local-view cards. The good detail, figures and matt surface are reminiscent of the French Lévy cards (*see* Chapter V). Postally-used in 1908 and 1909.

Many other very good photographic-view cards of Worthing bear the credit 'Stengel & Co. Dresden. Berlin' with a reference number such as 14643 which relates to an early view of 'The Parade, Worthing'. These quality German postcards were produced over many years, and by 1901 Stengel had produced over ten thousand different topographical cards, sold in Russia, Japan, Australia and most European countries. The Worthing shops took a small part in this worldwide trade.

Another of my Worthing-view cards, postmark dated 21 October 1904, bears the printed trade mark 'Dainty Series'. The photographic view of Worthing pier—a very popular postcard subject—bears the credit 'E.T.W.D.'. The 'Dainty Series' was issued by E.T.W. Dennis (& Sons Ltd.) of Scarborough. When this firm commenced in the 1890s only the initials were used, but the 'Dainty' trade mark had obviously been adopted by autumn 1904. This example is well printed on a good quality stout card.

Let us now consider the publishers of my local-view card, posted in 1905. One colourful view of Worthing Park (the Peoples' Park or Homefield Park) bears the surprisingly high reference number 22299. The address side includes in the lower left-hand corner a small crest of a bear's head and upper body. On checking this device in Anthony Byatt's section on trade marks, one learns that this crest was used by the Photochrom Company Ltd., of Tunbridge Wells. The firm originated in Zurich (which no doubt explains the crestmark); by 1900 its view cards featured most British towns, and by 1906 it claimed to hold a quarter of a million negatives. At the 1905 Earl's Court Postcard Exhibition the firm won a gold and two silver medals. The colour-printed cards with reference numbers over 22000 date from 1905 when the bear crest was introduced by this important firm, well covered in Mr. Byatt's book on postcard publishers. The Photochrom Co. Ltd. also issued Worthing-view cards in its 'Sepiatone Series' and in the full colour 'Celesque Series'; Worthing's South Street view is a version of number 22290, renumbered for the coloured card 35034 and E 35034.

A rather ordinary photographic beach scene card, posted on 19 June 1905, bears the credit 'Yes or No' series. This name is not listed by Mr. Byatt but *The Dictionary of Picture Postcards in Britain 1894-1939* by A.W. Coysh (Antique Collectors' Club, Woodbridge, 1984) states that such cards were related to Shurey's Publications magazine of that name—cards were seemingly given away to publicise their magazines. A related coloured view of Worthing Town Hall (plate 81) has a fuller credit: 'This beautiful Series of Fine Art Post Cards is supplied free exclusively by Shurey's Publications, comprising "Smart Novels", "Yes and No" and "Dainty Novels". The Finest 1d magazine is "Weekly Tale Teller".' The stamp-space contains further helpful information—'Printed by Delittle, Fenwick & Co. York for Shurey's Publications & British Throughout'.

One of my many cards featuring the Old Town Hall and town centre is the pleasant colour-printed card shown in plate 82. In addition to the brief caption it bears the identification 'J.W.S.1195'. The initials represent one of the marks used by Joseph Welch & Sons of Portsmouth, one of the larger local-view

Town Hall, Worthing.

81
A colourful local-view card 'Printed by Delittle, Fenwick & Co. York, for Shurey's Publications'. It is actually a free give-away advertisement card for Shurey's 'Smart Novels', 'Yes or No' and 'Daisy Novels'. We are told: 'The finest 1d magazine is Weekly Tale-Teller'. Shurey's produced tens of thousands of such cards.

The Town Hall, Worthing.   JWS 1195

82
A 1905 Joseph Welch & Sons colour-printed card showing in good detail the centre of the town ruled over by the Town Hall. A common (originally popular) scene duplicated on many cards, now available for a few pounds.

publishers, well detailed in Anthony Byatt's book. This card was posted at Worthing on 6 September 1905 and has a later dealer's pencilled price '5p' added. (Very good value but alas a little outdated now!) Some Welch cards bear the trade name 'Chrichromatic' or 'Trichromatic' and the imprint—'Printed at our Works in Belgium'.

My collection also includes unused and therefore undated cards of the 1905 period, credited on the front and reverse 'The Wrench Series' with reference numbers in excess of six thousand. Evelyn Wrench, according to his autobiography, was attracted by the high quality of the German postcards and his first orders for British view cards arrived from his German printers in November 1900. They cost a mere 13s. 6d. (less than 70p) a thousand, plus carriage to England. Sold at a penny each they would retail at ten pounds in total! Within two or three years

83
A local-event postcard produced by the Mezzotint Co. of Brighton. The card, one of a set, relates to Worthing's first Motor Carnival at Easter 1905. The written message relates to the carnival and postcard collecting and as such adds interest and value to a perhaps not inspiring card.

young Wrench was selling some three million cards per month and his stock comprised ten thousand different subjects. However, great as the market was, Wrench had over-reached himself and his company closed in 1906. My Worthing-view card of 'The Bandstand' is number 6414. Another Wrench depicting Holy Trinity Church, Worthing, was postally-used in August 1906 and bears the high number 9733. Heene Church in the same set is numbered 9737. These cards were printed in Saxony and their fronts bear the overprinted greeting 'Wishing you the Compliments of the Season', which may have been added in an attempt to sell some of his vast overstock of such mainly summer-season cards.

I have a rare and interesting photographic-based card relating to one of the early motor carnivals held in Worthing (plate 83). The bunting-bedecked arrival-point is shown with a greeting, 'Welcome. Sunny Worthing'. This card was postally-used on 28 April 1905 and bears an interesting message from a postcard collecting child to her collecting aunt:

> Dear Aunt Emm.
>   Do you like this P.C.
> It [the view] is where the arrival was held. How is your collection getting on? Thanks for Char's P.C. We had one from Bob the same time. With love from Mum.
>   Kit.

When these postcard messages relate to collecting or to the subject on the front great interest is added, which to my mind scores over a mint-unused card, even though it might well be in a cleaner condition.

This card bears the credit 'Printed and Published by the Mezzotint Co., Brighton', a firm not listed in Mr. Byatt's book, presumably because it was one of hundreds of publishers catering only for local trade. I will discuss later the rôle of Worthing in the days of the early motor car and also mention in Chapter VI some of the purely local postcard publishers. However, one may note here that several Brighton firms extended their coverage to nearby towns, and the Mezzotint Company certainly produced some interesting Worthing cards.

Moving forward to 1906, some very colourful view and heraldic postcards were issued by Brown & Rawcliffe Ltd. of Liverpool in or before 1906. One such

WORTHING

84
A Brown & Rawcliffe of Liverpool local heraldic card. The view of Worthing's South Street and Town Hall is reasonably standard, but it hopefully gave pleasure to a young lady in Hammersmith being 'the first one you have of Worthing'. Postally-used in September 1906.

card depicting South Street and the Town Hall is shown as plate 84. This bears the credit 'B&R's Camera Series'. I have already mentioned that in the previous century this Liverpool firm had printed Worthing-view albums, and now in the early 1900s they turned to decorative postcards. Those featuring the town arms were probably advertised in 1906 at seven for six old pence (*see* page 75) but several other sets occur with the arms. Sets of seven or more were sold in packets with 'envelope' covers of the general type shown in plates 59 & 75. A slightly larger, untrimmed version of the same photograph appears printed in black on a card number 2549 in the 'Victoria Series', and bears the postmark for 10 August 1906.

I also have a splendid photographic view of South Street looking up to the old Town Hall—termed the 'old' Town Hall after the imposing new building was built a quarter of a mile away in 1933. (Alas, the old Town Hall was demolished in recent years and a shopping-centre built on the site.) This view-card with its horse-drawn cabs is an unusually large size—twice as long as a standard postcard and nearly three times its height, measuring 9 x 10¾ ins. It is titled on the reverse 'Book Post. This Card may be sent by Post (abroad or inland) with Halfpenny Stamp, provided nothing further than Sender's name is on it, in addition to the address. If any communication is written, Inland postage is One Penny, and usual letter rate according to weight for abroad'. It is signed, 'Rush & Warwick, Art Printers, Bedford'. My large card and a companion of the sea-front are both unused. It would seem that these very large cards were purchased mainly for the photographic view, rather than for use in the post, as they were of a size that suggested a mount and frame for wall decoration. In the post they were very prone to damage from tearing, creasing or folding. To collectors of local history and topographical material they are of great interest but to postcard collectors they present difficulties of storage or display because of their size. The view of South Street looking towards the Town Hall appears, from the road markings and other features (but not the traffic), to have been taken within a few moments of the photograph used for the standard-size card shown in plate 84. This is almost certainly a further example of one photographer taking a series of photographs for sale to different postcard publishers.

A local-view card posted in March 1906 has the familiar name 'Boots' incorporated in the circular trade mark. This is one of the far-ranging 'Pelham

Series' cards. This nationwide firm of cash chemists first sold postcards in 1899, but the 'Boots Pelham Series' credit is normally found on cards of the 1904-14 period. A later mark features the capital letter 'B'; subsequently a large ornately engraved 'Boots—the Chemists' device was used. I assume that Messrs. Boots commissioned such cards from one of the large trade-suppliers, but their cards were only sold in their own shops. W.H. Smith's also published and stocked a wide range of local-view and other cards, usually bearing the identifying initials W.H.S. and/or the trade names 'Kingsway', 'Derwent' or 'Aldwych'.

Of course, most of the postcard publishers which I have noted on earlier cards continued to supply local shops in 1906 and in subsequent years. In particular, one finds Stengel & Co.'s cards, though now with a London address—39 Redcross Street, London, E.C. The 'Peacock Brand' cards issued by the Pictorial Stationery Co. Ltd. are also much in evidence. Although surprising to find old-style undivided-back postcards appearing in 1906, this can, I think, be attributed to the continuing sale of old stock held by some smaller shops with a slow turnover and no need of frequent reorders of replacement stock. Cards were mainly sold to the shops on a firm-sale basis, not 'sale or return', so shopkeepers were encouraged to keep unsold stock on sale for as long as it took to sell.

In 1906 picture postcards and other decorative types were widely available, but the post office was still stocking the earlier type of plain card with its pre-printed halfpenny stamp. These were sold at 10 for 5½d. (under three pence in today's money) or 10 for 6d. in a stouter card, inclusive of the inland postage.

One of my brightest colour-printed views of Worthing shows the then tree-lined Brighton Road with shops in the new 'Broadway' development erected on the site of former Warwick House in 1903. These new shops included a leading stationer and retailer of Worthing postcards. My Broadway card (plate 68) is over-printed in gold 'A Happy Christmas and a Bright New Year', so limiting the period of its sale but extending its use from that of a standard postcard. The printed credit is to 'F.C. Morgan & Co. Ltd., London E.C. Ser.202.2' who printed this Worthing card (and others in this 202 series) in Saxony. The card also bears the reference number 65128, suggesting it was actually produced by one of the German giants of the trade. This is one of the better cards in my collection that was not published by a firm listed in the standard modern postcard reference books. Perhaps, however, F.C. Morgan was only acting as a middleman and was not a true postcard publisher—no matter, I treasure the card.

One of my 1907 cards permits me belatedly to mention the major firm of F. Frith & Co. Ltd. Francis Frith (1822-98) became interested in photography in the 1850s. By 1859 he was established in Reigate (Surrey) where he published many travel books of photographic studies. The large and expanding business was taken over by Francis' sons, Eustace and Cyril, in the 1890s. The earliest Frith postcards were of the small court-shape and were printed in Germany. The post-1902 standard-size Frith cards were usually printed in this country and include a very wide range of local-view studies. These were often printed in sepia rather than full colour, but the quality of reproduction was very good.

Plates 85-6 show a good study of Worthing's Montague Street (now a popular pedestrian precinct) which was postally-used in September 1907, and an undated view of the 'Cinderella Coach' by the pier. The Frith firm continued to 1939, steadily adding to its hoard of photograph prints. After various takeovers the firm failed in 1971, after which the valuable prints were, I understand, acquired by Messrs. Rothman and resold a few years later. However, in the early 1990s the 'original master photographs' were being advertised for sale by 'The Francis Frith Collection Plc. Andover, Hampshire'. The earlier photographs (taken from glass plate negatives) numbered below eighty-nine thousand, and were offered at

Worthing, Montague Street.

Worthing, Marine Parade, "Cinderella Coach".

£25 on a 'first come, first served' basis. The later examples with a lettered reference were priced at £10. This firm held well over a hundred thousand original Frith prints, perhaps a unique coverage of pre-war Britain. One wonders if any of these scenes will be reissued in postcard form. Many have been marketed as blown-up photographic pictures, neatly mounted, to hang on a wall.

My postally-used 1908 selection of local-view cards includes an attractive coloured view of the beach at the aptly-named Splash Point. The front of the card bears the credit 'The Woodbury Series', with the reference number 2241. This trade mark was used by the royal printers, Messrs. Eyre & Spottiswoode Ltd. of London, who had entered the postcard trade in 1902 and continued to supply cards of various types for some twenty years. A special printing process was used, called 'Woodbury-type', hence the trade name. These cards occur both in monochrome and later (at least by 1907) in colour.

87
From goat-power to horse-power. The caption to this P.P.Co. card highlights the Parade and bandstand in the background; today the interest is more likely to be the pre-1920s taxis awaiting customers. Sold locally by I.K.C.

Parade & Bandstand, Worthing

Another of my 1908 cards bears the printed credit 'The Milton "Artletto" series, No. 158, Woolstone Brothers, London'. The 'Milton' trade name was registered in 1902. One of this firm's specialities was novelty cards (*see* Chapter VII) and their early cards were printed in Germany. My coloured view of South Street is blurred and below the standard reached by most firms by 1908, but perhaps the original low price reflects the poor quality.

I also have a monochrome pictorial card of St Paul's Church, Worthing, with the trade name 'The Wyndham Series' and the reference number 'W 8423'. The great but little-known publisher was Wyndham & Co. Ltd. of Acton, which published nearly ten thousand mainly topographical postcards from about 1902 onwards perhaps into the early 1920s.

Plate 87 illustrates an interesting card of early motor cars or cabs waiting just to the west of the pier. It is credited to 'P.P. Co's Copyright. no.1136'. These initials may relate to the Pastel Publishing Company (also known as the Pastel Postcard Company) of Gough Square, London, although the scene appears to be a photographic rather than a hand-drawn view. A coloured version bears the 'National' trade name used by Messrs. Miller & Lang.

Among other cards produced before 1910 a number bear the description 'The Charterhouse Series of Worthing Views'. The issuing firm was Julius Bendix of London. No doubt he also supplied many other provincial towns, perhaps like Valentine's, calling on the services of local photographers to supply suitable photographs to his national firm.

Earlier in this chapter I mentioned the London firm of Sandle Brothers who produced, or rather marketed, in the 1890s some of the earliest English view cards (*see* plate 36). This firm continued through the Edwardian era as publishers of topographical cards, taking over three postcard publishers as they progressed from engraved views to photographic-based types.

A Sandle Brothers black and white matt-surfaced printed card of Windsor Castle, used as an advertising card, gives details of their prices in, I assume, about 1905. As the industry was so competitive, not to say cut-throat, these prices will be representative of the terms offered by the leading postcard publishers of local-view cards. These are the prices charged to retailers, who would supply their own choice of photographs professionally taken by local photographers, such as—in Worthing—Walter Gardiner or Loaders.

This Sandle Brothers card gives the rates for producing local-view postcards reproduced from the customers' own unglazed photographs. The resulting cards were said to be 'good stout regulation size postcards printed with coloured view, name of same and retailers' imprint'.

The basic rates per thousand cards (the lowest number supplied from any one original) were £1 1s. 0d. for one view, £1 0s. 0d. for each of three views, i.e. an order for 3,000, and 18s. 6d. for each of six views, or 6,000 cards. These were presumably for black or one colour printed cards, for the list continued:

> Also supplied:
> Hand Coloured at £1-19-0 per 1000.
> Machine Coloured at £2-0-0 per 1000.

There was an overall reduction of one shilling per thousand if more than three views were ordered at one time, for example, a set of six or a dozen. These were presumably for sale as single cards, for no mention is made of sets or of packaging. These costs, to the retailer, work out at approximately an old farthing per monochrome card or a halfpenny for a coloured card. It is surprising to learn that the hand-coloured versions were slightly cheaper than the machine-coloured examples, a fact that underlines the low pay of the German female or child workers.

I have already made several passing references to Tuck cards and to the internationally respected firm of Raphael Tuck & Sons Ltd. Tuck is almost a household name, readily associated with very good quality greeting and other types of card. Almost every shop-front card of any form of stationers has a Raphael Tuck advertisement in the window.

It therefore came as a surprise when I came to write this chapter on local-view cards to discover that I had relatively few Tuck examples, and most were quite ordinary monochrome types. It cannot be denied that Tuck's produced some superb cards, often of novel and tasteful design. Such a card is shown in plate 88 for Eastbourne.

There is no doubt that this royal warrant holder who, as Anthony Byatt related, 'stands foremost in the history of Fine Art Publishing in Great Britain' stood for quality and leadership at a time of strong competition from the continent. Tuck's produced better than average postcards and were market-leaders. But even this great firm had to cater for market requirements—for most buyers this was for view cards available for a penny or less. The market for quality cards retailing at threepence or sixpence was restricted and was not aimed at trippers. Postcard production is all about long print runs, mass production and large sales.

Examination of reprints of early Tuck price-lists* shows that most of Tuck's cards were sold at a penny each, either in sixpenny packets of six, or shilling packets of twelve. But some, such as the 'Connoisseur' series, were twice the standard price. The 'Elite' series cost 1s. 6d. for a packet of six but the hand-coloured versions of 'Dainty Faces' in the 'Continental' series cost 2s. 6d. for six, or five (old) pence each.

In general, all hand-coloured versions of black and white subjects were double the price of the plain, literally a case of 'penny plain, two pence coloured'. The greatest range of prices occurs among birthday postcards. Packets of six were priced at 6d., 1s., 1s. 6d. or 2s. Obviously the difference in price reflected the quality of the card; the most expensive were probably superbly embossed and highly coloured continental productions. However, except perhaps for a few specialist Tuck collectors, these costly birthday postcards are not in demand with present-day collectors. The contemporary collectors were however in Tuck's mind for the price-lists comment: 'particularly interesting to the collector'; 'thus enhancing the value of this series for the collector'.

* The 1903 list was republished by permission in 1993, by Graham Leadly of 59 High Road, Wormley, Herts.

88
A typically good quality Raphael Tuck heraldic card (no.1003) 'Designed in England. Chromographed in Bavaria'. Cards of this Tuck format were made for many other towns, *c.*1905. *See* plate 29.

Tuck's 'Oilette' series is famous, the general intent being to emulate an oil-painting. These cards can be very decorative and charming, but are not always of great interest to the modern historian. From a historical point of view the original photograph, from which an artist made the painting to be mass-produced on postcards, would be more helpful.

The many black and white or one colour printed Tuck series include: 'Art Toned Sepia'; 'Sepia Plate-marked'; or the more glossy 'Glosso' and 'Silverette'. These were issued for hundreds of different towns. They are well produced but unexciting. Perhaps they had the edge over other cards as they were Tuck's—'Art Publishers to their Majesties the King & Queen'. Incidentally the approximate period of an undated Tuck card can be gauged by the royal warrant wording. That cited above relates to King George and Queen Elizabeth. In 1937 the wording was extended to include '... and to Her Majesty Queen Mary'. The form of royal arms was also amended and 'Ltd' appears after the firm's name. A revised royal arms appears on post-1952 Queen Elizabeth cards with the wording 'By appointment to Her Majesty the Queen, Fine Art Publishers'.

Plate 89 shows two typical Tuck local-view postcards that probably retailed for a penny or two. One helpful feature of these Tuck cards is a printed appreciation on the message side. That showing 'Worthing, the Front and Bandstand', for example, reads:

> Front and Bandstand. Worthing is a fashionable and popular seaside resort about ten miles from Brighton. It possesses a mild and pleasant climate, and is an excellent centre for viewing the beautiful country of the South Downs.
>
> The Front, a favourite promenade, extends for over a mile and includes among other attractions, a handsome bandstand, from which excellent bands discourse music daily during the season.

The text was amended for different views, and, of course, to suit other localities. Tuck's were not the only publishers to add such blurbs; Messrs. Waterlow & Sons' cards (produced for the old London, Brighton & South Coast Railway) went to town in their blurb:

> WORTHING is a select Watering Place and Residential Town and Winter resort for Invalids on the South Coast, situated amidst sylvan surroundings.

89
Two glossy Raphael Tuck 'Glosso' Worthing-view cards. The address side includes interesting information on the localities depicted, *c.*1910-15.

WORTHING. LAUNCHING THE LIFEBOATS.

WORTHING. THE FRONT AND BANDSTAND.

It is noted for its bright sunshine and genial climate. There are about thirty miles of glass-houses in use by professional fruit growers—a leading industry of the town and neighbourhood. Asphalted Promenade 1¼ miles long. Excellent train service and cheap ticket facilities.

Returning to Raphael Tuck & Sons, a feature to note is the Tuck mark—an artist's easel with the initials 'R T S' reproduced in miniature on the front of the card. It is repeated larger in the stamp box on the address side. The postwar Tuck cards usually also have the town initials on the front followed by the reference number. For Worthing these references run W T G 1, W T G 2 and so on.

Anthony Byatt's standard book *Picture Postcards and their Publishers* (Golden Age Postcard Books, 1978) devotes 12 pages to a history of the Tuck firm and its vast range of products. Various articles have also appeared in the magazine *Picture PostCard Monthly*.

Chapter V

The Lévy and Related Home-Town Cards

A typical Lévy local-view card, entitled: '20 Worthing – Parade from Pier Gates – LL.'. One of a very long series, several variations occur of each numbered view from *c.*1907 onwards. This French firm supplied thousands of different photographic-based view cards.

The purpose of this chapter is twofold. The previous chapter on the publishers of local-view picture postcards was, because of the vastness of the subject, becoming over-long. More importantly, I wish to give due prominence to one major firm. In the previous chapter the producers of the cards were mainly German or British; but there was at least one important Paris-based firm that had built up a worldwide coverage of their pictorial postcards and other view material.

This firm and its cards are special and have very many devotees. Most postcard dealers have sections or boxes of these French topographical photographic studies. These cards are often familiarly known as 'LL.s', for these initials appear on the front of each card, after the description of the scene. The second initial stood for Lévy, or perhaps originally, Levitsky. The christian name is open to some doubt.

Most English postcard publishers obtained their local-view photographs (the originals) from professional photographers who knew the district and could supply a selection of suitable prints taken under favourable conditions. From this commissioned portfolio the publishers could choose a suitable and saleable set. They ordered prints only when they needed them and so did not have to employ their own full-time photographers. The disadvantage of this system was that each national publisher tended to be supplied with very much the same stock views.

The greatest exception to this convenient practice was the Paris-based firm that seemingly employed its own talented team of photographers. This French firm covered at least the southern part of the British Isles as well as most of Europe—not that they stopped there. It was multi-national coverage.

Whilst most British and German suppliers of local-view cards would be content with perhaps two-dozen views of any medium-sized town, the French issued much longer sets. In the case of Worthing, with a population of only about 25,000 in 1905, they issued a hundred very superior named and numbered views of the town and the neighbourhood.

The Worthing Lévy postcards seem to date from 1907 but other towns were apparently covered from about 1905. Sales continued into the 1920s; indeed some originals are still being reprinted and used in various forms today.

The appeal and quality of these cards rests on striking, wide-angle photographs and on the printing process, which was usually a pleasing matt-black or sepia, but several other tints occur and also coloured versions of the same scenes. A further attraction is the large range of views, several of which are not depicted by other publishers. These French productions also tended to be more lively than other types: figures and children were well used to add interest.

The French, or non-British, Lévy postcards date back to about 1900. Some Russian-subject cards bear the unusual credit 'L. Levitsky'. It is not known if this was the original name or merely the Russian version of Lévy, amended to make the products more acceptable in Russia. These Russian market cards are important as they indicate that the photographs were taken by this L. Levitsky. The full credit reads: 'Photographié a Peterhof le 16 Aôut 1901, par L. Levistky Photographe de L L Majestés'. The French and English market cards, however, often (but not always) bear the publisher's name Lévy on the address side with the photographer's initials 'LL.' on the view side. Note the initials are rendered with only one final full-stop.

Over the years much research has been carried out on the Lévy cards but, even now, we are not sure of the basic facts. Do the double initials really relate to the photographer? Could one person have taken all the view cards issued by this one company? What was the Christian name of 'LL.'?

90
Two typical matt-printed monochrome 'LL.' French-produced Lévy cards, one of thousands of well-populated views of south coast English towns and resorts. Coloured versions also occur. Postally-used in 1916.

27 *BRIGHTON BEACH. — LL.*

8 *EASTBOURNE. — On the Beach. — LL.*

Many readers will be saying, 'Don't be silly, it was Louis Lévy'. Yes, indeed, for many years collectors have confidently referred to Louis, but from at least 1991 research has strongly suggested that the christian name was Lucien. I shall from this point refer to Lucien Lévy as the photographer of these charming French-produced view cards but there is much still to be discovered about these thousands of Lévy view cards. Each southern English town had its own series of numbered cards. The London views ran into hundreds (my London Zoo card is numbered 728) but the Paris views ran to well over a thousand.

Some years ago there was a 'Louis Lévy collectors' club' but this folded, mainly because most members were only interested in Lévy views of their own town, not in the overall story of the firm and its massive pictorial coverage.

It is recorded (by Anthony Byatt and others) that the Lévy firm came to London in 1905, engaging Max Alexander as its agent. The address was

4 BOGNOR. — Looking West from Royal Pier Hotel. — LL.

19 EASTBOURNE. — The Parade. — LL.

3 GODSHILL (Isle of Wight). — The Church and Old Cottage. — LL.

91
Three typical coloured versions of the usually monochrome, matt-surfaced, French 'LL.' local-view postcards. Postally-used in 1907.

92
A most attractive Lévy beach scene postcard, showing wheeled bathing tents and (over-)dressed holiday-makers. The 1909 message reads, in part, 'I thought you would like a card for your album'.

18   WORTHING. — Bathing Tents. — LL.

118-122 Holborn, in the Gamages block. While the Lévy continental view cards vastly outnumber the English scenes, the scope of their coverage—particularly of English south coast resorts—is astounding. In some specimens the caption and credit are at the bottom, at other times at the top, or to one side. Also various colours of paper were used and some fifteen or more different variations of the address side are to be found. All British subject cards that I have seen, however, are of the divided-back type. It has been estimated that this French firm issued over ten thousand British views, in all probability an underestimate. They also issued series of pictorial 'home-town' cards for well over a hundred English towns or cities, mainly in the southern counties.

The editor of the *Worthing Gazette* very nearly found a place in postcard history when he chose to reproduce a Lévy postcard, one of several views of Worthing beach, in his issue of Wednesday 28 August 1912. It is a classic example of a Lévy local view, and is my favourite Worthing example (plate 92) number 18, entitled 'Bathing Tents'.* It had the unusual 'LL.' signature, but no other credit to Lévy, the Paris publishers.

The *Worthing Gazette* editor was a gentleman; he gave credit for his illustration to the publisher of the card, in his article on 'Our Present Bathing Facilities'. The Lévy photograph had a new caption, 'When Family Bathing began to develop'. The following text reads, in part:

> We are indebted to the courtesy of Messrs. Lévy Sons & Co of 118-122 Holborn E.C. for permission to reproduce the illustration which accompanies this article. It is one of their excellent series of pictorial postcards and shows a condition of things that existed a few years ago, between Heene Terrace and the Hotel Metropole ...

* This was a popular view, reproduced in Ward Lock & Co.'s Worthing [and district] illustrated guide book of 1921-2, along with other postcard views, credited to Lévy Sons & Co., 118 Holborn, but with no personal credit to the individual photographer.

How important this acknowledgement could have been if the local editor had delved a little deeper or even followed up with an article on the suppliers of the popular picture postcards.

Turning to the production process, we were informed by Mr. Ian McDonald (*Picture PostCard Monthly*, July 1980) that Louis Edward Lévy, an American, invented in about 1899 a new process for the acid etching of photographic

81. *WORTHING — The Town Hall. — LL.*

93
A contrast in posing. The first card, a German Hartmann production is coloured but lifeless. The second example, a French Lévy monochrome card is full of life—the figures include several well-known local characters. Lévy studies of standard views such as Worthing Town Hall are usually superior to other makes.

printing blocks, resulting in improved clarity of the print. His brother Max Lévy had earlier introduced a half-tone screen printing process. The new 'acid blast' process was in use in about 1900. This information has more recently been superseded by Mr. Harold Gough's researches published in *Picture PostCard Monthly* of December 1991. Briefly, the tiny worm-like marks seen under high-magnification (rather than the dots observed in other processes) indicate the use of a collotype technique, based on a 'photogelatin' process in which the negative is exposed to light over a sensitised plate. It is noteworthy that none of the Lévy cards claim any form of patent for the printing or reproductive processes used. Whatever the technical details, the end-product is usually superb, even though it is matt and devoid of a glossy surface.

    The overall effect should be credited to the photographer (or photographers), for the views are chosen with care and in most cases the scene is enlivened with figures and traffic. They capture so well the bustle of a busy town centre or market-place. Plate 93 shows two postcards of Worthing Town Hall. The French-printed Lévy example is in this case printed in rather too dark a manner (this can vary from card to card) but it is so lively in comparison with the German-printed Hartmann version.

The period over which the Lévy cards were produced is great, ranging for Worthing as far as my present selection is concerned from the summer of 1907 (Brighton and some other Sussex town cards date from 1905) through the First World War and into the mid-1920s.

From about 1920 new printings of English subject cards rarely bear the name and address 'Lévy Sons & Co. Paris' (or 'Lévy Fils et Cie, Paris' on French subject cards) along the dividing line between the address and the correspondence sides. One of my later Lévy Worthing-view cards is postmarked June 1924 but, of course, such dates are evidence for the date of posting and not necessarily the month or year of production, for some shops would have held stocks for long periods, especially of the less popular views. Perhaps the ultimate example of the later use of a card is represented by a beautiful view of 'Worthing Parade from Pier Gates' with horse-drawn coaches and cabs (LL. Worthing series card number 20), not posted until 9 September 1965. The message, written some fifty years later than the view depicted, reads in part: 'On the other side of this P.C. is the Worthing of 50 years ago looks a bit square doesn't it? ... Dad'. Not at all. It looks delightful and these tranquil times can never return. I do not know if 'Dad' found the card in the bottom of a drawer or if he purchased a job lot and used the old card—it being cheaper than the cost of a modern product!* Perhaps the cards were being reissued? This is quite possible, for these 'LL.' photographs of Edwardian Worthing are masterpieces, and in their composition and interest outrival all my other local picture postcards. However, the stamp panel bears the correct contemporary printed postage charge of one halfpenny.

I must mention that several views were re-photographed two or perhaps three times so that one finds slight variations, mainly in the position of figures, when only a minute or two separated different exposures. This can be seen in the two views of Worthing Town Hall shown in plate 94. The lower version was photographed, according to the clock, at seven minutes past eleven, the less animated version three minutes later. One can understand a photographer taking several shots of any one scene to obtain the best possible picture, but it is strange that both versions were used, with the same reference number. This is a frequent practice.

The whole series of Worthing cards (opinions vary as to whether the set comprised 99 or 101) was not taken in the same period. The French photographer's first visit to Worthing was probably in spring 1907, for the earliest postally-used or dated example I have noted was in April 1907. (The photographs appear, however, to have been taken in high summer, in August or September; note the beach scene shown in plate 92. This is not a British spring, but high summer of perhaps 1906.) He may then have taken subjects numbered up to the late 70s. A fresh visit in about 1915 is evidenced by some cards from at least number 79 (plate 95) onwards, showing new shop owners' names or depicting the rebuilt pier which had been opened on 29 May 1914. This second visit would have been before the end of August 1915 for number 99 shows the 1910 Kursaal on the sea-front with that name displayed. The owner, C. Adolf Seebold—a colourful Swiss national, renamed this The Dome in August 1915 to avoid any seemingly German connection. This change is also conveniently commented upon on a LL. card in my collection dated 22 August 1915: 'Kursaal now renamed The Dome'. The Dome remains (just) as a wonderful reminder

*A Brighton lady, writing in *Picture Postcard Monthly*, November 1979, relates that, as a young girl holidaying in Boulogne and Le Touquet in 1959, she purchased old black and white First World War Lévy cards still on display over forty years later. They were understandably the cheapest cards available.

32 WORTHING. — *The Town Hall.* — LL.

3 1 WORTHING. — *The Town Hall.* — LL.

94
Two other Lévy views of Worthing Town Hall and Warwick Street. The clock shows they were taken four minutes apart, but both views were put in production under the same Worthing reference number. The Lévy cards display several such variations.

of an early cinema, although it was originally built as a roller-skating rink, a large hall or ballroom (originally called 'The Coronation Hall' café and Winter Garden). Quite a complex.

That card, reporting the new name on 22 August 1915, predated by three days the press announcement of the change. Mr. Seebold had announced a town competition to suggest a new non-Germanic name for his Kursaal a fortnight earlier. The prize was one pound! Over four hundred suggestions were received: 'The Cupola', 'The Rotunda', even 'The Khakidome', and Mr. Seebold was sensible enough to reject 'Seebold's Palace'—I bet somebody thought he would win a pound with this vanity name! The fact is that before the end of August 1915 this prominent building was called 'The Dome', not the 'Kursaal' as depicted on the LL. local-view card number 99.

95
Two different Lévy views of Warwick Street, taken from in front of the Town Hall. Number 79 was taken later than number 44; from a study of the local directories it is clear that the second version postdates 1914, while the first is *c.*1907.

79 WORTHING. — *Warwick Street* — LL.

44 WORTHING — *Warwick Street.* — LL.

The second (or maybe the third) visit by Messrs. Lévy's photographer to Worthing was, I am sure, between the opening of the new pier at the end of May 1914 and the renaming of the Kursaal in August 1915. The commercial likelihood indicates late spring 1915, in order to produce a new enlarged selection ready for the summer season.

It is probable that this photographer worked his way through other southern English resorts at the same period. He would not have visited only Worthing. Perhaps research on the pictorial LL. view cards of other towns will solve this mini-mystery. Perhaps, too, a study of posting dates will help to establish the likely dates for the new issues which enlarged the original series. The exact date might be discovered if I could trace why the Town Hall flag is at half-mast on card number 81 (plate 93): the death of a lifeboat man or perhaps a councillor—

99 WORTHING. — The Kursaal. — LL.

56 WORTHING. — Homefield Park. The Rustic Bridge. - LL.

53 WORTHING. — Broadwater Church (Interior). — LL.

96 *(left)*
A rare Lévy Worthing card, postally-used in August 1915. The message mentions that 'Kursaal is now renamed 'The Dome', no foreign names for Worthing'. Worthing-view card number 99, towards the end of a long series.

97 *(top right)*
An interesting version of a Worthing Lévy postcard, perhaps showing the French photographer posing on the bridge. Postally-used in Worthing in July 1909.

98 *(bottom right)*
Not all Lévy cards are of outdoor views—several interior church scenes were included in each town's set. These are not now universally popular, but this depicts the church where my wife and I were married and our son christened. It obviously has special personal significance. Any collection should include examples that have personal associations.

as yet I do not know. There is so much of interest in these French-produced view cards of southern England.

The Lévy view of the old rustic bridge in Homefield Park may be important in this study of these French-produced views of English towns. Two versions occur: one with a young lad leaning over the bridge, the other (plate 97) shows a middle-aged man. Local postcard collector, Geoff Pyle, has suggested that the man is in fact the French photographer. Geoff suggests that the bag in the foreground is the photographer's bag of equipment and that, not liking the first view with the boy, he asked the lad to activate the camera whilst he took up the position on the bridge to complete the composition. There may be other, simpler, reasons for the two different figures to appear, but it would be interesting to discover if this hatted figure makes an appearance in other Lévy cards, particularly in those taken in other towns covered by this photographer.

The rare colour-printed LL. cards were produced usually, but not invariably, from special photographs; they are not coloured versions of the standard monochrome scenes. Plate 99 shows two cards numbered 23; the seated figures, prams, deck-chairs, etc., are in identical positions, but the walking figures have changed, showing that the two exposures were made but a few moments apart. It must be admitted, however, that the quality of reproduction of the Lévy

99
Two coloured Lévy mass-market popular trippers'-subject cards of the same Worthing sea-front scene, but taken a few moments apart. Postally-used in August 1914.

23 WORTHING. — Marine Parade. — Looking West. — LL.

23 WORTHING. — Marine Parade. — Looking West. — LL.

colour-printed cards is not nearly as fine as the monochrome examples. They are very grainy—not as sharp as the one-colour examples. Nevertheless, the buyer was probably charged an enhanced price for the colour. I do not know of any contemporary references to the original prices for these French cards, but the one-colour standard examples were probably only a penny or slightly less (eight for sixpence, perhaps) in order to compete with all the other types of picture postcards on the market at the same period.

The coloured version of any Lévy scene bears the same reference number as the monochrome edition. One could build up two complete sets of the hundred or so Worthing views, plus all the many variations. Some towns like Hastings had even longer series than Worthing. I would love to illustrate all my hundred and more English 'LL.' cards but obviously this cannot be done in this book, so I must content myself with the examples shown in plates 100-3.

38 WORTHING. — Chapel Road — LL.

17 WORTHING. — Paddling. — LL.

45 WORTHING. — South Street. — LL.

100
A lively Lévy view of Worthing main street with not a motor car in sight. Message to Miss Nyria Thompson of Devon reads: 'Will send your stays as soon as possible, keep woollen coat on till the petticoat arrives'. Postally-used in August 1915.

101 *(left and below)*
Two typical matt-surfaced Lévy monochrome cards. Local shrimpers and fully-dressed paddlers are sampling the delights of the sands and shallow water. Also a remarkably peaceful South Street scene free of cars. Postally-used in 1907 and 1908.

102 *(right and below)*
Two typical Lévy local-view cards showing the sea-front east and west of the pier. *Warne's Hotel* is in the centre of the middle view, now, alas, an open car park site.

48 WORTHING. — *Warne's Hotel.* — LL.

72 WORTHING. — *The Bandstand and New Shelter.* — LL.

103
More delights of the coastal resorts which supported a number of small shows, concert parties, orchestras, bands and so on.

18 LITTLEHAMPTON. — *On the Common.* — LL.

164 TROUVILLE. — La Rue des Bains. — LL.

104
A classic Lévy home market card, Trouville number 164, showing in the foreground a postcard shop. Postally-used and sent to England in 1909 without a message.

I see from one of this selection that has become damp that they are not made up from a single thin card, but as a three-piece sandwich. A plain centre—the filling, with the printed view stuck to the top and the separately printed address side affixed below. No doubt this style had production and therefore commercial advantages.

My foreign view cards issued by this firm, like my Worthing views, can be beautiful and highly interesting—a typical French view is shown in plate 104. At least some of the Lévy local-view cards were issued in booklet form, the left-hand side of the detachable card being joined to the binding and having perforations so that each card could be torn out. Such booklet-bound detachable cards consequently have slightly rough left-hand edges. My partly-used booklet of views of Trouville comprises 22 cards. Strangely, the reference numbers are jumbled; that is, they are not bound in numerical order, and range between 1 and 296 with many gaps. These cards are credited 'Lévy Fils & Cie. Paris' (a trade-style in use by at least 1907 but not, it seems, fully used on postcards at first). They also bear a small oval monogram mark of the Union Syndicate des Maîtres Imprimeurs de France, as used from about 1916, and the French copyright working 'Modèle. Deposé'. The large initials 'LL.' can also occur printed within a laurel wreath.

Most of the 'LL.' cards do not bear a printed Lévy credit on the address side, although the stamp panel will bear the wording 'Made in France'. Some Lévy English view cards will, however, bear the name and address of local major retailers. A Hastings card, for example, may have the added imprint 'Salmon's Library, 33, White Rock, Hastings', a Folkestone card the imprint 'F.J. Thompson, 32, Guildhall Street, Folkestone'. Other cards may have a rubber-stamped indication of the point of sale. For example, 'The Watch Tower. Beachy Head' is stamped on a Lévy Eastbourne-view card of 'Beachy Head and the Lighthouse'.

Some Worthing and district LL. cards bear the initials 'R.B.W.'. I will return to discuss the significance of these initials later. Any Lévy card bearing the initial or name of a local retailer is relatively rare, as they were only sold at one outlet. They are not, however, any more valuable, only more interesting to some specialist collectors.

Most Lévy pictorial postcards bear a photographic scene that completely filled the card, except for a small area left for the reference number and caption

105
A third series Lévy card (*left*) using an existing photograph printed in a slightly recessed frame and with new simpler title but retaining the 'LL.' credit. These post-1920 examples are relatively scarce. The other example (*right*) shows the same view in its original format.

and perhaps a line or two of writing at the bottom. In other words the picture fills the entire width of the card (some 5½ ins.). However, a rarer series has a smaller picture (approx. 2½ x 4¼ ins.) set in a stamped slightly recessed framework. Above the picture is printed the name of the town with its caption and initials LL. below. In this smaller picture series no reference numbers appear. I show specimens of the two types in plate 105. The smaller variety was available in Sussex shops by at least 1911.

Various contributions to our understanding of the Lévy pictorial cards have appeared in the British collector's magazine *Picture PostCard Monthly*; indeed this subject seems to have cropped up more than any other. The following issues contain articles or correspondence relating to photographic cards believed until only a few years ago to have been taken by Louis Lévy. We now understand that the Lévy connection was the long-established Paris publishing and printing house and that Louis was non-existent. The leading light or perhaps the photographer during the picture postcard period was Lucien Lévy. See issues for October, November 1979; November 1981; October 1982; March 1983; January, April, June, September 1985; February 1986; January 1989; August, October, November, December 1991; May 1992; February 1993.

The most important and up-to-date account of the various and succeeding Lévy firms was that written by Harold Gough and published in *Picture PostCard Monthly* of December 1991. It is, however, unlikely to be the last contribution to our study of these popular home-town postcards.

The popular views—the pier, the sea-front, the Town Hall and other central views—are still quite common, having been sold over a ten- or fifteen-year period and can be found for a pound or two. Views of outlying districts sold in smaller numbers and were more likely to have been withdrawn from the series after a year or so. As a result they are decidedly scarce and expensive when found. Some in the Worthing series I have not yet seen and I, a keen collector, would obviously give a very good price should one of the missing subjects be reported to me.*

Yet, because these subjects were originally unpopular these rarities may well appear dull or uninteresting to the layman. The low numbers are usually the most common; they represent obvious local scenes, and were on sale for the longest period. The higher reference numbers often represent the outlying views or subjects introduced in later years. I will return to the strange commercial aspects of collecting in Chapter IX.

My experiences with the LL. Worthing cards can be mirrored in countless other southern English towns or districts. An interesting article by Clive Ponsford published in *Picture PostCard Monthly* of February 1993, for example, relates his

* The Worthing numbers that have eluded me so far are: 4, 15, 51, 66-9, 83, 85-7, 93, 95, 96, 100 or any higher numbers. Some of these may depict outlying districts rather than main town scenes.

experiences in collecting LL.'s Devon-view cards—a search which included a visit to Worthing, where he had to borrow £60 from his wife to pay for his new purchases at a local postcard fair, a good investment no doubt.

Back in 1912 the editor of the *Worthing Gazette* chose a five-year-old French-photographed view of Worthing beach to illustrate his article. Since then very many Lévy cards have been reproduced (usually without credit) to illustrate books and other material. I am happy to relate that a local charity-minded resident has illustrated an excellent large format 'Sepia Scenes' calendar mainly with reproductions of these old, Edwardian LL. views. The profits from this locally printed enterprise go to Mr. Wilf Hugill's charity work in Romania.

Few Edwardian photographs of local scenes can have given as much long-term, continuing pleasure as have these Lévy photographs. Today they please collectors, local historians, postcard dealers, and also some families overseas who are not able to enjoy the basic necessities of life.

The Lévy firm merged with another great French firm in about 1919. They then traded as Lévy et Neurdein. These cards of the 1920s will often bear the enlarged credit, 'Lévy et Neurdein réunis' or 'Lévy et Neurdein réunis, 44 rue Letellier, Paris', signifying that these two competing photographic firms had united.

Lévy & Neurdein cards of the late 1920s or early 1930s were issued in the now standard glossy finish. The new photographs are sharp and clear but lack the period charm of the earlier, traditional types. However, some matt-surfaced LL. views were issued by 'Cie des Arts Photomécaniques' of Strasbourg.

Some continental and Channel Island view cards produced in a similar matt-printed style bear the front credit, 'Collections N D Phote' whilst the reverse carries the fuller credit, 'Etablissements Photographiques de NEURDEIN Freres—Paris'. Some of these seem to predate the British subject Lévy cards and the earlier Neurdein 'Carte Postale' have the undivided-back or address side. However, very few Neurdein cards depict British towns; the rival Lévy Company seems to have monopolised the trade in England. Nevertheless Neurdein enjoyed a large trade on the continent, as did several other French firms who seem to have produced Lévy-type postcards. Interesting as these foreign views can be, they are not highly valued in this country; we are concerned mainly with pictures of our own towns.

I have mentioned that some Lévy cards bear (apart from the standard LL. credit) the initials 'R.B., W'. These occur on many other Worthing cards and are often preceded by 'Published by ...'. The punctuation can vary and there is often a dash before the 'W'. Cards with these initials are, in general, of a rather superior quality to the general run of local views. However, these 'R.B., W' cards are not wholly restricted to my town; other examples can be found for places such as Arundel and similar Sussex tourist spots. These initials warrant a passing mention in Anthony Byatt's *Picture Postcards and their Publishers* in relation to a Lévy Chichester-view card, but these R.B. cards are very much more commonly found with Worthing views. My endeavours to trace the significance of these initials cost me sleepless nights and many daylight hours—in the end I was rewarded.

As several of these cards carried double credits, one to well-known national publishers such as Valentine & Sons Ltd. of Dundee and the French firm of Lévy & Sons, I assumed that R.B., W referred to a retailer and I further guessed that the last initial stood for Worthing. This left R.B. to be identified. In most cases the second of these initials would be the surname, the first a Christian name. On this basis we might have Richard Burton. But I could not find any Worthing shopkeeper or photographer with these initials. I discussed the problem with other collectors and with old Worthing tradesmen, but none could come up with the answer.

The problem of these initials was raised at a Rotary meeting. By a fortunate coincidence there was seated opposite me at this lunchtime meeting a guest who also collected Worthing cards. Although initially unable to help with the mystery initials this guest, Robert Naunton, phoned that evening to say that on checking his cards he had come up with the answer. He had discovered a card bearing the full credit, 'Ramsden Bros, Worthing' and also a related card with the mystery initials 'R.B., W'. The initial 'B' was not the surname, but stood for 'Bros' or 'Brothers'.

This high-class firm of booksellers and stationers, situated at 11 Chapel Road, had always been known to me simply as 'Ramsden's', while the local directories I had consulted listed the firm as 'Ramsden's Library' rather than 'Ramsden Bros'. Local directories revealed that this shop (where before the war we bought our family Christmas cards and my parents obtained their lending-library books) first appeared in Chapel Road in 1922 and continued until 1957 when it was taken over by W.H. Smith and subsequently closed. In the 1930s I had been into Ramsden's hundreds of times but, being under ten years old, I cannot recall having seen any postcards. Perhaps by then they had ceased to stock such low-price goods. Still, the mystery was seemingly solved on that fateful Monday in February 1988.

On Saturday of that week, however, I began to have doubts for, on re-checking my 'R.B., W' cards, I found several depicting the storm-wrecked Worthing pier and the reopening of its successor. The dates of these events are well recorded on postcards—23 March 1913 and 19 May 1914—eight or so years before Ramsden's Library opened at 11 Chapel Road. Could the helpful Robert Naunton have been wrong? Were his two cards not directly related after all?

That same Saturday afternoon in the Worthing Reference Library I was examining its local history collection and there—right before my eyes—were two cards which clinched the basic point. They were picture postcards of 'The Bandstand & Pier, Worthing' as it appeared in about 1914. The cards bear on the address side the tell-tale initials, but they are overprinted with the sales blurb:

> This is a View of Bandstand and Parade
> as it used to be.
> For Views of Worthing as it is to-day,
> see RAMSDEN'S DISPLAY,
> at RAMSDEN'S LIBRARY,
> 11 Chapel Road,
> Worthing'

Apparently the management, having a quantity of out-of-date cards, used some to publicise their new stock of up-to-date views. But, importantly for me, this new overprinting for 'Ramsden's Display' neatly tied in with the initials 'R.B., W' which appeared on the same card.

However, this still left me with the problem of how Ramsden's were able to sell event cards well before the firm appeared in directories at the Chapel Road address which I had known so well. Directories in the Reference Library revealed that this family business had earlier traded as Ramsden Bros., Stationers, at 7 The Broadway, Brighton Road, Worthing. The local directories for 1909-21 include this entry. In 1921 Charles E. Thomas, bookseller, was occupying 11 Chapel Road but, in the next issue of *Kelly's* local directory, Ramsden Bros. are in occupation having left their Broadway address. Charles Thomas had carried on much the same type of high-class stationery and bookselling business. There is an interesting photographic record of the double-fronted shop in the Worthing Museum collection—it is, of course, a real-photograph picture postcard.

The 'R.B., W' Ramsden cards can therefore date back to 1909. Indeed, I am not at present sure if they could not date back further to 1903 when this Art Nouveau-style terrace of shops was built at the beginning of Brighton Road, just to the east of the town centre (plates 68 & 80). The local directories of the 1903-8 period all list at 7 The Broadway 'J. Armsden, Stationer'. I rather suspect that this is a recurring printer's error for 'J. Ramsden', the first two letters of the name having been transposed, especially as in the 1909 directory the entry for the same shop became Ramsden Bros. Ramsden as a local stationer and possible source of postcards, could well date back to 1903.*

Having carried out my own elementary research, I thought to contact an old school colleague and leading member of our local church—Herbert Ramsden—as I had hoped he was related to the Ramsden family, although not directly connected with their business. He was able to tell me that the two brothers were James (b.c.1872) and William. Apparently these brothers sold the business in the 1930s to the owner of an old-established firm of printers (Paines) although the Ramsden name remained and the take-over seems to have been kept very secret.

I had at first assumed that all the 'R.B., W' cards were merely retailed by Ramsdens at one of their two successive shops. It now seems possible, however, that they both produced these cards and supplied some to other outlets. Firstly, I found one 1912 card in our reference library which bore the credit 'Ramsden Bros. Printers'. Secondly, a card showing the popular and well-known 'Old Houses at Tarring. Built about 12th Century' has the normal credit 'R.B., W', but with the following helpful information handwritten on the reverse:

> Purchased this card in old cottage (marked X) on Sept. 13th 1916. King Henry (the Sixth) granted a Charter to Tarring to hold an open market weekly for ever.

This Ramsden Brothers' card was therefore on sale at the tourist attraction depicted on the card, not at their own shop in the centre of the town. This dated note reminds us that then, as now, picture postcards were available not only at post offices and shops but also at many other places.

The Lévy view of the old Worthing library (plate 106), number 75 in this series, is interesting on three counts. Firstly, it does not bear the usual LL. initial credit on the front, only the Ramsden Brothers' credit. It is certainly part of the Lévy set of Worthing views and was posted in August 1922. Perhaps other Lévy views of other towns bear only the initials of local retailers, but 99 per cent or more of such cards bear the standard Lévy initials.

The second point is that the rough left-hand edge shows that this card was torn from a packet or booklet of such cards available at Ramsden's, enabling them to sell cards in groups of a dozen or more, rather than individually. It is in my experience very unusual to find Lévy's English-view cards in booklet form.

Thirdly, you will have noticed that the overseas-rate postage stamp is affixed to the view side of the card. This is a deplorable French or continental practice! In this case a young Belgian lady was writing to her parents in Antwerp, praising the delights of sunny Worthing.

It is surprising how many Worthing-view cards were sent overseas by foreign visitors. With the increasing trade in postcards many of them are finding their way back to their original country or town. Possibly some English postcard dealers buy on the continent, or European dealers might send their English contacts selections of English view cards. These would then either be bought or exchanged for continental views, which can be found here in quite large numbers. With this Lévy card, the French photographer travelled to Worthing to take the photograph as one of a series. This was then processed and printed in Paris. The completed cards were then sent back to Worthing. This example was sold in Ramsden's shop

* To illustrate the dangers of assumption, very much later I discovered a local press report of a fire at Mr. James Armsden's premises at 7 The Broadway. Furthermore this was followed by a signed letter of gratitude to the fire brigade for their smart and prompt appearance 'only a very few minutes indeed elapsed between the time the alarm was given by Councillor Gardiner and their arrival thus allaying what might have been a very disastrous fire'. This was signed 'J. Armsden'. Nevertheless, there does seem to have been a link with the slightly later Ramsden firm. It was not unknown for local tradesmen to change their name for one reason or another, *see* page 160.

106
A local-view Lévy card with perforated left edge, showing that it was originally sold in booklet form. The 'LL.' French credit has in this case been replaced by the initials of the Worthing retailer. The overseas postage stamp is on the view side in the continental manner—a pity.

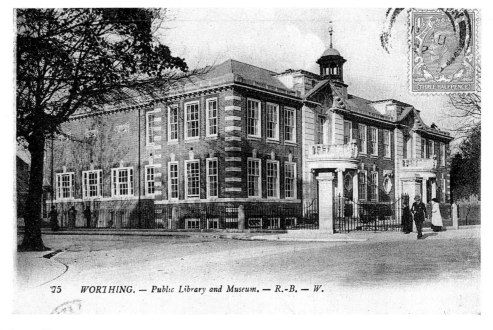

75   WORTHING. — Public Library and Museum. — R.-B. — W.

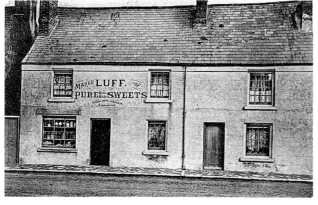

107
A local 'Chatsworth series' picture postcard showing a justly celebrated sweetshop. The card, which bears a related message, was probably sold from this shop. Postally-used in September 1907.

* This view of Luff's sweetshop was reissued by the West Sussex County Council Library Service in 1993 as part of a set of six on Broadwater. An interesting potted history of the shop has been added but with no credit to the original publisher or its source. Strange for a library service! They even date the view to *c*.1920, whereas my example was postally-used in 1907.

to a young visitor from Belgium who duly sent it home to her parents. Some seventy years later it found its way back to Worthing where I purchased it from a local postcard dealer. The postcard market is truly international.

I have just revisited Ramsden Brothers' first shop at 7 Brighton Road. It is now a newsagent's and carries a good stock of Worthing-view cards as well as a more general display of seaside humour and pretty floral and animal subject cards. It is good to know that for some ninety years this shop, under its different owners, has continued to supply Worthing residents and visitors with colourful postcards.

I have spent some time discussing these hitherto unidentified initials 'R.B., W'. They demonstrate one of thousands of minor points that can help us build up a more complete story of postcard publishing and retailing. In this case three persons gave me assistance: Robert Naunton (a respected local solicitor), my school chum, Rotary colleague and fellow postcard collector, Geoff Pyle (who I should also have mentioned in connection with the Lévy research), and Herbert Ramsden. Any research is made easier if you can enlist the help of like-minded collectors or local historians.

Continuing my résumé of Worthing-view cards, I must mention that the real-photograph cards bear the rubber-stamp mark of another much-loved Worthing shop, but one much smaller than Ramsden's and altogether more 'homely'— Luff's—famous for its home-made sweets. Here the added imprint is simply 'Published by Luff, Worthing'. Alas, it is no more. This tiny shop facing Broadwater Green is immortalised on various photographic cards, pictured in one above the caption 'The Celebrated Broadwater Sweet Shop, near Worthing' (*see* plate 107).* This 'Chatsworth series' card bears the September 1907 message: 'The reminder of the dear shop where your Dad and I visited, hope you will enjoy the special sweets I sent you'. They were special too. I think it more than probable that the card was purchased in the shop, along with some Luff's sweets, and sent to a Miss B. Harris in South Kensington.

108
A rare and desirable real-photograph postcard showing the interior of a small pre-1914 café and shop, with open boxes of Rowntree's biscuits and chocolates on the counter. Stamped photographer's credit: H.F. Goodden, Park Road, Worthing. Dated *c*.1911.

The once separate and ancient village of Broadwater is now very much part of Worthing. Another local shop was Pollicutt's—a newsagent-cum-sweetshop. Various cards can be found with the stamped credit 'J.H.W. Pollicutt, Broadwater'.

I have other Worthing-view cards with the printed credit 'H.A. Foyster, Worthing'. This relates to Henry Albert Foyster of 10 South Street, two doors from Walter Bros.' fancy bazaar. Henry Foyster was a stationer and bookseller who as early as 1901 had sold interesting mounted photographs of Worthing. His later stock of picture postcards was, however, mainly purchased from large English or continental suppliers (*see* page 74). He died in about 1909 and his business was taken over by Miss M.L. Shirtliff.

Another South Street-view card I have bears the name and address of the vendor—'C.F. Worsfold, Steyne Bonbonniere, Brighton Road, Worthing and at 31 Marine Parade, Worthing'. This 1906 example is interesting in that the ordinary card is overprinted 'With Seasons Greetings', yet was used purely to send birthday good wishes.

Other Worthing-view cards purchased from the approximate period 1910 onwards bear a horseshoe trade mark containing the description 'The Arcadia' Bazaar Series. I think these were produced for and sold at The Arcadia Bazaar at 6 Warwick Street, Worthing. These premises had, until 1909, been occupied by Miss E. Brigden's Berlin Wool Repository, before they were taken over by The Arcadia Bazaar in 1910. My grandfather's advertisements recorded his premises at 5 Warwick Street—within a stone's throw of the Town Hall—as being opposite the penny bazaar, that is, this Arcadia Bazaar, seemingly a well-known landmark.

The Worthing 'Arcadia Bazaar' may have been but one of a series. Mr. Coysh mentions the Arcadia Bazaar Company of Ramsgate, which published postcards bearing the initials 'A B Co.' within a horseshoe device. Davidson Bros. issued an Arcadia series of cards but these are not related to the Worthing or Ramsgate Bazaar Company. It has been suggested that the Worthing penny bazaar was owned by Mr. Marks, who later went into partnership with Mr. Spencer.

Other Worthing cards bear the name 'The Criterion, 3 West Buildings, Worthing'. This is the name of a small café just off the sea-front. I mention the imprint of this café to show the variety of establishments that stocked picture

109
An A.W. Wardell of Brighton glossy real-photograph card showing the wreck of Worthing pier after the storm of 22 March 1913. This subject proved very popular with local photographers and even with the larger postcard firms. Most of these are not particularly rare as the cards were kept as mementoes.

postcards. The café interior card (plate 108) may depict this small establishment, but local residents hold differing views on this.

Some Worthing cards bear only the title 'Chatsworth series'. This trade name could relate to a local printer or publisher, particularly as the *Worthing Gazette*, one of the main local papers, had offices and printing works in Chatsworth Road and ran a weekly sporting feature under the name 'Chatsworth'. However, should this trade name also occur on non-Sussex view cards I will be proved wrong.

Most of the postcard publishers mentioned in this chapter have been national or international concerns, and even cards bearing credit to a local retailer will also have been produced by such publishers. There is one local firm which should, however, be recorded especially; it is still in being and has produced a wide range of many glossy photographic views from the 1920s to postwar days. The firm dates back to at least 1913 when it issued a good, sharp view of the storm-wrecked Worthing pier (plate 109). This card bears the central A.W.W. initial trade mark and the full credit: 'Photographed and Published by A.W. Wardell, 4 Clarence Street, Brighton', with the reference number 201. Later cards of the 1950s have an amended credit 'Copyright A.W.W. Brighton & Worthing'. Tens of thousands of Wardell cards were produced over a long period and, until I began to write this, I was under the impression that the firm was very much in being. Alas I cannot trace the company today. It is one of many postcard publishers that seem to have disappeared, leaving only their picture postcards behind. In this connection I could also mention D. Constance Ltd. of Littlehampton; *see* Chapter VII.

Apart from use on standard postcards, the same photographs or engravings were often pressed into service in other forms, such as 'lettercards'. I have a very special postally-used (July 1927) Worthing 'Lettercard—Programme'. The inside of the front and back cover is left clear for written correspondence, and the basic details of postal information are given: 'The telephone Call office is open all night for urgent telephone calls'; details of the public library and museum are also given. The inside booklet contains four postcard-type photographs of the Pier Pavilion and bandstand. There is a good map of the centre of the town, with the major attractions pinpointed. There are also 16 advertisements for local firms or services.

The Southdown Motor Services Ltd. advertised its daily trips—starting times and return fares—'Monday 09.30 all day trip to Windsor Castle, 10/-ᵈ; Saturday 09.15, 16.15 & 17.15 London (Victoria) 11/6ᵈ' and so on. The swimming baths also advertised: 'Adults 6ᵈ, children 4ᵈ. Mixed bathing after 2 p.m.'.

Ramsden's Library in Chapel Road, the local family firm that published and sold hundreds of postcards, took a page to list recent additions to the library. The standard subscriptions for the year's reading was 15s. 6d. but there was also the choice of a de luxe subscription to the 'newest books in Fiction, Travels, Biography, etc.'. This special service cost £1 11s. 6d. and gave one access to the shelves containing new publications.

The order of the various military and other bands playing at the Parade Bandstand from early June to late November—the Season—was also listed, as were general details of the delights of the Pier Pavilion: 'The most popular rendezvous for residents and visitors. Cool in summer—warm in winter'. This large pavilion at the shore end of the pier then housed 'Worthing's super show. The Charleston Follies'. The pier's attractions included steamboat and motor launch trips, fancy diving, dancing in South Pavilion, Punch and Judy, ventriloquism, conjuring, etc., for the children. Refreshments. What fun!

All these features comprised the basic Lettercard-Programme but the centre two pages detailed the week's entertainment, giving all the events for the week of 3-9 July. Apart from all the municipal entertainments, the picture houses were showing *That Model from Paris* (the Rivoli), *Spanish Passion* (the Picturedrome), *The High Flyer* (the Dome) whilst *Dracula* was delighting the theatre-goers. The Odeon and Plaza cinemas were to come in the 1930s.

All the picture houses and the theatre changed their programmes on Thursdays. This was presumably so that the weekly visitors—Saturday to Saturday—could see two different shows during their short stay and the proprietors could reap their reward twice. Surprisingly, however, two of the cinemas were open for two shows on Sundays.

This publication does not bear any credits. I am not sure if it was prepared by a private individual or firm, or if it was the brainchild of the town's 'Entertainments Department' which then consisted of two persons (the Entertainments Manager, Frank Cooper, and his secretary), their combined wages costing the town under ten pounds a week. There are no details of the cost of purchase of this lettercard, but the postage was 1½d. It, and similar publications, may not interest purist postcard collectors but they offer an outstanding insight into the attractions of British seaside resorts in the 1920s. The town gave its visitors value for money; you were invited to purchase a 'Combined annual ticket' for 25s. For this one could enjoy:

1. Music twice day throughout the year in the Pier pavilion—the most comfortable Hall on the Coast.
2. First-class Military Band performances in the Parade Bandstand in the summer.
3. Admission to the Pier throughout the year.
4. The use of a deck chair on the Parade or Beach.

All these attractions and very many more are depicted in the thousands of local-view postcards or lettercard publications of that period. The very neglected pictorial lettercard (originally rendered as two words 'Letter Cards') can be very helpful to the collector, as they usually include a set of views taken at the same time and also issued as a set of postcards. One can perhaps recreate an original set by referring to the lettercard publication. Likewise the local historian is treated to the set of pictures usually as taken by a single photographer. They will, however,

110
A reasonably standard, uncredited, glossy real-photograph local-view card. Postally-used in 1929 and as such of personal interest to me. Another slight bonus is the one penny special Postal Union Congress stamp.

PIER PAVILION, WORTHING.

be standard views of popular tourist sights or sites! In booklet form they are not as easy to display as individual local-view postcards.

If one did not wish to collect the whole range of topographical cards depicting one's home town, one might collect just those posted in the year of one's birth. This idea was prompted by a Worthing card before me now—a good glossy photographic view of the Front and Pier Pavilion (plate 110) including, in the road, three wonderful open charabancs and a newsagent's awning advertising postcards. This card bears a clear postmark for 17 August 1929 (my year!) and a special 'Postal Union Congress London 1929' stamp. The card and the unusual stamp are only worth pennies, but if the stamp should be one with a sideways-placed watermark it would be worth several pounds, as would the card if it was postmarked on the first day of issue of the stamp, 10 May 1929. My interest is that I have enjoyed so many events—summer shows, concerts, lectures, dances and recently antique fairs in the Worthing (Pier) Pavilion—that this birth-year card has a very special value to me. Even mass-produced cards can have a real, if individual, interest outside that of commercial value or rarity.

I cannot list all the many later postcard manufacturers that were producing local-view picture postcards in the 1930s and beyond. These are outside the scope of the present book. However, whilst it is generally thought that the postcard boom had ceased by the 1920s this does not seem true of the resort cards. Folk were still streaming to the seaside and they were still happily sending off picture postcards of standard types. However, the standard mass-produced usually glossy-surfaced photographic postcards of the 1920s and '30s are not now in great demand.

What had come to an end was the collecting craze. Postcards were now only being purchased to be postally-used, not merely to be added to an album. This meant that the cards on sale in Worthing and elsewhere were becoming more and more standard. Pier and beach scenes outnumbered all others, with, of course, the ever popular McGill-type comic cards (*see* Chapter VII).

Indeed, the selection popular in the 1930s was very similar to the cards available in the 1990s, is it really sixty years later! Many shops in tourist or seaside areas still sell attractive, glossy, local-view cards. These are usually displayed outside the shop or in the window. They are stocked today for the same commercial reason that they were always sold—profit—but also to encourage folk to enter the main shop, perhaps to make a more expensive purchase.

These modern cards still have interest; they are the old-fashioned, even 'antique', cards of the future! It is interesting to purchase at little cost a selection of comparative modern view cards, showing scenes as they are today for display with like views of the 1900s, or the 1910s or '20s. All these old cards were once new. If you do purchase a selection of these modern cards for your collection, do add a little pencilled note. Record for the future where and when you purchased the card, its cost, the current postage rate and perhaps if you can ascertain the information, something about the publisher or photographer—I think you will find that many modern cards are still produced abroad.

You may well also find that some of the modern cards are reissues of old Edwardian local-view postcards, still made and sold because of nostalgia. Our local museum and the county library both display and sell packets of cards reproduced from originals.

You can find many other reissues of Edwardian postcards. Some old Worthing views are reissued by 'Collectorcard' of Croydon. I have before me now two sepia-toned cards depicting Worthing pier. These were purchased in February 1988 for 25p each. They bear the imprint 'Leo Nostalgic Cards of Eastbourne' and the credit is to the Robert Jeeves Postcard Saloon Collection. Like many of the original pre-1914 cards they were printed on the continent, but now instead of (perhaps) 'Printed in Saxony', we find the all-embracing initials EEC. These stand for European Economic Community—rather faceless and uninformative.

Yet these new cards continue to cater for our love of old times, the good old days, nostalgia. Have we perhaps entered upon a new picture postcard age?

'Tell Rosie I will send her a card later on, I have used up all I bought yesterday'
(Worthing sea-front view, May 1908)

'This is the first instalment. I have several more for you, which will follow'
(Worthing-view card, August 1910)

Chapter VI

Home-Town Local-Event
Cards and Publishers

'I don't think you have this one, ta, ta.'

'I thought you would like a card from Worthing.'

To this point this book has been concerned with the mass-produced cards printed by large national or international postcard publishers and sold to local firms, who often added their own name and address, for sale in their own shops. There exists also a very interesting class of cards wholly produced by local firms, photographers or even by individuals. These tend to be one colour, usually 'real-photograph' cards, but their interest can be far greater than the mass-produced coloured examples.

To this point, too, the printers and publishers of the postcards depicted have mostly been of at least national standing, and their names are generally recorded in the standard reference books available to postcard collectors. We now turn, however, to local photographers and others, who served their community very well but failed to gain a wide reputation. Your city, town or community will also have been served by such professionals.

The professional photographers on the spot could produce photographic cards depicting local events within a matter of hours. The photographers could print, say, two dozen such cards and then dozens more if the demand warranted the extra cost. (National firms also could rush out new cards if the occasion demanded. I have a Valentine's Coronation view card which states 'Prints flown to Dundee by aeroplane on Coronation Day, May 12th 1937. Post cards on sale in London by 11 o'clock on the 13th May!') Local photographers could easily beat this; their event cards were often on sale the same day!

These highly interesting, locally produced postcards are usually of the type we call 'real photographs', a descriptive term often abbreviated to 'RP' in catalogues or dealers' lists. They were mainly produced by local photographers, the earliest of whom would have produced mounted local views or event photographs for local sale well before the days of picture postcards (see Chapter I).

These (usually) glossy-surfaced real-photograph cards can be far more interesting than the mass-produced standard views issued by the large national firms. They are certainly far rarer, being issued in very limited quantities—tens rather than thousands. They fall into three main types:

(i)   Scenes or events photographed by professionals for resale, mainly in their own homes.

(ii) Sponsored or commissioned. For example, shop-fronts, groups of school children, groups of entertainers and the like. The photographer would have been invited to attend and then to supply real photographs mounted on postcard backs for the use of the person depicted or for sale by them—perhaps as a form of publicity. A large proportion of local real-photograph postcards fall into this category.

(iii) Amateur or non-professional photographic cards. This little-known but important subdivision can be very dull, for it covers purely personal photographs or snapshots which, by request, were printed onto postcard blanks. Such cards exist in large numbers in family photograph albums, in odd boxes and so on. Only six or a dozen of each image may ever have existed, most of which will have been lost or destroyed.

Before dealing with each of these subdivisions, we must mention the rôle of the local photographers. They were likely to have been highly professional, of artistic inclination, and in possession of expensive up-to-date equipment and good processing facilities. Their main trade, as now, would have been in portraiture, for we all love to record good looks or likenesses. We are used to having photographs taken at various stages of life—as a baby, as growing children, at school or at play, in the countryside or by the sea. Wedding photographs have always been the bread and butter of the local photographer's livelihood. Later landmarks are also recorded as new family groups and grandchildren start the circle afresh. Similarly some record of advancement in business or in the town's affairs is often required. Such portraiture is needed or at least expected of one. If you wish for a professional result you obviously consult such artistic craftsmen.

An Edwardian advertisement card helpfully lists photographer's charges, assuming portrait photographs of various standard sizes in the approximate period 1905-7. The last price relates to photographs mounted or printed as a postcard. The full list of prices reads:

This Post Card entitles the holder to ...	
3 Highly-finished Cabinets for	5/-
12 Highly-finished Cabinets for	12/6d.
Including handsome gold frame	15/6d.
A 12 in. by 10 in. Water Colour Enlargement	
and 3 cabinets	12/6d.
A 20 in. by 16 in. Enlargment, beautifully finished	
in crayon, in massive walnut frame	21/-
Your photograph on a Post Card	
12 for	3/9d.

Given that this advertising postcard was in effect touting for business, it could well be that these prices were slightly below average for the period, but even so small numbers of postcards made from a studio-posed photograph were priced at 3¾d. each. However, this price is not far from the pre-1914 price of having a negative enlarged and printed on a postcard blank. A leading Worthing photographer at this period was advertising snapshot enlargements on postcard blanks at 6d. each, or three for a shilling (that is 4d. each). Larger prints were 10d. or 1s. 3d. each and these were not as useful as the smaller postcards. The reduction for quantity obviously meant that many folk would order three postcards rather than a single example. The quality of such non-professional photographs was, of course, variable and some subjects—family portraits, etc.—would have been of restricted interest. Some, however, represent very rare records of events, locations or interesting features.

Apart from portraiture, these professionals also sold photographic equipment and tended to augment their income by photographing local scenes for sale in their shops. Portraits of buildings were extremely popular. People were proud of their homes and, of course, in the case of hotels or boarding-houses photographs were taken for publicity.

The advent of the picture postcard proved an added bonus to these photographers. It greatly expanded the market for the photographic recording of local events. Locally produced photographic cards for restricted sale over a short period were, however, slow to arrive in Worthing. It would be difficult to trace a pre-1905 example, but in the 1906-10 period the town was all but flooded with such cards.

In the early days of this century local papers were devoid of photographic illustrations, apart from portraits taken by local photographers and presumably lent by the subject to be reproduced in the local press.

In May 1901 SS *Indiana* was wrecked off Worthing. This was a well-remembered local event—thousands of oranges were cast up on the foreshore and the local inhabitants took liberally of the unexpected fruitful harvest from the sea. As might be expected, local photographers recorded the scenes. The *Worthing Gazette* of 22 May 1901 carried the following advertisement:

WRECK OF THE SS *INDIANA* OFF WORTHING

The following series of half plate mounted photographs with printed titles,
can be seen at Mr. Foyster's bookseller, South Street.
1. Oranges cast up on sands
2. Shumac bags piled up on beach
3. Crew of the salvage cutter *Invicta*
4. Crew of *Invicta*, with a diver
5. A diver being dressed
6. Diver waiting to be undressed, attendants arguing
7. Salvage cutter *Invicta*
8. The *Indiana* looking towards the bows

What a set of photographic picture postcards these mounted event photographs
would have made, yet as far as I am aware no postcard depicts this 1901 disaster,
a few years too early in the development of the picture postcard.

Likewise, the next issue of the *Worthing Gazette* reported another momentous
event well recorded by local photographers. This large hotel fire (*see* plates 15 and
111) warranted an all too rare but very poor photographic reproduction in the
Gazette of 29 May 1901. In addition to the photographs (taken by W.E. Carter)
of the fire, the paper contained a lengthy verbal account:

> At no former period in the history of Worthing has so destructive a fire
> occurred as that which was witnessed in the early hours of Friday morning
> May 24, 1901, when in a very short space of time the Royal Hotel—the
> largest in the borough was reduced to a total ruin ...

The fire was discovered by the manager, Reinhardt Datz, at four o'clock in
the morning. Seeing that it was too great to be controlled by the small local
brigade, Mr. Datz phoned for assistance from the Brighton brigades. One of the
Brighton steam fire-engines was loaded on to a railway truck and by this means
was transported the 10 miles to Worthing!

No postcard exists of this fire or of the burnt-out hotel, although various
local photographers took and published interesting photographs. These were usually
on thick cards and sold as mementoes of the event or local disaster. It is a human
failing that we revel in disasters—much to the benefit of photographers and
newspaper sales. To cater for this failing I include a pre-postcard photograph
(plate 111) of the gutted Worthing hotel. One hopes the freshly-installed electric
light system was not to blame. The hotel was never rebuilt; the prime plot
remained vacant for about fifteen years before an arcade of shops was built on the
enlarged site. This existing development is shown on many postcards, such as
those in plates 112-13.

Many local folk were involved in this development, either as investors,
shareholders or directors of the Arcade Company; one was Walter Gardiner, the
famous Worthing photographer. We can therefore conveniently switch to this
important figure in local postcard history but one not, as yet, mentioned in
postcard literature.

Mr. and Mrs. Walter Gardiner came to Worthing in 1893, when they took
over the existing photographic business of E. Pattison Pett, who in turn had
succeeded Russell & Sons in Bath Place, near the pier and the *Royal Hotel*. Like
some other high-class photographers, their trade description harked back to earlier
times, for they described themselves as photographers and 'miniature painters'. He
was, perhaps, a little naughty in claiming in advertisements that his business had
been established in 1849 but he was certainly not alone in claiming the earliest
possible date for such an event, going back to the original founder of the business–
Russell & Sons.

111
A local-event photograph of the burning *Royal Hotel* on the morning of 24 May 1901, before the days of real photographic local-event or disaster postcards.

112 *(left)*
A real-photograph card showing The Arcade which replaced the *Royal Hotel* c.1930.

113 *(above)*
The northern entrance to The Arcade—a 1930s development which remains today with different traders.

Walter Gardiner, who with his wife settled here after a number of years in Australia, quickly made his presence felt in the town and was soon elected to the council. He was an outspoken councillor and an important figure in the photographic world—both he and his wife were members of the Royal Photographic Society. His large publicity photographs of Worthing formed part of a holiday resort exhibition at the Crystal Palace in 1903. Earlier, in January 1896, both partners had received a very lengthy and highly-praised write-up in *The Practical Photographer* monthly magazine. His postcard activities were, however, in the nature of an iceberg—largely unseen.

Plate 114 shows a very rare Walter Gardiner local-view postcard. This is admittedly a dull card which one might find in a dealer's tray for a very reasonable price. I was, however, happy to pay £25 for this example. Let me explain why it is of particular interest in the development of local postcards, even though it has not been postally-used so is not dated, nor is it exactly datable.

It is obviously quite early, being of the pre-November 1899 tubby court shape and size, as

114
A rare, locally designed, court-size, local-view card incorporating the Worthing industries—grape and tomato growing. Signed 'Designed by Walter Gardiner', *c.*1894.

explained in Chapter II. The three small photographic-based vignetted views obviously hark back to, or were inspired by, the traditional continental 'Gruss aus'-type postcards (plates 26-7). The right-hand view of the lake in Worthing's Homefield Park was a Walter Gardiner photograph which appeared in the *Worthing Gazette*'s Queen Victoria Jubilee 'Worthing Souvenir' of 1897. This suggested that 1897 represented the date of the card, but in fact recent research has revealed that it dates from 1894, making Walter Gardiner a pioneer designer of British local-view postcards. It certainly demonstrates the truth of the statement made in the January 1902 copy of the *Stationery Trades Journal* under the heading, 'View Cards':

> A sign of the times, and one indicating a healthy growth of the movement,
> is the increasingly large number of local printers and stationers who print
> and publish their own postcards illustrating their own cities or districts.

This opinion would have been penned probably in December 1901.

Two other points make this Walter Gardiner card noteworthy. Firstly the fruit and foliage relate to the important local industry of growing grapes and tomatoes. Such 'Worthing grown' crops, as I have explained in Chapter I, enjoyed a national reputation and were sent (usually by rail) to markets all over the country. This aspect of Worthing was little commemorated on later postcards which were mainly angled on the seaside, for the benefit of summer visitors.

Lastly, the printed credit added beneath the beach scene is most unusual. It reads 'Designed by Walter Gardiner'. (If only other designers had thought to add their names.) Many early continental and British publishers added credits but these usually relate to the printer, wholesaler or retailer, rather than the designer. Perhaps these Gardiner cards were issued as a set of six or a dozen, with different views, rather like the early cards illustrated in plates 41 and 45. I would obviously be most interested to hear of the existence of other similar Walter Gardiner Worthing-view cards, or of datable examples. As local products of a photographer and his printer, they are in monochrome rather than colour-printed—a process almost certainly not available in Worthing at that period. As the coloured Pictorial Stationery Company cards were widely available at less than a penny (in packets of eight for sixpence), one wonders at what price Mr. Gardiner was able to sell his monochrome cards.

At even a penny each, the demand for these cards, in competition with more colourful nationally produced cards, must have been small and the profit margin almost non-existent. Had it been otherwise, Walter Gardiner and other such photographers would have progressed to become national figures in the expanding trade. Gardiner's elevation to the status of pioneer in the design of local-view postcards has come about through the discovery that this card was part of a set of 11 similar cards which was registered for copyright purposes at the old Stationers' Hall in London on 8 October 1894. Incidentally the registration also covered letterheads although the postcard version was sent to London in the name of Charles Fibbens, a private resident who may have initiated the idea. The complete set of postcards with over forty vignetted views was discovered in the Public Record Office Stationers' Hall archives by Mr. Tony Byatt and was reported by him in *Picture PostCard Monthly* of August 1995.

This early dating is quite startling. Private postcards bearing adhesive halfpenny stamps had only been sanctioned by the British post office on 1 September some five weeks earlier. The earliest recorded British local-view cards were two engraving-based Scarborough cards, one of which was posted on 15 September 1894. Yet here in Worthing our local photographer was about to issue a set of 11 photographic-based cards showing the delights and main buildings of this modest south coast resort. What is more he added his name to at least two of the set as the designer. Perhaps the Worthing typhoid epidemic of 1893 and the Corporation's subsequent efforts to publicise the town in the summer of 1894 (*see* page 4) prompted the issue of these cards which seem to have been produced locally rather than by a national or continental firm. As yet no postally-used examples have turned up, only a very few unused examples and one that was posted with a message but within an envelope. Walter Gardiner of Worthing may well have been the first British photographer to have produced and credited himself with designing local-view postcards. Perhaps, however, time and further research will suggest other claimants.

Walter Gardiner and other local photographers were also engaged in the national postcard publishing business in a second-hand manner. They supplied photographs to various newspapers and publishers of journals and directories. Likewise they supplied on request sets of local views to the major city-based postcard publishing firms. These photographs and the reproduction rights were purchased by the publishers; in most cases the published postcards do not bear a credit to the local firm which supplied the original print. Walter Gardiner and other Worthing firms such as Loader's supplied hundreds of photographs which were reproduced en masse by specialist postcard publishers.

In July 1900 Walter Gardiner opened new enlarged premises in a new development in Brighton Road. This is reported in the *Worthing Gazette* of 25 July:

The Broadway Studio

Mr & Mrs Walter Gardiner ... their well known premises in Bath Place are far from sufficient for ordinary purposes and they have accordingly displayed considerable enterprise in supplementing the accommodation by means of a very handsome and suitable establishment in what is very aptly named The Broadway, in Brighton Road ... The new Studio ... is now fully completed and will be formally opened tomorrow ... (Thurs 26 July 1900)

The firm's advertisement does not mention postcards. Incidentally, in the Victorian period the Gardiners were considerate employers, being one of the earliest Worthing firms to adopt a half day early closing. The new Broadway Studio was closed at two o'clock on Wednesdays. Today in the 1990s many local shopkeepers are open seven days a week.

Walter Gardiner had his own postcards for business and private use early in the century. A particularly interesting example is plate 115. This undivided-back card was written in October 1902 and part of the message addressed to Miss

Carrie Noakes in Mayfield noted: 'The boys are sketching some postcards of their own, it keeps them out of mischief'. This early interest in postcards was later to do more than keep them out of mischief, it would earn them good money. Incidentally, this 1902 (or earlier) Walter Gardiner postcard commences by stating, perhaps in reply to an earlier card from Carrie, that she was 'getting on famously with your collection'. What minor treasures would she have gathered together?

Walter Gardiner's large studio and shop in the tree-lined Broadway can be seen to the right in the undated view (plate 116). A vertical row of photographs or postcards can just be seen in the window. Later Walter Gardiner shops did not display postcards—the photographic business had become too important to be concerned with objects selling for pennies. In recent years the firm has concentrated on commercial photography, and Derek Gardiner and his partners have won many national awards. A far cry and a century from the little local-view penny postcard of the 1890s.

Derek, the grandson of Walter Gardiner, has held a centenary exhibition of the family business, which has retained so many interesting old negatives or prints and has recorded a wonderful photographic image of the town, its interests, pastimes and inhabitants. The first baby photograph of me was taken in the Gardiner studio lying naked on a carved table; likewise my wife, Jean, was separately photographed there. Our son Jonathan was also captured on Gardiner equipment. Every president of the Rotary Club of Worthing has been photographed by a member of the Gardiner family. The list is endless, the material priceless, from a local history point of view.

Plate 117 shows two typical Walter Gardiner credited postcards; very many more do not bear his name. Indeed, the signed cards are scarce and, like the examples, appear to be special commissions, or sponsored postcards, carried out for, in this case, a school and not for general sale throughout the town. The Gardiner cards were not angled at the tripper.

Important contemporaries of Walter Gardiner were Messrs. Loader, who, over a very long period, traded from several different addresses in the town. Local newspapers were often illustrated with Loader photographs and, when the local-event 'real-photograph' postcards came into fashion Loader's issued a long and interesting range, some of which are shown in plate 118. Apart from these Loader credited postcards, the Loader family business also, like the Gardiner's, supplied photographs of the locality to various national publishers.

Whilst Walter Gardiner specialised in portrait photography, Loader's specialised in outdoor work, which explains their greater interest in event and other local postcards. These cards, including the highly interesting local-event cards, were displayed and sold in Loader's retail shop, and further batches were processed as required. All such cards were sold in relatively small quantities over a brief period. Most of the Loader pictorial postcards were issued within the period 1911-25, but some were produced later, including some postwar examples.

This firm of Worthing photographers and dealers in photographic materials and equipment was established in 1911. The set of 12 cards commemorating the

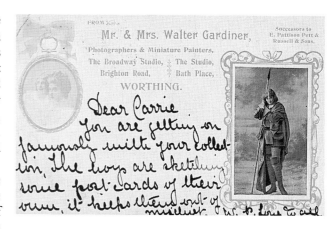

115 *(top)*
A rare advertising or personal use card designed and used by the local photographers Mr. and Mrs. Walter Gardiner, with postcard interest message. Postally-used October 1902.

116 *(above)*
A colour-printed card of the 1901 Broadway in Brighton Road showing, on the right, Walter Gardiner's window with rows of picture postcards.

117 *(above)*
Two Walter Gardiner examples taken for Steyne High School, typical of sponsored or commissioned picture post-cards. Very many schools were similarly featured by different local photographers.

118 *(right)*
Two real-photograph cards, part of a set taken and sold locally by Messrs. Loader, depicting the opening of the new pier in May 1914. The different perspective of the second card was captured by the photographer standing on a ladder.

opening of the rebuilt pier in May 1914 bears the white credit on the front 'Loader's Series' without any reference number. Later, post-1918 cards often have a neatly printed credit on the address side 'Loader's Photo Stores, 24 Chapel Road, Worthing'. Later still, in the late 1920s or '30s, the photographs were printed on blank Kodak postcards to which a rubber-stamped local credit was added: 'Loader's Photo Stores, Worthing'. The Kodak blank cards bear a 'K Ltd.' logo in the stamp box, and presumably they were sold in thousands to photographers up and down the country or even abroad—the 'post card' caption is in both English and French. Cards with this 'K' logo usually signify a locally produced photograph.

Derek Loader remembers carrying equipment for his father, as he went about the town and the surrounding district before the Second World War taking photographs on a half-plate camera. The resulting negative was on a glass plate which had to be masked to postcard size, and the caption and prints were printed, fixed, washed and trimmed before being displayed in the shop for sale. Fresh supplies could be prepared quickly. Loader's, and presumably other leading photographers, also supplied prints to national postcard publishers and photographs to the London newspapers. Photographs of the 1913 wreck of the pier were put on a train that day and appeared in the national press the next morning.

119
A non-postcard photograph of the shop-front of the Worthing Portrait Company with many of its postcards displayed. Note the upstairs daylight studio.

Far scarcer are Worthing postcards produced by 'Spencer's Photo Stores' at 24 Chapel Road—the shop was taken over by Mr. Loader in 1911.

Many Worthing local-view and commissioned or sponsored postcards bear a credit to the Worthing Portrait Company in Railway Approach. This company is linked to Walter Gardiner's arrival in Worthing, for the manager and main photographer, Miss Rewman, had been employed for many years by E. Pattison Pett, whose photographic business Mr. and Mrs. Walter Gardiner took over on their arrival in Worthing. Mrs. Gardiner then replaced Miss Rewman.

The Worthing Portrait Company occupied premises which had been specially built and equipped (plate 119). The *Gazette* noted late in July 1898 that the new company had 'secured the services of a most efficient operator'. This and later announcements suggest that a group of local businesses or backers set up the new company but that they themselves were not skilled photographers.

The following is the first announcement of the company, and is taken from the *Worthing Gazette* of 30 July 1898. We have so few details of the beginnings of local firms, or indeed of any photographers or postcard publishers:

WORTHING PORTRAIT CO. 4 RAILWAY APPROACH

The Worthing Portrait Company are opening their new premises early in August under the management of Miss Rewman (for 13 years with the late E. Pattison Pett) who, with the assistance of qualified artists, will give her immediate supervision to the business and spare no pains to give personal care and attention to every individual sitter. Satisfaction Guaranteed

Views, groups and all out door work undertaken. Best work only, at moderate prices. Children and groups a speciality.

Like all photographers of the late Victorian era, the emphasis was on portrait work, but in its first month the new Worthing Portrait Company expanded its

120
The pride of my mother's collection! A family snap printed on to a Kodak postcard blank. (I am the one seemingly feeling a little pressed!)

coverage to local events: 'Some very successful photographs have been taken by the Worthing Portrait Company, which are on sale at a low price. The Five Mile Championship Race, start and finish are particularly interesting'.

Incidentally by 1898 photography in Worthing was making great strides. William Lauri-Dickson of the Mutoscope Company had taken early movie films of the launch of the Worthing lifeboat and members of the Worthing swimming club playing water polo in the local baths. These local events were soon being shown to astonished audiences all over the country and abroad.

The Worthing Portrait Company prospered and from March 1899 its photographs were being reproduced in local newspapers. We, however, are concerned with the later postcards produced by this local firm. These cards include portraits, groups of individuals, sponsored cards of all types (private residences and business premises), as well as the view and event cards (plate 164). These always bear a printed or impressed credit to the company, either on the front or on the message side. Occasionally an additional credit relates to the retailer. The company seems to have continued in Railway Approach until about 1926, after which a Mr. Ernest Burton succeeded, but most of the W.P. Co. cards relate to the period 1905-18. A few coloured examples were issued.

The Godden family photo boxes contain many one-off real photographs printed on postcard blanks. Some may have been taken by my parents with simple box cameras and then printed by Loader's. One such card (plate 120) shows me and my young brother on Worthing sands in about 1934. Such snaps are only of interest within the family (if then) unless the setting or background later proves of interest. The smock-like dress of my brother might be of interest to students of social history. There exist tens of thousands of such amateur photographs printed onto postcard blanks. The resulting snaps were far more useful than normal prints, as they could be sent to friends with a simple message for a halfpenny. A Kodak advertising postcard is inscribed: 'The kind of Postcards you can make if you have a 3A folding pocket Kodak'. The address side has a small sideways note: 'The No 3A Folding Pocket Kodak. Price £4 10s. 0d. may be obtained from all Dealers or Kodak Limited, 57-61 Clerkenwell Road, London E.C.'. Kodak and other firms greatly benefited from the popularity of DIY photographic postcards. Professionally-taken scenes were of superior quality and usually depicted more interesting subjects or events—for, of course, they had to be sold to the public.

Other Godden family postcards were taken by street photographers who were such a feature of pre-war seaside resorts. A 'Sunny Snaps' postcard print is shown in plate 121. These are dated to the year and are normally taken in busy thoroughfares. This 1933 family group of my mother, brother John and myself was taken in Montague Street, a major shopping street just inland from the Parade. (The old wood block roadway still lies under several coatings of tar. Afterwards it took two-way traffic but in the postwar period it became a one-way street to deal with the inrush of motor traffic; later, vehicles were banished and it became Worthing's earliest pedestrian precinct.) This family card is of interest, for example, to students of dress—note, only the two charming children are hatless. The newsagent on the corner (now a massive new Boots store) stocked a good selection of conventional comic seaside cards and pictorial views.

There is much debate about the correct classification of one-off real photographs, which were printed on postcard blanks, rather than on plain paper. If such examples have been postally-used, they should be accepted as true postcards. Even if they were not posted, many of these photographs feature buildings, persons or events that might not otherwise have been photographically preserved.

One of the most interesting types of these real-photograph postcards features local traders. These belong to the sponsored or commissioned variety. The view of Green Bros. Dairy premises (plate 122) in Ambrose Place is outstanding. Milk and cream were hand-wheeled around towns in little carts and ladled from gleaming churns into the customers' jugs. A couple of new-fangled glass milk bottles are in the window. Of the pottery ornaments in the window the ornate milk-maid and the heron are now quite valuable collectors' items, as would be the churns and indeed this postcard itself.

The photographic view (plate 123) of one of Potter Bailey's several Worthing shops is also of great interest. This branch was in Crescent Road, just down the road from my own shop. The utilitarian hardware of the 1920s is of historic interest—the carpet beaters hanging by the door, for example. Some local cards bear the rubber-stamped credit, 'Potters Series'. These could well have been sold at the several branches of Messrs. Potter Bailey, a firm known locally simply as 'Potters'.

Other Worthing real-photograph cards, including those showing the storm-damaged pier in 1913, bear the double credit, 'Photo J. Howell. Published by F. Coppard, Worthing'. I know nothing of J. Howell—perhaps he was a local photographer drawn to the beach the morning following the storm. Mr. Coppard ran a general printing business in tiny premises at 8 Crescent Road, opposite my father's shop. The printing was done in the basement and he had to leave his work and trudge upstairs (none too happily) whenever the doorbell rang, or when he chose to answer the customers' summons. The business was carried on by his son Fred after the war; all our business printing was done at Fred Coppard's. He retired a few years ago and the enlarged shop now sells Japanese office machinery; all my photocopying is done in Mr. Coppard's old shop.

The next illustration of a real-photograph postcard shows the interior of a bar or licensed hotel or restaurant, with its pottery oval spirit barrels (plate 124). Threepence is rung up on the cash register—what might this sum have purchased? The postmark is 20 June 1905 and the individual quality of the view is underlined by the start of the message: 'Snap shot taken of the bar ...'. This snap was postally-used and must be considered a true postcard. The unnamed bar has not been identified.

Worthing entertainments could form the basis of an interesting postcard collection. There are the free seaside amusements—regattas, Punch and Judy shows, early aeroplanes landing on the sands, bands, parades and the like. Announcements and proclamations from the Town Hall steps drew large crowds

121
A Worthing 'Sunny Snaps' photographic postcard of my mother, brother and myself (left) in 1933. The newsagent on the right sold local-view and comic cards but the main interest is in the street scene, now a pedestrian precinct with large modern shops.

122
A superb commissioned, real-photograph advertising card showing the Ambrose Place dairy shop of Green Bros. The social history interest is in the polished metal milk churns and the hand barrows, *c.*1920.

123
Another local shop-front commissioned, real-photograph card showing the stock of Potter Bailey's Crescent Road shop, frequented by me in the old days. A good social history document and rightly in some demand.

(plate 125), and major local events were featured on real-photograph postcards. Park views often depict tennis, or the beginnings of Worthing as the bowls centre of England! (The venue for 'World Bowls' in 1972 and again in 1992, as host to teams from 28 countries.) The town football team was also depicted each year on real-photograph cards and the Worthing Borough Band was similarly honoured. The Salvation Army Band appears on a card in 'The Salvation Army Series of Pictorial Post Cards', published by Messrs. Milne, Tannahill & Methven, who specialised in Salvation Army work.

Several very interesting real-photograph Worthing postcards of the pre-1914 period bear on the face the impressed name and address 'W.J. Knowles, 23 Warwick Street, Worthing'. These are local photographic records, for example, of the August Bank holiday children's fête of 1910.

124
A rare and interesting real-photograph of a local pub interior with colourful pottery spirit barrels. The taller barmaid, Kate, posted this card in June 1905.

125
A typical real-photograph card of an election proclamation in front of the Town Hall. The card is helpfully inscribed 'The arrival of Sir Henry and Lady Fletcher at the Town Hall Worthing after the result of the Election had been proclaimed Saturday Jan 29th 1910'. Of considerable interest to dedicated local historians.

126
One of a series of real-photograph cards depicting local entertainers, in this case 'C. Adolf Seebold's Worthing Whimsies 1914', taken in the ornamental gardens behind Mr. Seebold's Kursaal. Credit: Otto Brown.

Concert parties were also featured. Plate 126 shows a splendid photographic postcard of C. Adolf Seebold's 'Worthing Whimsies' of 1914 in the colourful Winter Gardens behind the Kursaal. There are also real-photograph cards of 'The Comets, Kursaal Gardens', taken by Otto Brown. He had a well-known photographic studio in the Kursaal complex, and was therefore well placed to take photographs of the many bands, including the Royal Navy Ladies Orchestra, concert parties and other entertainers who performed at the Kursaal and at the Winter Gardens, just behind the main building. (Actresses appearing at the local Theatre Royal were also depicted on postcards. These could have been used in other towns with changed captions as the touring company travelled around the circuit. However, in most cases theatre advertising cards were produced by national companies and not by local photographers.) The real-photograph cards of local entertainers and concert parties depicted by local photographers are now of great interest—part of our ever-changing social history.

Worthing Corporation also dabbled in advertising postcards. Plate 127 shows a card featuring the Municipal Gentlemen's Swimming Bath, and the rates for various services—first- and second-class slipper baths, pails of hot seawater etc.

There are many more types of Worthing-view cards—from photographs of large town houses set in park-like grounds (plate 128) to rather ordinary side-street scenes with their terraces of small dwellings. The very dreary-looking real-photograph postcard is in fact far rarer than those more showy cards depicting the main buildings, major shopping streets or the sea-front. The back-street is a valuable source for social historians. 'Street scenes' form an important classification for postcard collectors. Each has different points of interest—the buildings, the traffic, the pedestrians and their dress.

Other real-photograph cards of Worthing events bear the stamp of H.F. Goodden [sic] of Park Road and are normally of the pre-1914 period. Mr. Goodden's cards are among the rarest local views and all dealers who have mentioned his name to me, asking if I am related, have professed total ignorance of him.

However, research into local newspapers will usually uncover background information or at least help to fix the working period of any photographer or businessman. By November 1910, H.F. Goodden was residing at St Mary's Lodge in Park Road. He was described as a portrait and landscape photographer and postcard publisher. He had recently moved to Worthing from Tunbridge Wells in Kent where he had practised as a photographer for many years. Like so many others, Mr. Goodden moved to Worthing on account of his wife's ill-health.

His elder son F.W. Goodden, then aged 21, accompanied E.T. Willows on his famous London-Paris flight. The Gooddens were still in residence in Worthing in mid-January 1911, when the local papers recorded the death of their younger son, aged only eighteen. The family was dogged by ill luck; their elder son, Lieutenant F.W. Goodden was injured in a flying accident near Shoreham in July 1915 and was (I believe) killed later in the war, but by this period this local photographer had left the town.

Another Worthing photographer whose local-event cards are quite scarce was G.W. Tuft. His scenes, usually of the approximate period 1905-10, are merely signed 'Photo Tuft' on the front.

Another important and very prolific Worthing photographer and publisher of real-photograph postcards was Edward Edwards and his son, trading as Edwards & Son. This firm produced some highly interesting, mainly local-event, cards depicting life in and around Worthing. Cards of village life and events are far rarer than those relating to towns. The Edwards cards relating to small villages such as Clapham, Findon or Patching were produced or sold in very small numbers and

WORTHING CORPORATION BATHS, HEENE ROAD.
Salt Water (Interior of Gentlemen's Swimming Bath.) Direct from the Sea.

1 Offington Park, Worthing

Photo: Tuft

127 *(top left)*
An interesting local advertisement card giving details and prices for the old Corporation Baths containing 'Salt Water direct from the sea'. Pails of sea water were delivered each morning—hot: 4d., cold: 3d. per pail!

128 *(top right)*
A real-photograph postcard of Offington Park, early in the century the site of many military summer camps but now completely built over with hundreds of houses—a story that can be repeated nationally. The card is inexpensive but of special interest if you now live in a house at Offington in Worthing.

129 *(right)*
Another Town Hall scene relating to a mid-Sussex election in 1906. An interesting real-photograph card showing dress of the period, shops, buildings and horse transport.

would not have been sold in the Worthing shops. There is a special study of Edwards & Son in Chapter VIII.

Several cards with photographic views of Worthing were not published by local firms or photographers, but by others located in nearby towns. Presumably they advertised in county papers or had agents in different towns and were therefore able to compete with Worthing photographers. For example, a view of the now defunct Seabury School at West Worthing carried the printed credit, 'Photographed and Published by Marshall, Keane & Co, Hove, Sussex'. A series of real-photograph cards illustrating events at Wykeham House School, Worthing, was published by P.A. Buchanan & Co. of Croydon.

Other real-photograph cards depict Sompting Abbots School, in this case published by A.J. & F.W. Baker of 210 Church Road, Hove. This firm and C.V. Travers of the same address issued various real-photograph cards of territorial army regiments encamped at Broadwater in the years before the First World War.

Other Worthing cards were published by 'Comptons, Photographers, High Street, Old Town, Eastbourne'. The list of firms supplying Worthing with picture postcards seems almost endless, and the subject merits further research.

Chapter VII

Humorous and other Popular Subjects

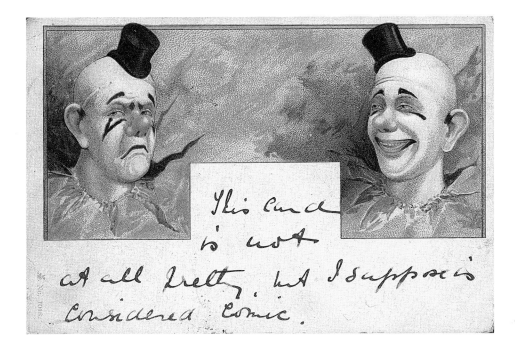

'Dot doesn't like the plain postcards, she wants Bill to send the funny ones.'

'Another vulgarity. Thanks to both of you for yours.'

It must not be thought that local-view picture postcards were the only type on sale or to be found in albums. A brief look at any postcard collector's price-guide, more general reference books or collectors' magazines will reveal hundreds of different categories. Any postcard fair will likewise show that major dealers have boxes of different types of postcard. As these selections are taken from fair to fair, it can be assumed that there is a market (however small) for all these subjects, far too numerous to list. It would be hard to think of any subject that is not depicted on picture postcards.

130
An amusing Worthing card, printed in Saxony and published by Wildt & Kray of London. This and similar cards could obviously be easily adapted for sale in any other town. Postally-used in May 1910.

This chapter mentions only some of the major subjects that were available in Worthing (or any other town) in the approximate period 1900-20, and which proved popular with the visitor or with the local population. These are the types of cards that all the stationers, the newsagents, the sub-post offices, the bazaars and kiosks kept in stock.

Many of these categories are obvious and still exist today; for example, the typically British seaside humour cards of the McGill type. There are very many other groupings that are highly collectable. An obvious way to discover the subjects selling in, say, 1910 is to study old family albums which will contain a range of cards purchased or received within a period of a few years. Unless the original collection belonged to someone only interested in one subject—cats, horses, flowers etc.—the subject range will be very wide. Over the last few years I have searched for cards that were posted in Worthing, that is, postally-used cards with a Worthing cancellation. Such cards were almost certainly purchased locally, demonstrating the available stocks and the taste of various casual purchasers.

Old postcard advertisements, price-lists and catalogues are helpful sources, but are now extremely rare. One has to examine as many albums or loose collections as possible, seek out dealers' stocks and use one's common sense! Most of the postcards produced today mirror the types popular sixty or more years ago. The taste of trippers or tourists seeking to send home a simple message has varied little over the years. In many seaside resorts or towns, humorous or comic cards were and still remain extremely popular and we tend to think typically British. An enquiry to *Picture PostCard Monthly* in October 1991 sought the earliest postally-used British comic card. His earliest was a so-called 'Write-away' example designed by Lance Thackeray posted in August 1901. Later research in 1996 has dated reports back to December 1899.

I am, however, quite sure that earlier continental humorous or comic cards exist. It is necessary to define what one means by 'comic'. Probably we have in mind the popular McGill cards with their amusing captions. There are also humorous cards without the need of a caption or associated wording, as, for example, that in plate 131. Some amusing cards were being produced in the Victorian period; not all were simple views or the popular German 'Gruss aus'-type of pictorial and topographical cards.

The December 1898 issue of the *Stationery Trades Journal* reported on 'Pictorial Post Cards' and noted in particular the new types published by Messrs. Blum & Degen of Paternoster Row. These included not only packets of seven landscape subjects at sixpence but new attractive subjects, such as 'Ladies sports illustrating cycling, rowing, skating and shooting, as practised by graceful figures in fetching costumes'. It also stated that this early firm of postcard publishers issued two sets of 'humorous' subjects. These proved popular, for a further set was added to the range in 1899. Other publishers obviously soon followed suit and published cards

131
An early German 'Smiler'-type seaside card depicting a lady in bathing costume being ogled by men—a timeless subject. This example was postally-used in November 1899.

132 *(above)*
A 'Smiler'-type tripper card—fun for a penny. Printed in Germany and postally-used in September 1912.

133 *(right)*
Another 'Smiler' card—good for students of Edwardian dress, if nothing else. 'Stop it George' is from J. Asher & Co.'s 'Kismet' series, postally-used in 1909.

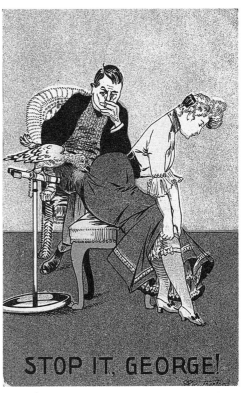

that would make folk smile or laugh and, more importantly, buy the cards, perhaps to send off to their friends as a joke.

One of the most successful of the humorous novelty cards, and one which seems to have been a British invention, was Tuck's 'Write away' cards, introduced perhaps in 1899. The idea was that a well-drawn sketch prompted the sender to add an appropriate message or caption.

The 'Write away' cards proved exceedingly popular, and trade journals in 1902 and 1903 made many enthusiastic references to new sets of Tuck's 'Write

135
Two Raphael Tuck 'Write away'-type cards drawn by Lance Thackeray and chromographed in Saxony. Series 288, nos. 3 and 4 in the set, c.1904.

away' postcards. The basic idea was copied by several other publishers; John Hassall's early series, issued by C.W. Faulkner, can be very attractive, whilst Albert Pirkis drew amusingly for Messrs. Hildesheimer (*see* plate 136). Humorous cards drawn by Tom Browne, often published by Davidson Bros., can be a delight. These cards were usually issued in a related set contained in a publicity envelope, as plate 134. In later years the comic cards were displayed outside shops in revolving stands of the type still in common use, and could be sold individually.

Raphael Tuck examples in particular are attractive, amusing and tasteful. As the firm correctly noted on their 1903 price-list, '"The Write Away" series has established itself at one bound as the popular series *par excellence* among every species of Post Cards ... The subject depicted is in each case accompanied by the commencement of a sentence intended to give a lead to the sender ... the Write Away series is intensely humorous without a spark of vulgarity'.

By 1903 Tuck's had issued nearly forty different 'Write away' sets, on sale at sixpence for a packet of six. Within a few years hundreds more had been issued. They were designed by leading popular artists such as Phil May and Lance Thackeray and most if not all were colour printed in Germany. As with other attractive cards, many were purchased solely to be added to an album and relatively few remaining examples bear a message. This imbalance, of course, may be because the examples preserved in albums have passed down to us, whilst most of the postally-used examples with inconsequential wording were quickly discarded.

The early 'Write away' cards lent themselves to the pre-1903 undivided-back cards, where the message had to be added to the pictorial side. The design was simple and was drawn especially for these cards. The Tuck examples, in particular, are restrained and tasteful, and as yet they are very modestly priced.

Plates 135-6 show some of the typical prompt words or starters. My album of these cards is great fun. They undoubtedly sold well in Worthing, and indeed had national if not international appeal in the first decade of the century.

These popular 'Write away' cards were tasteful. But once the market for comic or humorous cards had been established standards rapidly dropped—at least in some places. Nevertheless, they remained exceedingly popular; the more vulgar they were the better they sold.

134
Four of a set of six Tom Browne humorous postcards, with their envelope. Research has been carried out on the source of the 'On the Knee' novel quotation.

I must not suggest for one moment that the well-known McGill comic cards are vulgar but they are the leaders of a large class that can be rather near the knuckle, even by today's standards. Cards of this type were on sale in Worthing, and, if they were here, they would have been welcome at every other resort.

The firm evidence that such questionable cards were available lies in letters to our newspaper editors. One protest was prompted by a letter in *The Standard*,

I have arrived at the conclusion. Dykes are no place for dog carts or cars

136
An S. Hildesheimer & Co. 'Write away'-type card, printed in Austria. Many humorous subjects related to early motoring adventures. Postally-used in 1904.

11 September 1909, which appealed to readers to induce proprietors of newsagents, railway bookstalls and libraries to withdraw these undesirable cards from sale and, if necessary, threaten to remove their custom 'and to deal elsewhere if they continue to be stocked'. Locally, this national appeal on 'The Picture Post Card Nuisance' was underlined by a West Worthing resident:

> Sir,
> A perusal of the enclosed cutting from *The Standard* of the 11th inst. [this was quoted in full] has induced me to crave the use of your columns to suggest to the *Borough Recorder* that he shall take a stroll around and inspect the postcards exhibited for sale in our shops, some of which are frankly indecent, others merely suggestive and very simply vulgar and in bad taste.
> His opinion, if he confirms mine, would probably carry weight and might induce the vendors to overhaul their stock with a view to eliminate at any rate the most outrageous.

The complaint did not have any long-term effect, for three years later a similar letter was published in the *Worthing Gazette* of 12 June 1912:

> Pictorial Postcards
>
> Sir,
> Will you allow me ... to utter a few words of earnest protest against the exhibition in certain shops in this town of picture postcards the sentiments of which are a disgrace to our present civilisation.
> If a Censor be deemed necessary to guard the best interests of the Theatre-going public, surely he is more urgently needed to prevent the seeds of impure suggestions being sown in the minds of the youth of this place.
> Personally I revel in real humour, but the cards in question are not only devoid of this but are evil.
> A visitor to the Town

Unfortunately, neither this visitor nor the editor described fully or illustrated the offending cards, so we cannot tell how prudish or over-sensitive were these complaints. The reasonably innocent 1909 card shown in plate 146 has at the start of the written message 'Another Vulgarity'. It is a sad fact that in much more

137
An amusing and harmless seaside comic postcard drawn by Donald McGill, but without a publisher's credit. Postally-used at Great Yarmouth in August 1913.

I'M LIVING ON THE FAT OF THE LAND

recent times Donald McGill found himself in court over some designs and some authorities, such as those on the Isle of Man, did censor the designs intended for sale on the island.*

The fact remains that such cheap and cheerful postcards were on sale and remained on sale, because they sold well, especially to 'trippers'. Most were sold nationally, so the publisher's print run was huge. Consequently prices were kept down and profits were enjoyed by the manufacturers and the retailers, even though the cards were only sold for a penny!

Today such cards are still on sale; they have been the subject of many recent books. For example, *The Comic Postcard in English Life* by Frederick Alderson (David & Charles, 1970); *I've lost my little Willie—a Celebration of Comic Postcards* by Benny Green (Elm Tree Books Ltd., 1976) and Ronnie Barker's *A Pennyworth of Art* (The Herbert Press, 1986). All are great fun and there are several more similar well-illustrated books.

It is appropriate to record something of Donald McGill's career, for this artist is so associated with seaside cards. His work, however, ranged over many subjects and the well-known cards do not represent his earliest work. Nevertheless, he will always remain the 'King of the Saucy Postcards'. Many articles have been written about McGill. He is featured in postcard literature and in specialist books such as Elfreda Buckland's *The World of Donald McGill* (Blandford Press, 1984). Donald McGill was born in January 1875; he grew up with two brothers and three sisters (he needed his sense of humour) but did not start to draw until prompted by one of his brothers early in 1904. The earliest known postally-used example was posted on 13 July 1904. Initially he drew designs only in his spare time for the Pictorial Postcard Company, but his work was soon noticed and started to sell extremely well. The *Picture PostCard Monthly* of December 1905 carried the comment that this young artist's comic subjects 'will soon become widely popular'. Not only popular; he was to become a market leader. He turned to full-time professional postcard designing in 1908.

His classic was undoubtedly the young girl kneeling by her bed saying her prayers. The bold caption reads 'Please Lord, excuse me a minute whilst I kick Fido' (plate 139). The first version of this was drawn in 1906; Donald reworked the design several times over the years and I understand that more than three

* The banner front-page headline in my local paper, the *Worthing Herald* of 10 September 1993 read: 'E.C. could ban our saucy seaside postcards'. A newsagent was reported as stating that European visitors to his shop claimed the cards were banned in their countries and he feared the seaside tradition could be stopped in the U.K. ... Is nothing sacred!

"I'M SURE YOU'LL ENJOY FEEDING THE BIRDS ON THE PIER!"

138 *(left)*
A rather late Inter-Art Co. 'Comique' McGill resort card. Again this should not have troubled a 'Watch Committee'. Harmless fun for a penny. Postally-used August 1925.

139 *(below)*
The ever-popular McGill comic card 'Please Lord ...'. This version was published by Inter-Art Co. in their 'Comique' series. Postally-used in September 1918.

million copies had been sold by 1962, probably over four million by now. The Worthing retailers would have sold their fair share of this amusing mass-produced card. It is, as I say, a classic of its type, but as so many were sold it is not rare nor costly. Probably you can find one for less than the price of a pint of beer.

McGill, once an established postcard artist or designer, was reputedly paid six shillings for each accepted drawing, so that if he completed five or six a week his income was under two pounds. A few colourful McGill cards are shown in plates 137-9, but these are only the merest flavour of the whole repertoire. McGill cards could be overprinted or adapted to suit various events or anniversaries, Christmas, birthdays or other greetings.

Donald McGill, who had one artificial leg since his youth, may nevertheless have helped to win the First World War, just as Jane of the *Daily Mirror* won the Second. At this period he was producing up to ten new designs a week. He continued to produce quality designs up to the 1940s, when the shortage of paper and the bombing of his publisher's London premises forced him to join the Ministry of Labour. He returned to the drawing board in 1944, aiming, he stated, by the amusing drawing and the clever caption with its double meaning to sell over 50,000 copies of each design. In most cases his cards achieved that target.

Over the years McGill worked for several publishers, but from 1936-62 McGill postcards were produced and marketed by Messrs. D. Constance Ltd. of Littlehampton in Sussex. They continued to sell after Donald's death in 1962 until the production of

Please, Lord, excuse me a minute while I kick Fido!

140 *(top left)*
A Davidson Brothers 'Write away'-type card, overprinted in the usual message space for use as a Christmas card. Posted on 23 December 1904.

141 *(top right)*
A Tom Browne 'Smiler'-type card published by Davidson Brothers. This example has printed on the address side: 'This Design is ONE of Davidson Brothers GREAT SUCCESSES. See our stands nos 34 and 65', which advertised a trade exhibition.

142 *(above left)*
A simple and clean comic card that could be sold nationally. This artist 'Comicus' (Harry Parlett) was very prolific.

143 *(above right)*
A typical posed Bamforth & Co. card of the type issued by this Holmfirth company in their thousands. Sent from one lady to another in September 1911 and described as 'another nice one, hoping you will like it'. Inexpensive.

144 *(above)*
A Watkins & Kracke 'Burlesque series' card, printed in Germany and postally-used in September 1909, sent to a Miss Poole without any message!

Everybody's doing it.

It's not the miles you travel
but the PACE that kills at Worthing.

145 *(left)*
A typical Mabel Lucie Attwell design issued by Valentine's and posted in July 1914.

146 *(above)*
A well-produced B.B. (Birn Brothers) localised card printed in Germany. The April 1909 message commences 'Another Vulgarity ...' and the card was seemingly welcomed as such.

the new McGills ceased six years later. The remaining stock of this firm and many of the original McGill drawings were sold by auction in Worthing, some other material having been sold previously at Sotheby's. What a stir the main Worthing sale caused, what prices the drawings commanded. More importantly what amusement his penny cards, in some 10,000 different designs, afforded the original buyers over such a long period.

In the highly competitive postcard world, other publishers sought to emulate McGill's style and success. Few artists had the master's flair, although some McGill-type cards published by Messrs. Bamforth are of this high standard. It seems almost certain that the complaints regarding the 'indecent' cards on display in sunny Worthing were prompted by imitations of McGill's technique and style, not by the artist's cheeky but not vulgar designs. Plates 140-2 show a small selection of non-McGill comic cards. The number of designs runs into thousands, each selling in tens of thousands. Seaside resorts would not have been the same without displays of these popular postcards.

A far more innocent but hugely popular form of humorous card of a slightly later period is typified by the neat children drawn by Mabel Lucie Attwell. Again hundreds of individual designs were published and most dealers have a selection of Lucie Attwell cards, quite modestly priced. As with all subdivisions of our subject, some designs will be common.

Another very popular type of inexpensive, mildly humorous postcard, mainly relevant to the seaside, was the multi-town special or 'localised comic postcard'. Here a standard design, that could be sold nationally, had the message completed by the addition of the name of the town, for example, Worthing. These were, perhaps, distantly related to the German 'Gruss aus' cards, except that, in those cases, each design was unique to one town. Here the design, the message and the humour were universal.

147
Three multi-town classic cards produced by the large-scale publishers Messrs. Millar & Lang Ltd. for its 'National' series. These popular cards were overprinted for sale in a multitude of towns.

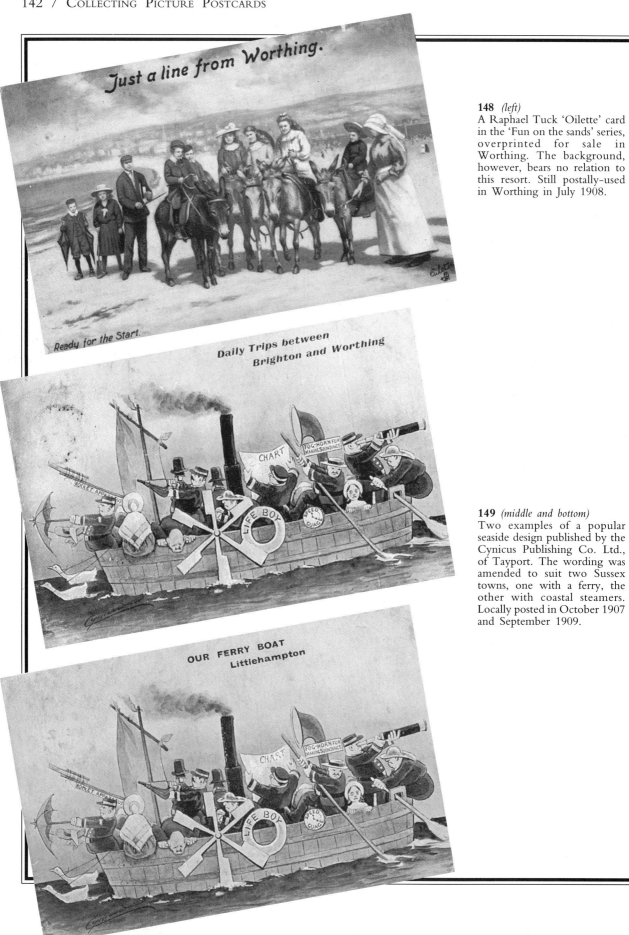

148 *(left)*
A Raphael Tuck 'Oilette' card in the 'Fun on the sands' series, overprinted for sale in Worthing. The background, however, bears no relation to this resort. Still postally-used in Worthing in July 1908.

149 *(middle and bottom)*
Two examples of a popular seaside design published by the Cynicus Publishing Co. Ltd., of Tayport. The wording was amended to suit two Sussex towns, one with a ferry, the other with coastal steamers. Locally posted in October 1907 and September 1909.

150 *(left)*
A popular type of localised multi-view card. The postman's bag contained a folded string of Worthing views. Full postage required if a message was added.

151 *(middle)*
A well-produced localised multi-view card published by the Photochrom Co. Ltd. in their 'Celesque' series. Posted in Worthing in August 1915.

152 *(right)*
A 'Pocket Novelty Card', 'Elsie at Worthing'. Her bag contains 12 miniature local views. It was sent 'with love from Jan' in August 1912. There were hundreds of such novelties.

One postcard printer and wholesalers of such 'localised comic' cards, John Thridgould & Co. of London, issued their own advertisement for such novelty designs. In about 1910 this firm was marketing a 'splendid variety of designs ... printed with the name of your town on each 6s. 6d. gross'. That is a fraction over an old halfpenny each, giving almost 100 per cent profit on cost. Such prices and mark-up were probably normal.

These mass-produced cards were printed with the name of the town as each order was received, in much the same way that a national charity will print your address on ordered Christmas cards. In some cases the cards were sold with a blank space, so that the purchaser had to add the town's name. In general these cards are not well produced; they were made to a price, and it is not unusual to find the town name added in a different typeface or size to the main wording (plate 154).

Nevertheless such 'multi-town' cards were extremely popular, and many comic or novel designs were produced. My bulging albums of such nonsenses are great fun, and typify the seaside tripper's basic mentality in the period *c.*1905-20. Other 'neutral' cards might leave out the town name, the caption reading only: 'This is an ideal place'.

Few serious collectors or dealers would trouble with these unsophisticated trifles of British postcards. The field is therefore wide open! You could build up a colourful collection of such cards bearing the name of your town, and the collection would probably run to hundreds.

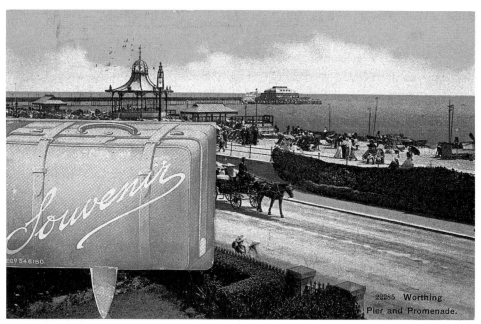

153
A Photochrom Co. Ltd. (of Tunbridge Wells) local-view novelty card. The 'Souvenir' suitcase bears a design-registration number for 1909. Posted in Worthing in December 1911.

Equally, you could choose one popular design and collect examples of that card bearing the names of different resorts or towns. In this case, the collection would have an element of repetition, but it might be fun to seek out examples from rare towns—presumably the smaller and less fashionable places with relatively few visitors to buy and send cards. Some of the most popular standard designs were issued not only with different town names but also with different wording (plate 149). Plates 147-54 show a few examples of these town cards. Today, they are plentiful and inexpensive—few should cost more than a drink or packet of cigarettes.

A subdivision of the 'multi-town' cards is novelty cards, incorporating in the card a pocket or other container for a concertina-like strip of miniature views of the town. A selection of these 'pull-out' cards is in plates 150-4. Again, there were standard designs mass-produced for the whole country but localised by the addition of the name of the town and the affixing of the narrow folded line of local views. In most cases these were standard views already used on full-size picture postcards. There are hundreds of such novelty cards, amended for sale in every sizeable locality.

These cards, with the addition of miniature local views, violated the half-rate postcard postal rate, unless only the name and address were added. If a message was written on these novelty cards, the full rate, then one penny, was required! In a few instances a localised card was enhanced with pocket views, as the Lucie Attwell card shown in plate 154. Some cards were produced or sold by large, very respectable firms such as Valentine's or the Photochrom Co. Ltd., the latter the publishers of the famous 'Celesque series'. These 'Mail Novelties' were probably more costly than the simple mass-produced localised town-name cards.

Many other novelty cards were produced. Their popularity rested on their novelty. Some were termed 'mechanical', in that moving parts made the card work. A typical amusing example is shown in plate 155. The card on sale looked as the contented upper image. The end of the card lever at the base turned, by means of a wheel-device, the picture to show a bawling baby and an anguished father. A situation understood worldwide! Again such mechanical cards were relatively costly—in postcard terms, perhaps selling at tuppence each and needing

GOOD LUCK IN A SHOE
AND ALL FOR YOU FROM
WORTHING

What's in the Post From
WORTHING

S.O.S.—L.S.D.—R.S.V.P. to WORTHING

154
Three typical Valentine,
overprinted Worthing, novelty
cards, each with a pocket of
miniature local views.

155
A German-produced novelty
lever-action simple mechanical
card of an amusing type.
Postally-used in March 1907
and accepted with a halfpenny
stamp.

156 *(right)*
Two attractive cards of the type on sale nationally. Both were published by Tuck's but were embossed and colour-printed in Saxony, *c.*1905-10.

157 *(below)*
A signed Tuck Valentine card of a general type on sale in all localities. Unused and perhaps purchased solely for a collection but copyrighted in 1907.

158 *(bottom left)*
A basic type of greeting card earlier in the century often took the form of specially designed postcards. This Christmas card was posted in Worthing on Christmas Eve 1909, for delivery on Christmas morning.

159 *(bottom right)*
A glossy real-photograph Easter card produced by E.A. Schwerdtreger & Co. of London and printed at their works in Berlin. It was sent from Littlehampton to nearby Worthing at Easter 1912.

160
The publicity cover for a pack of Tuck's Gramophone postcards. The miniature records were affixed to scenic postcards. Not very suitable for collecting in a standard album.

a penny stamp—real money. Consequently, such elaborate examples are now quite scarce. Also, such thicker cards, usually with a protruding lever, were not suitable for the old-fashioned album, made to contain standard postcards. Thousands of other novelty cards exist: for example, the 'hold to light' cards with pierced cut-out sections. Tuck's even issued real miniature gramophone records as postcards, on sale at four for a shilling. There are woven silk, printed silk and embroidered postcards. A non-specialised selection of novelty postcards, in Worthing (or any other town) in pre-war days, was produced by well over twenty different national publishers.

If, by chance, it did happen to be raining in 'sunny Worthing' you could have spent a good few hours browsing over thousands of colourful postcards on offer in this typical English seaside resort. What other hobby could give so much information or offer so much visual pleasure?

'I thought this rather good, not a bad idea'

'Here is a pretty picture, this is how we bathe here. Lovely place, lovely sea, lovely band in fact everything is lovely'

Messages on Worthing humorous novelty cards.

Chapter VIII

Local Research on
Your Postcards

'Kursall [sic] *is now renamed "The Dome" − no foreign names in Worthing'*

(Postcard view of 'The Kursaal' on Worthing sea-front, dated 22 August 1915)

In this chapter the pleasure and interest that can be gained from inquiry into local-event cards are demonstrated. Most pictorial cards have a story to tell, if you do but enquire.

The following story came about by accident or lucky chance. The happy ending is that I enjoyed a most interesting few weeks and ended with a far greater knowledge of my town.

The adventure began in November 1992 when I wrote to the editor of my local Friday newspaper, the *Worthing Herald*, asking for information about the Worthing photographer Edward Edwards (*see* page 129), or his family. I enclosed copies of three typical local-event Edwards postcards. A few days after my request was published, a member of a long-standing Worthing family telephoned to say that, while he did not have any information on the Edwards family, he did have an old card which depicted a 1908 fire just around the corner from my business premises. I expressed keen interest and the card was brought round to me within the hour.

This card is shown in plate 161. The subject was quite new. I had never heard of the fire nor of the firm that had suffered such damage over eighty years previously. I stated how I would like to add it to my collection of Edwards cards, and to carry out basic research on the event. It is now in my collection, and both the vendor and I are happy.

The very clear postmark on this local-event postcard shows that it had been sorted and stamped at 7.15 on Monday, 1 June 1908. Now the fire occurred early that very morning. Mr. Edwards had to attend the scene, and well after the fire was out, take his photograph, process it, print a supply on postcard blanks, and put the result on sale. Then, this example had been written and posted to another local inhabitant (of my vendor's family), collected and processed at the post office well within twelve hours of the photograph being taken! It was probably also delivered that same evening (*see* page 158).[*]

Some eight months later, in summer 1993, at a local Postcard Fair a friendly dealer drew my attention to another Edwards photographic card depicting the same 1908 shop fire. This splendid card (plate 162) was probably more interesting than my first purchase, as it included some of the Worthing firemen who had attended the blaze. The first card prompted my research into the event but showed only the burnt-out shop surrounded by young lads and other sightseers.

This second card had not been postally-used. It had probably been purchased as a memento of the fire. Within eight months I had come across two Edwards cards recording this minor local event; others may have been taken and await discovery.

The story has hardly begun. I visited the Worthing Reference Library to see if I could trace a contemporary account in a local newspaper. Nowadays such records are stored on micro-film; a whole year's run of the *Worthing Gazette* (a predecessor and relative of the *Worthing Herald*) is contained on one small roll of film.

The report published on Wednesday, 3 June 1908 was remarkably full and of great interest. It read:

Destructive Fire in Montague Street

An early morning outbreak.
Confectioners Shop completely destroyed.
Rescue of the Inmates.

In the early hours of Monday morning Montague Street was the scene of a most destructive fire, by which a shop was completely gutted ...

The shop is no 116, in which a sweet and confectionery business was carried on by Mrs Sarah Jameson. There were eight rooms attached to

[*] This is not, however, a record. Real-photograph cards depicting the proclamation of King George V on 9 May 1910 were on sale at Spencer's Chapel Road Photo store by 3.30 that afternoon.

161 *(left)*
An Edwards local-event real-photograph card captioned '116 Montague St. Worthing. Destroyed by Fire, June 1st 1908' and posted at 7.15 the same evening. A simple event card that triggered interesting research.

162 *(right)*
A further Edwards local-event real-photograph card showing some of the local firemen posed in front of the destroyed confectioner's in 1908. Such cards are highly interesting and valuable to local history collectors or students.

the house and sleeping on the premises were Mrs Lavinia Barker, a boy named Harold Eveleigh, aged thirteen and Samuel Goff (who were lodgers) and Mrs Jameson.

Between three and half past three o'clock P.C. Jeffrey was on duty in Shelley road, when he saw smoke ascending and hurrying to the shop he found the place alight. He blew his whistle ... P.C. Jeffrey sent one of those present to the nearest telephone, which was at Mr Leggatt's, to give the call to the Central Fire Station. This message was received at half-past three.

In the meantime Mr Clark procured an extension ladder which he uses in his business [he was a nearby window cleaner] and raised it to the top storey of the house, and with commendable pluck ascended and assisted by P.C. Jeffrey and others succeeded in getting the occupants of the rooms away without injury ... One of those rescued was Samuel Goff, who is said to be aged eighty-four and is bedridden and blind ...

This exciting incident of the rescue had just occurred when the members of the Fire Brigade, consisting of the Chief Officer (Mr. H. N. Collett), Second Officer C.F. Haines, Station Officer J. Allmark and sixteen firemen arrived on the scene with the escape, three hose carts and three hydrants.

Having seen the big flames from some distance away Station Officer Allmark, on the way to the fire, had dispatched a messenger with instructions for the manual to be brought to the outbreak ...

A good pressure of water was obtained, and the firemen were soon battling with the flames ... It was apparent that the shop and stock could not be saved, so main attention was centred on the task of preventing the flames from spreading to the property on either side ... After working with great energy for upwards of an hour the fireman got the upper hand of the flames but it was not before the entire premises were gutted ...

The cause of the origin of the fire is a complete mystery ... All that remains of the shop are the outside walls, portions of two floors and the roof. The shop is filled with a heap of charred wood and debris ...

The spot was visited by a large number of people throughout the day.

The *Worthing Gazette* did not carry a photograph or illustration of the fire; indeed the paper at that period was almost devoid of illustration apart from photographs of local dignitaries. The newspapers supplied the words, the local photographers supplied good photographs, usually in the form of postcards.

Picture poor 84-year-old, blind and bedridden Samuel Goff being rescued from a first- or second-floor window, above the blazing shop! He was born in the reign of George IV, had lived through the complete reigns of William IV and Queen Victoria and was now in the Edwardian era. Consider also the other lodger, young Harold Eveleigh, born in the 1890s, a Victorian. What would he live to see, what postcards would he send, from where, to whom? At least his name is not included amongst those on the Worthing War Memorial, so perhaps his luck held.

When did the telephone come to Worthing?—Mr. Aston, the chemist, was the subscriber given the number 'Worthing 1', a distinction he or the firm retained for many years. At the time of the fire in 1908 the system was run by the 'National Tel. Co. Ltd.'. Apart from private and trade subscribers, there were three 'public call offices'—one at Aston's the chemists, one at the railway station, and one at the company's office in Bath Place.

While reading the contemporary press report on the micro-film in our Reference Library, I happened to notice the report of a Council meeting held on Tuesday 2 June, the day after the fire. Under the heading 'Our Fire Appliance', the Chief Fire Officer, Mr. Collett drew attention to the 'great disabilities under which the Fire Brigade laboured in promptly responding to calls, consequent to the delay which now took place between the receipt of the call and obtaining the necessary horses for the conveyance of the men and appliances to the scene of a fire ... The Chief Officer ... advised the purchase of a motor propelled cart* and fire escape, similar to that now used by the London Fire Brigade'.

The mayor stated that, 'having heard that there had been a serious delay in the attendance of the members of the Fire Brigade at the fire in Montague Street on Monday morning he had taken it upon himself to invite an explanation from the Chief Officer'.

In his reply Mr. Collet said it did not seem to have occurred to any of the numerous people present to give the brigade a call! The first intimation they had of the fire was the receipt of a telephone message sent from Mr. Leggatt of Montague Street. This was received at half past three o'clock.

The men residing at headquarters turned out immediately with the escape and hose cart and had left in a little over two minutes from the receipt of the call. A message was sent for horses to bring on the manual (which also carried four lengths of ladder, each of six foot and six inches) in case more hoses were required.

The escape and hose cart had just left when he [Mr. Collet, the Chief Officer] reached headquarters and he proceeded to the fire on his bicycle, passing the appliances on the way. He met the first man coming to call the brigade near Mr. Ashdown's premises at the corner of Liverpool Gardens.

* Mr. Collet's 1905 annual report to the Council had even then requested a 'motor-power hose cart'.

According to the police the escape and hose cart were on the scene of the outbreak at twenty minutes to four and when it was taken into consideration that the men had to dress and turn out the appliances, that the escape and hose cart were hand-propelled and that the distance was approximately eight hundred yards, he failed to see how the time in these circumstances was to be improved upon.

It seems almost inconceivable to us today that in 1908 a town with a population exceeding 25,000 should have relied on fire appliances which were hand-drawn (or at best, dependent on horses supplied by a tradesman) and that the Chief Officer on his bicycle should overtake these appliances on the way to the blaze.

This concern was indeed felt at the time; the *Worthing Gazette* of 10 June published a reader's letter, under the heading 'Protection from Fire':

> Dear Sir,
>
> The disastrous fire which occurred in Montague Street last week ... surely calls for an inquiry into the fire protection of the town ... I feel I am not out of place in saying that the methods here are totally inadequate to the requirements ...
>
> To commence with, our appliances are kept at a distance from the class of property which is at greatest risk ... from this point of view even to a fire escape, these have to be dragged by hand to the scene of the outbreak. What is required is a light horse escape and reel; horse kept on the Station, ready, not dependant on calling an outside jobmaster; a fully qualified Fire Superintendent of London ... at the head of affairs to look after things and advise the authorities on what is practically required.

All the above was gained from under an hour's research. Another basic source of information on all fires is provided by the published minutes of the Town Council and in particular those of the General Purposes Committee, to whom the Chief Fire Officer had to report on every turn-out and its cost to the town! One can read in the June reports:

> Called 1st June at 3-30am to 116 Montague Street, occupied by Miss Jameson—confectioner. Attended by three Officers and 18 members of the Brigade with Escape, three hose carts and manual.
>
> Building of three floors and contents severly [*sic*] damaged by fire, etc. Messrs. Barker, Goff and H. Everleigh rescued by J.W. Clark, G. Newman and P. Jeffries before the arrival of the Brigade.
>
> Slight damage also occasioned to nos. 143, 145, 147 and 118 Montague Street, adjoining.
>
> Expenses incurred, £6-6-0.

At the same meeting of the General Purposes Committee Mr. Collet reported that he had enquired of 20 other Chief Fire Officers possessing motor appliances and that consequently he recommended that the Council 'should acquire a motor fire escape in preference to one to be horse driven'.

One could well research further the history of your town's fire service. In Worthing progress was quite slow. In fact Chief Officer Herbert Norman Collet remained in command for a further 20 years, until 1928, receiving various long-service medals. He did not receive the requested motor fire engine until October 1910. This machine, the 'latest pattern of fire fighting appliance in the form of a powerful motor engine and escape', is shown in plate 163 outside the central fire station which had been opened in June 1904. The building of a special fire station had first been mooted in July 1902, when it was agreed to purchase Warwick Hall at a cost of £3,510, the loan being repayable over 50 years!

At this 1904 period, however, the firemen were dependent on procuring a horse to transport the equipment. On one occasion they had to wait twenty minutes before a horse could be supplied! This fact is evidenced by a complaint to the editor of the *Worthing Gazette*, published on 17 August 1904:

> Sir,
>
> In a borough of 25,000 inhabitants it is perfectly monstrous that our Fire Brigade could not get away on Wednesday last for half an hour after a call was received, because no horses were available.
>
> The ratepayers have a right to demand that we should not be dependant upon the local livery stable-keepers to loan the horses for the engine, but that the Corporation should purchase and keep two horses for the purpose ...

This correspondent also requested the purchase of a steam engine. This suggestion was by no means new, but the Fire Brigade Committee stated in July 1902 that 'it is not necessary, the water pressure is too good to require it'.

A combined motorised fire engine and fire escape was not a new invention at the time of this 1908 fire. The *Worthing Mercury Directory* of 1906, prepared and printed in 1905, includes a photograph of such an engine, and the caption states 'a considerable advance has been made in the direction of rapidly reaching the scene of the fire'. Worthing acquired such a machine in the next reign, seven years after the Corporation had first viewed a new London motor fire appliance.

Worthing's first motor fire engine did not arrive before the matter had been debated at length by the Town Council. One such discussion took place just five weeks after the Montague Street fire, on Tuesday, 7 July 1908 and was reported by the *Worthing Gazette* as follows:

> ... the public will learn with gratification that the Town Council are taking steps to improve the equipment of the Borough Fire Brigade ...
>
> Having carefully considered the matter the Committee ultimately expressed the opinion that as it was essential that a new escape should be obtained for the proper protection of life in the borough, it was desirable that the Council should acquire a motor propelled escape in preference to one to be horse driven and recommended the Council to accept an offer made by Messrs Merryweather and Sons to supply a petrol motor combined hose tender and fire escape, with chemical fire extinguishing apparatus attached, at the price of £945, subject to the Local Government Board sanctioning a loan.
>
> Councilor [sic] Ellis pointed out that the motor they proposed to purchase would enable the Brigade to get away from the Station in one minute, whereas the quickest time in which the horsed engine had been known to get away had been ten minutes.

The case for the purchase of the new engine was clear cut, but we learn that:

> Councillor Jackson proposed as an amendment that the Council should purchase a horsed escape from Messrs Bailey. For one thing he did not consider Worthing was a suitable town for motor-propelled vehicles of this description and another objection to purchasing one of these appliances lay in the fact that at present they were still in the experimental stage.
>
> Councillor Baker could not understand what they wanted all these elaborate engines for, when they had standpipes all over the town sufficient to meet all their requirements. They had quite enough motors in the town already, he added, and quite enough fads.
>
> Councillor Cook suggested that this matter should be referred back for fuller information.

163
A non-Worthing real-photograph card showing magnificent London horse-drawn fire engines, fine when the horses are readily available. Postally-used May 1906.

A Turn Out — Streatham L.F.B.

The matter was indeed referred back and referred back and referred back! During one of these later debates a councillor 'defied any man at the present time to say that motors were efficient'. It must be admitted that special horse-drawn fire engines of the period were very efficient and probably nearly as fast as early motors, but one needed trained and readily available horses—as shown on the real photograph of the Streatham turn-out, a postcard postally-used in May 1906 (plate 163).

The research prompted by my first postcard reveals that this new machine was built by Dennis Ltd. (still producing appliances for this and other authorities) and cost £837, a sum which included the new 'Patent front-wheel brakes'. This sum was obtained as a loan to be repaid over a 10-year period—the subject of local rejoicing, as it spread the burden on the rates. A demonstration was arranged in Beach House Park, with the old horse-drawn manual pump also performing, to show the advantages of the new wonder machine.

The *Worthing Gazette* of 2 November 1910 reported that the new engine could send a stream of water 180 feet, that four jets could be worked, and that the motor carried its own supply of 40 gallons of water and a 300-foot hose. (Modern appliances carry 400 gallons). The escape ladder extended to 50 feet (the present-day platform raises to 85 feet). At the handing-over ceremony the mayor remarked that the new motor would enable the firemen (now termed 'fire-fighters') to arrive at a blaze fresh, not out of breath from manhandling the apparatus through the streets! Regarding the original large escape, Mr. Collet had earlier reported in all seriousness that he had not turned out on one occasion because 'the escape was of a very heavy pattern' and the 'danger of sending men up a ladder after running from the Station and pushing an escape weighing fifteen hundred weight' was too great! Local fire-fighters, however, had been assisted by the purchase early in 1909 of one of Professor Tyndall's smoke respirators. This could not have been complicated apparatus as the cost was estimated at £2 0s. 0d.

The *Worthing Gazette* illustrated their November 1910 report on the new fire engine with the photograph at plate 164; this was credited to Worthing Portrait Company in Railway Approach as the local papers did not then have their own staff-photographers. The fire brigade then used this photograph in postcard form. My example contains a message to Councillor W.G. Tree to the effect that a fireman and a messenger would call that evening to be measured for

164
A real-photograph postcard published by the Worthing Portrait Co., showing the new motor fire engine and brigade. This card was used by the Chief Officer in November 1912.

their uniforms. Councillor William Tree (a leading figure in the town, mayor 1935-6, and president of my local bowls club) is depicted on many local-event postcards and was a tailor by trade. He fitted out the fire brigade and perhaps also the local police force.

This postcard was signed with the initials 'H.N.C.', those of Chief Officer Herbert Norman Collet, who received his 20-year service medal at the same time as the new motor engine was handed over to his brigade. Apart from this use of the fire engine postcard, copies may also have been for sale at the fire station, just as a selection of lifeboat postcards was available at the lifeboat station. This fire brigade card bears the impressed stamp 'Worthing Portrait Company' on the front with the printed credit on the address side 'Published by The Worthing Portrait Co. 4 Railway Approach, Worthing'. It is postmarked 1.10 p.m. 8 November 1912, over two years after the photograph was taken and used in the *Worthing Gazette*. The message referred to a visit that evening. I am not sure whether Councillor Tree was then on the telephone at his business premises, but he certainly was towards the end of the next year—the 1914 Directory included his telephone number. Perhaps the card plus the halfpenny stamp was cheaper than a telephone call to say that two firemen would be calling that evening. How fortunate that the card, rather than the telephone, was used as we now have a very good picture of Worthing's first motor fire engine and its crew.

The newly acquired motor fire engine was insured against fire but it soon caused difficulties—nobody in the brigade could drive! It had been delivered and demonstrated by Dennis' own driver—seen standing by the station doors dressed as a chauffeur in plate 164. The *Worthing Gazette* of 7 December 1910 reported that a new motor fire engine mechanic, driver and Station Officer from Birkenhead had been appointed at £1 10s. 0d. a week, with free quarters and lighting. This person, Mr. A.W.C. Bristowe, was reported to be a trained driver and 'expert mechanician'.

Having invested in the new driver, the Council saw fit to dismiss the existing Station Officer Allmark, who had attended the 1908 fire. Poor Mr. Allmark could not drive but, although many town councillors expressed sympathy and stated that he could learn in a couple of weeks, the experience of the imported new driver-mechanic won the day. Given time and patience once could perhaps endeavour to trace the future fortunes of Mr. J. Allmark and of the imported Mr. A.W.C. Bristowe.

The Council had taken over the responsibility for the town's fire protection in 1891-2. From 1869 to this period the inhabitants had been protected by volunteer fire brigades—three of them! At that time and until 1904 the 'Fire House' was at the back of the Town Hall, the keys to the underground room being kept 'at Mr Chas Cook's, South Street'. However, by the time of the 1908 fire featured on my Edwards' postcard the local brigade was described in the following brief terms:

> Worthing Borough Fire Brigade which is under the immediate control of the Town Council has a membership of 31 of all ranks, including the Chief Officer (H.N.Collet), the second officer (C.F. Haines) and the Station Officer (H. Finnis). The Head Quarters are at the Central Fire Station, High Street, where rooms are provided for the Station Officer and three cottages for occupation by firemen.

This 1904 building was understandably described in July 1938 as 'hopelessly inadequate' but it remained in being until the 1960s when our present large station was built on a new site, judged to be the centre of a now very diverse area. Before I purchased this local-event postcard I knew next to nothing about the history of our fire service—these facts have been prompted by that 1908 card.

We can research the 1908 postcard much further. What about that very small shop (the frontage is less than six yards) with the four inhabitants? What sort of confectionery did it display? This research into Edwardian edibles must be left, as I have not yet found a Worthing postcard showing the interior of a confectioner's. The nearest is a local café whose counter shows boxes of biscuits or sweets (plate 109).

What happened to the fire-damaged shop? Was it re-equipped and continued by Mrs. Jameson? What of it now? Does it still exist?

The fire-damaged shop was repaired and refurbished. By March 1909 it had been reopened, for on the night of Wednesday 24 March Jameson's shop suffered another fire! This was a minor affair, caused by a gas-burner, but this report shows how quickly the gutted premises were rebuilt and trading continued.

The whole row of small shops remains intact today. Number 116 has a new shop-front with a centrally-placed door. It now sells television sets and radios, and the top windows are guarded by a satellite dish to pick up pictures via the heavens. Times have changed in other aspects, too. This shop and all others is 'on the phone', it has a burglar alarm that might also help to warn of any fire. The proprietor no longer lives over the shop; indeed, no one resides on the premises. The eight or so rooms that there were in 1908 are now used to store spare stock. The residents have mainly moved out from the centre of the town—as has the fire station.

You could extend your research to your town's postal services. It will have been extremely efficient. One of my 1908 Worthing cards bears the unremarkable message:

> Lily and I will call and see you this evening, if convenient to you.

This card was written on the morning of 6 February, posted and received locally the same day. The writer expected this service, hence the 'same-day' message, and received it for a halfpenny. Basic information on local post office services can be gleaned from most old town directories. Cards might even feature some of the postmen or the various post offices.

165
The Worthing escape ladder in its normal place leaning against the Town Hall, waiting to be pushed to a fire. An E.T.W. Dennis & Sons 'Dainty Series' local-view card, posted in 1908.

The 1906 *Worthing Mercury Directory* shows that the 'chief office' in Chapel Road was open from 7 a.m. to 10 p.m. including Bank Holidays, but on Sundays, Good Friday and Christmas Day the office was only open for two periods—between 8 a.m. and 10 a.m. and between 5 p.m. and 6 p.m. These long weekday (including Saturday) hours were no doubt general, not restricted to Worthing. The town was also serviced by 18 in-town sub-post offices and 14 others in outlying villages. These were all open, Sunday excepted, between 8 a.m. and 8 p.m. All would almost certainly have sold picture postcards.

Worthing enjoyed five deliveries each weekday. These were at 6.30; 9.45; 12.30; 16.30 and 19.30; personal callers at the chief office could collect later mail at 8.15 p.m. Alas, on Sunday there was only one delivery at 7.00 a.m. The post-box at the main office was 'cleared for local letters 5 minutes before the commencement of each delivery'. This means in effect that, if that Montague Street fire card (plate 161) was posted by 7.24 p.m., it would have been cleared, postmarked and delivered that night. It was in fact postmarked 7.15 p.m. so the event took place, the result was photographed, processed, put on sale, sold, written, posted and delivered on the same day. Not bad service from all concerned.

The present-day postmaster has informed me that these hard-working pre-First World War local postmen would have earned from 17s. (85p) to 25s. (£1.25) a week according to their grade or age.* This is for a six-day week with deliveries alone commencing at 6.30 a.m., continuing to 7.30 p.m. quite apart from the pre-delivery sorting. (Perhaps this book should have been dedicated to the postmen.) I have no figures for the proportion of letters to postcards delivered, but in the summer halfpenny cards probably outnumbered penny letters. The service certainly increased as the town grew. There were, for example, 56 street letter-boxes in 1899 but by 1912 this number had nearly doubled to 107.** Most of these were cleared seven times a day, starting at 5 a.m., and twice on Sundays. Some of this increase may be due to the popularity of the postcard as a reliable and inexpensive means of communication. For an old halfpenny the Edwardian resident certainly received value for his money.

What might we also discover about Mr. Edwards, the photographer? How could he, and others like him, earn a living by photographing such local events, and then processing and preparing such postcards to sell at a penny at time? Did

* These rates for a postman are much the same as those paid to a police constable. In May 1912 their minimum weekly wage was to be raised to £1 2s. 9d.

** In 1993 the larger town has 191 pillar-boxes and 28 sub-post offices.

they sell such local-demand cards at this standard price to compete with the popular fast-selling commercially produced local-view cards? Did Mr. Edwards charge interested parties threepence or even sixpence for their 'real-photograph' cards? It could not have been very remunerative work. We are the winners when we purchase over eighty years later the fruits of their labour. At least we receive some reward, if we research the local history behind these humble cards.

We should research these local photographers for future generations. The search for background information is relatively easy if the firm, or its successors, is still in business. In Worthing, I am lucky in that the sons or grandsons of the photographers of the Walter Gardiner and the Loader cards are still active—I was brought up with them and have done business with their firms over a long period.

It does not follow, however, that after two world wars, salvage drives, moving premises, modernisation and so on that their old records are still available. The owners of such business records or archives should deposit them with their local library, museum or County Record Office. What may be unwanted space-wasting files and records can prove of the greatest interest to future generations. For example, I do not know of any surviving records of the many other local publishers or suppliers of picture postcards. Such lost records could have been saved with little or no trouble.

Such feelings are prompted by difficulties in tracing even basic details of Worthing's noteworthy local photographer and publisher of real-photograph postcards, Edward Edwards or the firm known as Edwards & Son. It may be of interest to other researchers into local photographers if I detail how I set about tracing Mr. Edwards' history.

From previous experience I started my quest for information on Edward Edwards (or his son) by writing to local newspapers. I wrote to the editor of the county paper, the *West Sussex Gazette*, and to the editor of the *Worthing Herald*, enclosing samples of typical Edwards local-event cards. Both editors published my letter and the different illustrations, but nobody came forward with information. I still needed to trace the person behind the camera.

The search for Edward Edwards proved extremely difficult and perplexing. I was thrown back into local directories and newspaper files. The directories included E. Edwards as a photographer at 94 Belle Vue or Chapel Street from 1888 to 1896. Chapel Street was long ago renamed Portland Road, a fact that might have warned me of difficulties to come. From 1891 onwards Mr. Edwards was listed at New Street down by the sea-front.

The reverse of the early Edwards photographs usually bears one of several different printed publicity labels. One Victorian example was printed in Paris; others describe E. Edwards as a portrait and landscape photographer. The reference to the Belle Vue Studio should have been deleted from about 1895. Halfway through the 1890s Mr. Edwards was not engaged in the postcard trade. He did, however, supply most of the local-view photographs for an interesting pre-1902 publication *The Standard Picture Guide to Worthing*, published at a penny by 'The Standard Picture Guide Company' of London, which produced similar booklets, with local information and advertisements, for many towns.

These photographic postcards seem to have been produced from *c.*1905 onwards. He had produced at least one set of standard local-view cards by December 1905; but he and other local photographers are better known for their special-event or commissioned cards, than their more commercial view cards, which would have been sold over a long period.

A full-page Edwards' advertisement in *Kelly's Directory* of 1904 informs us that the firm, then trading as Edwards & Sons, was established in 1887. The small

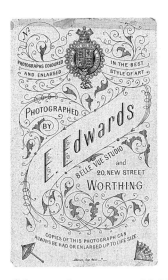

fisherman's cottage at 20 New Street was by 1904 grandly entitled the 'Excelsior Studios'. Today it is used by a partnership of 'Chartered Physiotherapists'. Although the premises look much as they did in say 1910, the only contemporary view is that shown on the postcard illustrated in plate 167. This was sent to Mrs. Tree in July 1908 with the simple note 'Dear Aggie. Have sent you the promised card, can't remember to give it to you when I see you'. The man leading the pony could well be one of the Mr. Edwards.

The Worthing directories listed Edwards & Son at 20 New Street until 1919. In 1920 we find listed at these premises 'Mr & Mrs W.G. Lawson, The Fine Art Studio, 20 New Street. Outdoor Photography Experts'; perhaps the end of the Edwards story. The directories had proved helpful, and I moved to the files of local papers with high hopes of tracing an obituary notice that would fill in some of the missing details. After hours of plodding I had to acknowledge that Mr. Edwards had vanished without trace. Only their work remained as evidence that these talented photographers served the town and its inhabitants for over thirty years, from 1887 to c.1919.

One very important source of local information had not been tapped—local census returns. British censuses have been carried out every ten years from at least 1841, but they are unseen by private researchers for a hundred years. The 1891 census returns were published and available on micro-film in the Worthing Reference Library when I carried out my enquiry.

Local directories had led me to believe that Edward Edwards was living in Worthing in 1891 and that he should be shown in the census returns as living at 20 New Street. I was in for a great surprise.

The census returns show that the name 'E. Edwards' was merely a commercial trade name. My elusive photographer was an Edward Bex! The entry for 20 New Street, read: 'Edward Bex, aged 45, Photographer Widow born at Lympsfield, Surrey.'

At this period he had a live-in housekeeper—Fanny Churcher aged 50, a son—Edward Charles Bex, who was described as a 'Photographers assistant', although he was only sixteen. A younger son, Percy W. Bex, was aged eight and was at school. In addition, this small terraced house or cottage sheltered a boarder, Ann Smith.

166 *(left)*
The printed label on the reverse of an early Edwards portrait photograph. Edwards and all such local photographers were important professionals in any town.

167 *(right)*
A rather faded but rare and interesting real-photograph postcard showing Mr. Edwards(?) and a child passing in front of his premises in New Street, Worthing. Photographic postcards are displayed in the window. Posted on 13 July 1908 to local 'Dear Aggie'.

168
A Bex local-view card postally-used in July 1938; it is a standard view of the Beach House boating pool in keeping with the Edwards family tradition. The reference number is high—2176.

From the basic census details we learn that Edward Bex was born in about 1846/7, that at the time his son was born in about 1875 the family was living along the coast at St Leonards, but by *c*.1883, when Percy was born, the family was in South Lambeth, moving to Worthing in 1887. At this time Edward Bex (or Edwards as he was then calling himself) was approximately forty-one and had presumably previously practised as a photographer at St Leonards and South Lambeth.

Edward Bex died in March 1928. He had retired from the business some years before this, and his son continued to trade as Edward Edwards & Son. He was buried in my local cemetery under his true name of Edward Bex. The death certificate, a copy of which was obtained for me through the professional help of Lady Teviot, confirms his date of death as 8 March 1928, his true name, his age at death and his occupation as a photographer. I have not traced an obituary or other note of his death in the local papers. His photographs and photographic postcards, however, bear witness to his professional skills and to his interest and the many events that occurred in the town in the first 15 years of this century.

Edward Charles Bex (born *c*.1875) who, according to the 1891 census, was already assisting his father at this period, took over the business as his father became infirm. He moved from the family house in New Street in about 1920, when the 'Edwards' business was taken over by Mr. and Mrs. Lawton, who traded for a few years under his name.

Edward then appeared in local directories under the Bex surname at 150 Tarring Road; real-photograph postcards occur with the Bex credit from the early 1920s up to *c*.1940. These tend to be general views of the type shown in plate 168, rather than the special-event and commissioned cards favoured by his father earlier in the century.

Edward Charles Bex died at Worthing on 13 February 1941, aged sixty-five. The *Worthing Gazette*, which earlier had published many 'Edwards' photographs, printed in its slim wartime issue a brief notice of his death:

> ... Mr Bex was a photographer in Worthing for nearly half a century, first in New Street where he was in business with his father and since the War at 150 Tarring Road, where he specialized in portraiture work and the production of picture postcards of local views and incidents.

169
A good sharp Edwards real-photograph card recording General Booth's visit to Worthing on 16 August 1907. This local-event card cost £30 and cannot be called over-priced because of its interest and quality. There is certainly another interesting story here—that of the Salvation Army in Worthing.

170
An Edwards & Son Worthing-event card depicting a conflict of horsepower in August 1908. This photograph was also published nationally in *The Car*. In fact, the new-fangled automobile could be stopped quicker than a horse pulling a loaded cart.

Even this brief contemporary note gave an incorrect date for his move to Tarring Road which took place in the 1920s. Efforts to trace any surviving family have not borne fruit. The 1941 funeral at Worthing Baptist church was attended by his widow and his younger brother, Percy, an eight-year-old schoolboy at the time of the 1891 census. No sons or daughters attended, but this was 1941, when his family might have been serving in the forces. Now, over fifty years later, the scent has dried up; Mrs. Edward Bex and Percy have long since passed away.

Census returns for 1911 or 1921 might shed some light on a family, but these records, under the hundred-year rule, will not be available to me until the next century.

Apart from collecting the Edwards event, commissioned or local-view picture postcards, I have experienced great pleasure from trying to learn something of the man behind the camera.

171
A good morning-after local-event card taken by Otto Brown, showing the crowds looking for the storm-destroyed pier. The marooned landing stage and pavilion was henceforth called Easter Island!

172
Another Otto Brown local-event card showing the effects of a fire in a Worthing timber yard in October 1919; a house was also destroyed. Another fire, another story that could be recorded by a postcard. Fire subjects are strangely popular.

Two further Edwards photographic cards (plates 169 and 170) are reproduced from my collection. The conflict between horse and car is famous and therefore not all that rare. This photograph was published in several newspapers and some people wrote to Worthing for copies of the postcard which were on sale here for a period of weeks. This was one local-event that attracted wide publicity. Some other Edwards real-photograph cards are illustrated in plates 1, 167, 169, 170 and 190.

My Edwards album is full of interesting photographic studies showing a good range of events that took place mainly before the end of the First World War. This collection of Edwards cards could be replicated for any of the local photographers practising their craft in Worthing or in any other English town.

Edward Bex was but one of several such local photographers. Otto Brown was another who produced some highly interesting photographic postcards (plates 171 and 172). He was a contemporary and rival of Edward Bex or Edwards.

Every town in the land had one or more such professionals, whose lives deserve even belated recognition.

The Edwards 1908 event postcard that prompted my research and this chapter is not an isolated example. Several other cards feature local fires (plates 172), for such events aroused great interest. Fires, accidents, and other disasters were very much part of the postcard scene. Such disaster cards form an important subdivision and are eagerly collected. Some can be very costly, whereas the next category is generally obtainable at low cost.

———————————

The story of that 1908 fire related mainly to some of the town's services—the fire service, the police, the post office, and one family firm of photographers. We now turn to one important industry of any resort or town—hotels. Without adequate accommodation for visitors a resort cannot prosper. Wealthy holiday-makers and business folk will patronise places where their comfort is provided for. The success of a holiday town relates in some measure to the number, quality or range of available hotels. In the Golden Age of postcards, the Edwardian period, the middle-class or wealthier family tended to choose one resort for a week's or a fortnight's holiday by the sea. To this place they might well return year after year.

The Worthing hotels, guest-houses, boarding-houses and so on certainly continued to commission cards featuring their imposing premises and the delights of the neighbourhood. Hotel cards of the 1910-30 period are not in great demand. This is especially true of those depicting the larger, prominent hotels, of which the cards may well be readily available for a pound or so.

To an enquiring mind such cards can give untold pleasure. A classic case relates to Worthing's *Warne's Hotel*. This building is depicted on more Worthing cards than any other hotel. The story behind its rise to fame is again prompted by research into postcards.

Warne's Hotel (not 'The Warnes' as it is sometimes called), or rather its founder Mr. Warne, has done more to publicise Worthing than any other person. We all know *Warne's*; many have wined, dined and danced or attended one of the thousands of functions that were held in its large public rooms. Some claim to know its history but few know much about its founder.

He was a mystery figure, ambitious (probably too ambitious) and a great publicist. Perhaps he did not fit into Worthing, but Worthing surely owes a great debt to him, which I do not believe has ever been fully acknowledged. He has not yet been granted an entry in the reference library's listing of notable personages. Here is an outline of his early career.

The 1891 Brighton census returns show that he was born at Greenwich in about 1864 (he was aged 27 at the 1891 census). He was married to Mary from Lewes and they had a son, Frederick, who was then aged three. This young couple were listed as 'Lodging Housekeepers', at Biskra House, 38 Regency Square, Brighton. They employed at least a resident 'Parlour Maid' and a 'House Maid'. The small Warne's establishment had great competition in Regency Square, for nearly all the sixty-odd houses are listed in the 1898 Directory as boarding- or lodging-houses.

At this period, however, he was on the move, west to Worthing, to make his mark—if not his fortune! Local press reports provide the basic facts but not the personal details, the events or accidents that led George Warne to move from thriving Brighton to the more sedate and smaller town of Worthing, when he was in his mid-thirties. But move he did and sought in his own way to enliven and improve the town.

He enjoyed excellent write-ups in the local papers. It is a matter of wonderment to me today to understand how he managed to have the following glowing account published in the *Worthing Gazette* of 2 August 1899 without paying for his own separate advertisement. No doubt he entertained the then editor extremely well!

The result is a wonderful account of how George Warne commenced to play monopoly in Worthing, and how he firstly acquired a single house or boarding establishment in one of the several terraces that face the sea in Marine Parade.

The report read:

THE SPIRIT OF MODERN ENTERPRISE
A NEW PRIVATE HOTEL

... Private hotels and boarding houses are comparatively recent innovations from the point of view of local experience, but they have arisen in response to a distinct demand and we have no hesitation in declaring that the existence of half a score of such establishments that may now be found along the Front has gone far to remove a reproach which hitherto existed as to paucity of superior accommodation ...

In availing ourselves of an invitation to make a formal inspection of Warne's Private Hotel we were simply actuated by a desire to see for ourselves the result of a very spirited enterprise ...

... Mr. G.H. Warne, who has embarked upon the present enterprise has secured for his purpose one of a row of houses familiar for several generations past and has extended his capital lavishly in adapting it to the uses to which it is at the moment being put. No 1 York terrace is the house in question, and the extent of the accommodation there available will be little understood except by those who, as we ourselves have done, take an opportunity of making themselves familiar with the main features of the interior of this hospitable abode.

We cannot give a detailed description of the many handsomely appointed apartments but we must repeat the substance of what we have already stated and declare that money would seem to have but a secondary consideration ...

The house has practically had to undergo a process of reconstruction and all that has been done in accordance with the design of Mr. Warne, the proprietor. Drawing room, dining room, billiard-room and smoking lounge are among the more notable apartments, and each of these is furnished and fitted with a richness and completeness that must surely tend to support the claim that this is one of the most elaborate establishments of the kind in the kingdom.

The dining room is on the ground floor and is furnished with separate tables, an arrangement that commends itself to private hotel patrons in general. A conspicuous object is the magnificent mantel-piece of polished oak and walnut, the dado having been designated by Mr. Warne. The ceilings throughout the house are of or anaglypta, and in this particular instance it is a specially noticeable piece of work.

The drawing-room on the floor above, apart from the richness of the decoration and furnishing, commands a view that if equalled is not surpassed, and the adjoining verandah, well provided with shades, furnishes a cool and comfortable lounge in this tropical weather.

Satinwood, walnut, ash and other woods are brought into use for the specially designed bedroom-suites, which exhibit—as, indeed, does every thing visible—a richness and beauty that lend to a general condition of sumptuousness. Panelled Lincrusta, with a mahogany rail, is to be found on the staircases and the paper hung there was specially obtained for the purpose from Japan. Carpets, suites, curtains and papers throughout are found to be in perfect harmony, the general scheme having doubtless entailed a considerable amount of thought and supervision. The carpets are by Cardinal and Harford and Tapling and Belfast linen of the finest manufacture has been obtained for the bedrooms. Mr Warne has travelled all over the world and in the eight hundred pictures or thereabouts that are to be found throughout the house, together with many curios and objects of art, are interesting souvenirs of his extensive journeyings.

The billiard room, well lighted by day and night, is fitted with one of Burroughes and Watt's steel block vacuum cushion tables and all the surroundings are in keeping with it. There are two bath rooms, in one of which—they are both by the way, fitted with Shanks' apparatus—spray, plunge, douche and other forms of bath are obtainable. Complete sanitary arrangements are to be found on every floor, Winser & Co. being responsible for this section of the work.

Mr Warne has a very cosy and comfortable private office in the neighbourhood of the billiard room, and by the introduction of the 'Homacoustic' a new speaking tube apparatus which he first saw in operation at the Chicago Exhibition [of 1893] he can place himself in the most easy and rapid communication with either floor.

Mr Warne was for some years in Regency Square, Brighton, and he embarks upon his newer enterprise with the good wishes of a very numerous clientele both at home and abroad, among whom are numbered one of her Majesty's Judges, several Q C's, clergymen and others occupying high positions in society.

Mr Warne—who is to have the assistance of Mrs. Warne in the active management of the establishment—has shown himself not only abreast but even in advance of the times, for he has made every preparation for the introduction of the electric light the moment it is made available by the Corporation; and altogether he has shown himself so possessed of the true spirit of enterprise that we cannot refrain from the publication of the present tribute, coupled with the hope that the future will yield him a rich reward for his courageous anticipation of Worthing's wants.

In the following week's *Gazette* the formal application for a drinking-licence was published. This short notice is important as it suggests the middle name was Ilbery and informs us that the house was 1 York Terrace or Marine Parade and that it was owned by Montague Soames Pilcher.* Mr. Pilcher had lived there for some years and moved further along the terrace when George Warne turned number 1 into the first unit of what was to become *Warne's Hotel*.

The required licensing notice was published on 8 August 1899 and read:

I George Ilbery Warne of no 1 York Terrace, Marine Parade Worthing ... Private Hotel Keeper, hereby give notice that it is my intention to apply to the General Annual Licensing meeting in the Worthing Division ... for a license to hold any of the Excise licenses that may be held by a publican for sale retail at a house situate at and being no 1 York Terrace, Marine Parade, Worthing, aforesaid, known by the sign of Warne's Private Hotel (of which premises Mr Montague Soames Pilcher is the owner) of intoxicating liquor to be consumed on and off the premises.
Given under my hand this 4th day of August 1899.
George Ilbery Warnes

Study of local directories shows how Mr. Warne enlarged his hotel by gradually taking over the whole terrace, of what was originally separate homes. It would be out of place for me to record this gradual progress but such information on any similar building or group of buildings can easily be ascertained from local records or directories.

George Warne's commercial progress in the hotel trade was helped by other's ill-luck. His greatest potential rival establishment, the large *Royal Hotel*,

* Different contemporary accounts and references give different middle names or spellings for Ilbery. Many contemporary references give the name as Hilbery. I have in all cases complied with the spelling originally used, but in my account I shall not use the troublesome middle name.

173
A real-photograph card of the half-completed *Hotel Metropole*, 'Worthing's White Elephant', that remained in this state for years.

centrally positioned opposite the pier, suffered a major fire during the early morning of Friday 24 May 1901. The local press report stated:

> At no former period in the history of Worthing has so destructive a fire occurred as that which was witnessed in the early hour of Friday morning, when in a very short space of time the Royal Hotel, the largest Hotel in the borough, was reduced to a total ruin ...

Despite optimistic plans for a replacement 'Grand Hotel' to cost £100,000— a large fortune in the early 1900s—this was not proceeded with. Luck was also with our new hotelier, Mr. Warne, as the *Hotel Metropole* (commenced in 1898) was never completed, the owners having run out of funds.* The half-completed building known as Worthing's White Elephant is to be seen on many a local-view postcard (plate 173). It remained roofless for a long period and the southern end was only completed in the postwar period, over fifty years after the would-be magnificent hotel was started. Thus George Warne's enterprise in buying up York Terrace and turning single houses into one large hotel could continue without much opposition.

Early in the century houses and other premises along the sea-front called Marine Parade were renumbered. York and other separately named terraces were included in a continuous numbering scheme. Number 1 York Terrace became 11 Marine Parade. By 1901 George had expanded to take in number 12 and by at least 1910 he had taken over the whole of the sea-front terrace—the new *Warne's Hotel* comprised 11, 12, 13, 14 and 15 Marine Parade. Warne's family moved out and lived in a separate house, 'Biskra', just round the corner in Steyne Gardens. The name was the same as his previous residence in Brighton.

This full mid-1899 account of George Warne's costly efforts to turn a modest sea-front three- or four-storey terraced house into a superior private hotel can be amplified by a non-postcard photograph of one room in the early 1900s.

The 1899 report, however, does not mention an important interest of Mr. Warne's, one which was to have important consequences for the development of his growing hotel and for the town in general.

George Warne was an early motorist, reputedly the first car owner in the town. More importantly, he was the first British hotelier to have a hotel garage fully equipped for the convenience of travelling motorists. This innovation was to reap great rewards for Mr. Warne and Worthing.

* The partly built hotel was sold at auction in May 1904 for £10,300, having reputedly cost the developers around £60,000.

George Warne was elected to the Automobile Club of Great Britain and Ireland in March 1899 (which became The Royal Automobile Club [R.A.C.] in 1907). The hotel garage was officially appointed in May 1900. The ornamental frontage to the garage is shown on several special *Warne's Hotel* postcards (plate 174); this historic corner was destroyed in recent years.

The garage frontage made a typically extravagant claim—that it or the hotel was the headquarters of the pioneering A.C.G.B. & I. or Automobile Club of Great Britain & Ireland. It was certainly an extremely important garage with the highest rating. For years in the early 1900s *Warne's* was the only British hotel garage to have an 'A' classification, and it was the only local garage of any sort to be listed in the R.A.C. handbook.

WARNES HOTEL, WORTHING.   TELEPHONE NO. 365.

174
A *Warne's Hotel* commissioned publicity photograph showing the entrance to the garage—the first hotel garage in the country. It also (falsely) claimed to be the headquarters of the original Automobile Club of Great Britain and Ireland, later the R.A.C.

In the early days there were very few automobiles outside London and motorists had great difficulty in finding petrol or spares. The 'A' rating required that such a first-class garage was equipped to:

1. Undertake general repairs
2. Offer storage accommodation
3. Have plant for charging electric accumulators
4. Have an inspection pit
5. Ensure a stock of petroleum spirit is always available

The last requirement was the most important but it also presented the most difficulty as very stringent laws were introduced to regulate the safe storage of the motor spirit. George Warne took full-page advertisements in the R.A.C. Year Book showing his new south coast hotel with rows of cars parked outside, claiming to be 'Headquarters and Repairers to the following Clubs; R.A.C., M.U., R.C., A.A., Storage for Cars, 1/- per night'. Indoor storage for open cars was very necessary, and, as only reasonably rich folk could enjoy the luxury of a new-fangled automobile, a shilling a night added to the hotel bill was not a difficulty.

Local reports and letters from the public underlined the public spirit of George Warne in bringing motorists and good publicity to the town—'publicity not only in the motoring world but in every place where newspapers circulate'.

The motoring world knew both *Warne's Hotel* and the growing town of Worthing. The archives of the Royal Automobile Club in London include a most interesting set of photographs showing interior shots of *Warne's* as it appeared in 1902 (plate 175).

George Warne was perhaps the first to coin the description still used in the town's publicity—'Sunny Worthing'. This 1902 advertisement was headed:

SUNNY WORTHING
WHY GO ABROAD. RIVIERA OF ENGLAND
HOURS OF SUNSHINE 2,500.7 (1901)
WARNES HOTEL

The Automobile Club (later the Royal Automobile Club or R.A.C.) included *Warne's Hotel* as a staging point in all its major trials. These were important in the history of the development of the motor car, for proven reliability of various makes greatly affected car sales and encouraged the manufacturers to make better and more dependable machines. The runs also encouraged the setting-up of

175 *(above)*
A real-photograph view of the interior of Worthing's *Warne's Hotel*. A celebrated centre for early motorists.

176 *(right)*
A pair of commissioned real-photograph luncheon invitation cards showing a fine array of early automobiles lined up in front of *Warne's Hotel*, dated 1905. These represent east and west views of the hotel and the cars.

garages to sell petrol and carry out repairs. In 1903 the famous 1,000-miles trial contestants stayed at *Warne's*, so naturally picture postcards and commissioned cards of *Warne's* showed various automobiles (*see* plate 176).

The Edwardian magazine *The Motorist and Traveller* of 3 May 1905 carried a recommendation in its 'Hotel and Restaurant' feature:

> One of the most popular motorists' hotels in England is Warne's at Worthing. Mr. Warne, who is a member of the Automobile Club, has fitted up a most excellent garage, and, furthermore, has several cars which he hires out to his guests. His hotel is decorated with the trophies of many years of travel in far lands and thereby has an individuality which adds to its excellence in all points. It has a very good cook and its 'fond de cuisine' is of the best. I think I am right in saying that I have never been in any other hotel where the bed-linen is so fine—a very exceptional recommendation.

This 1903 report was illustrated with a photograph captioned 'Warne's Hotel, Worthing: Mr Sousa on one of Mr Warne's cars'. This picture occurs as a real-photograph postcard and the magazine illustration was probably taken from one of the postcards.

George Warne, now a town councillor, organised a Motor Carnival and Battle of Flowers to take place over the Easter weekend in April 1905. This was arranged under the auspices of the Sussex Automobile Club and Worthing's Excelsior Cycling & Athletic Club. Valuable prizes and trophies were awarded and magnificent pre-event advertising insured that the town, indeed the country, knew of this novel event in Worthing. The reports and results of the various competitions sold local papers at an all-time rate. A local inhabitant wrote to the *Worthing Gazette*, expressing typical delight:

Sirs,

I think Worthing residents, one and all, must heartily thank Mr Councillor Warne for his happy thought in providing such a great treat for our Easter holiday.

It has been the means of bringing hundreds of visitors into the town; therefore tradesmen, boarding-houses, etc., must materially benefit by it. And likewise it will be the means of advertising Worthing.

I admire his up-to-date ideas and thank him for his arduous work.

The Motor (or rather transport) Carnival was undoubtedly a resounding success but from a postcard point of view it was also important as I believe it marks the first 'event' recorded by a series of picture postcards. Several cards were quickly produced by the Mezzotint Company of Brighton (plates 177-8). Perhaps Mr. Warne invited this Brighton firm to send a photographer to record the occasion, or he commissioned a local photographer to record the scenes, whose prints were turned into monochrome non-glossy picture postcards by the Brighton specialists.

Further 1905 Easter Worthing Carnival postcards were produced by other photographers. A glorious shot of a very controversial entry is shown in plate 179. This does not bear a Mezzotint Company credit and it is printed on a different type of card blank. The semi-glossy photographic card, shown in plate 181, records a car at the presentation stand on the sea-front. This too is not credited, and is on a different type of card blank from the others in my collection.

These April 1905 Carnival-view cards were pioneer examples recording interest in local events. Other carnivals were held in the town and many decorated cars or other subjects are preserved on postcards. A small selection is in plates 182-5. The cards, though only on sale for a short period, proved very popular because so many local inhabitants sent them to their friends or added to their own albums. Local-event cards tend to interest only present-day collectors in that locality, but similar events were held in other towns. Brighton, of course, is well known for its early association with the development of the motor car. Many Brighton cards depict speed trials, as a 1905 Mezzotint Company card in plate 186, but my Worthing Carnival cards predate this by a few months. George Warne's Motor Carnival is still in being; there is the annual Rotary 'Grand Carnival' procession through the town on August Bank Holiday Monday. This is made up of gaily decorated cars, lorries, buses and still the townspeople turn out and line the streets, applauding the more fanciful and contributing to the charity boxes. Alas, although the event is well recorded in local papers, nobody produces event postcards as in the Edwardian era.

Over a long period from its Victorian birth to its death in the 1980s, the hotel has played a lively part in the town's activities, tens of thousands of folk have dined and danced in its ballroom or entered through the old garage. That pioneer hotel garage and the whole hotel site is now an open car park. How times change! The good old days are still available to us as picture postcards; for a small selection see plates 187-9.

It is now time to mention sporting activities available to townsfolk and the way that sport can attract visitors or new inhabitants to reside in your town.

Real-photograph postcards of any town include a selection of various sports. Most comprise posed group-photograph postcards of local teams (plates 190-1), but action shots also occur. Group-photograph postcards were mainly purchased by the people depicted, and enjoyed a small, restricted sale, especially when the

177 *(top left)*
One of a set of Mezzotint Company (of Brighton) local-event cards showing decorated cars entered for our 1905 Easter Carnival.

178 *(top right)*
A further 1905 Worthing Motor Carnival card, showing vehicles lined up for inspection. Postally-used in May 1905.

179 *(middle left)*
Another 1905 Motor Carnival card. This entry caused great fuss when it was reportedly disqualified. Another card with a story.

180 *(bottom right)*
Crowds gathered on the front outside *Warne's* to see the dressed motors—a novel and popular event. Nicely captioned by the sender: 'Easter Monday Attraction' and dated 26 April 1905—two days later.

181 *(bottom left)*
This real-photograph card shows an award being presented to one of the dressed cars on the front opposite *Warne's Hotel*. Postally-used on 27 April 1905, three days after the event.

MOTOR CARNIVAL. WORTHING.

MOTOR CARNIVAL WORTHING.

OTOR CARNIVAL
WORTHING.

Easter Monday Attraction

182 *(top left)*
Dressed bicycles ready for inspection before the September 1908 Worthing Carnival. Postally-used with related message three days later.

183 *(top right)*
Another study of a 1908 Worthing Carnival entry with Willow Pattern wheels.

184 *(middle left)*
An attractive local event-card relating to the Children's Fête at the September 1908 Worthing Motor Carnival. Alderman Tree is on duty on the left. A good social history card.

185 *(bottom right)*
A superb 1908 Worthing Children's Fête card, showing the 'Dolls Parade'.

186 *(bottom left)*
One of a series of the Mezzotint Company's motor trials. These postdate the Worthing Motor Carnival cards, but these vehicles are not 'dressed'. Dated July 1905.

187
Two similar commissioned *Warne's Hotel* publicity cards. The left-hand (coloured) example is by A. Matthews & Co. and was postally-used in October 1911. The right-hand monochrome example is by Walter Gardiner of Worthing.

188
A rare real-photograph card showing the *Warne's Hotel* orchestra in the dining room, later used for balls. The palms were famous as 'the finest specimens of their kind in Great Britain'. Impressed imprint 'Bristow, Worthing', dated 15 May 1911.

189
Two of a set of *Warne's Hotel* commissioned publicity postcards showing interior views of about 1920. Alas, it is no more.

photograph is dated. A cricket team of 1905 would have little interest in, say, 1910, for the majority of the players might have been replaced by younger lads. Now these shots have a social history angle, if only because of changing modes of dress.

The sport particularly connected to Worthing is the ancient game of bowls, the flat-green version, rather than the crown-green version favoured in the Midlands. Worthing made a belated, tentative introduction to bowls but subsequently made up for the initial lack of enthusiasm. In modern times, it has hosted three World Bowls events and is widely considered to be the 'Bowls Capital' of England. The English Bowls Association has its headquarters in the town, adjacent to the famous Beach House Park.

The earliest Worthing postcard to depict the game is reproduced in plate 192. This interesting scene is available locally in an enlarged, framed and glazed version. I will explain shortly why this postcard is so interesting. Outline research into the history of bowls was sparked by my purchase of the postcard.

The first reference I have found to bowls in Worthing is an appeal by Mr. E. Lake of East Chichester. On 18 August 1897, his letter was published in the *Worthing Gazette*:

1st CRICKET ELEVEN.
STEYNE HIGH SCHOOL, WORTHING.

A BOWLING CLUB FOR WORTHING

Dear Sir,

As a frequent visitor to the beautiful town of Worthing, I have often felt surprised that with the lovely greens you have, a Bowling Club has not been started.

I can assure you such a Club is a great attraction to a town which so many visitors frequent. It is a game which can be indulged in by gentlemen who are past playing lawn tennis, cricket etc., and I am quite sure such a club would be a means of prolonging the stay and be an attraction to visitors.

I am writing as Captain of the Bowling Club of the Priory Park in the city [Chichester], the members of which number over ninety. The pleasure which is derived and gentle exercise which is inducive to health need no comment of mine.

I am, yours truly,

E. Lake.

The writer referred to the existing 'lovely greens you have' by which he meant that the town had good parks and open spaces where bowls could be played, if there was a bowls club or the sport was organised. There is a possibility that bowls was being played at a private club by 1899.

The commencement of municipal bowls in Worthing is well documented in the official minutes of the 'General Purpose Committee' of the Town Council. Most matters relating to the running of any town are outlined in such records, which should be available in your town or county library, on request. The following records were stored in the reserve stock of the West Sussex County Library at Worthing, and were produced for me in a matter of moments. Other sets of bound minutes exist in the Town Hall.

190 *(left)*
An Edwards & Son real photograph of a local football team. Such commissioned cards would be retaken each season but had a small restricted sale. Postally-used September 1914.

191 *(bottom left)*
An interesting local commissioned picture postcard of the Steyne High School first eleven ladies' cricket team—they look business-like, and no doubt knocked a few men for six in their day!

192 *(right)*
An uncredited real-photograph local-view card of the early municipal bowling green in Homefield Park, looking south. The start of great things, as Worthing later hosted the world championships. An interesting but much reproduced postcard.

44. Bowling Green, Homefield Park, Worthing.

I had already discovered from the files of the *Worthing Gazette* reports of the proposed new municipal bowling green under the heading 'BOWLING GREEN IN HOMEFIELD PARK'. These records covered the period of development; how did the idea come to fruition? A group of bowlers wrote to the Corporation which was reported to the General Purposes Committee, under the chairmanship of the mayor-elect, Councillor James White, on 26 January 1904:

> Read memorial signed by Mr W. H. George, Downview Road and ten other residents, suggesting the desirability of arranging for a small portion of the Park to be prepared and set apart for the playing of Bowls in the same way as Tennis and Cricket are now provided for, as a means of affording further attraction to the town.
> Resolved, that the memorial be referred to the Park-keeper, with instructions to report whether it is possible to make such arrangements as will meet the views of the memorialists on the subject.

Progress was relatively rapid for a fortnight later the minutes record:

> Resolved that a report from the Park Keeper on the subject of making provision for the playing of Bowls in a portion of the Park be referred to the Borough Surveyor, with a request to report as to the cost of carrying out the suggestions made therein.

At the meeting on 23 February 1904, the committee all but provided the bowlers with their new green or greens in Homefield Park:

> The Borough Surveyor reported with respect to the provision of ground in the Park for the playing of Bowls, that the piece of ground at the south-east corner which is recommended for the purpose, has a fall from south to north of five feet and that he estimates the cost of carrying out the necessary work of levelling and re-turfing, and including the erection of a wire fence where necessary, at £85.
> Resolved—That the Council be recommended to comply with the memorial recently presented to them, and to direct that part of the Park referred to be appropriated as a Bowling Green and to direct that the works referred to in the Surveyor's report be carried out next Autumn, it being in the

opinion of the Head Gardener inadvisable to execute the work at the present time, and that in the meantime such part of the piece of ground as may be necessary for the purpose of one green be appropriated and set apart for use in the coming season in its present condition.

This was only agreed in committee whose recommendation had to go before the full Council for approval. The matter seems to have been given full approval. The *Worthing Gazette*'s report is more helpful than the committee's printed minutes, for it comments briefly on the chairman's introduction to the subject:

Councillor White, in introducing the subject yesterday, explained that the outlay in preparing two greens would not be money thrown away, as there would be revenue from them, a charge being made for their use. [The initial charges for the 1905 season were three-pence an hour per player, a weekly season ticket was half a crown (12½ pence) or ten and sixpence (52½ pence) for the summer season ticket.]

They would no doubt, be an attraction to the town, and provide pleasure for many residents and visitors.

The worthy Councillor James White was certainly correct when he stated that the greens would 'be an attraction to the town and provide pleasure for many residents and visitors'.

Bowling greens, however, do not grow overnight. The new municipal facilities were not available until 1905. In the interim there was a progress report in the local paper, the *Worthing Gazette*, of 5 October 1904:

BOWLS

The New Green in the Park

I notice that the bowling green to be added to the attractions of Homefield Park is being prepared with all dispatch, and will have been levelled down, re-turfed and fenced in a few week's time, so that it will probably be in good condition at the commencement of next season.

The casual observer of the piece of ground that is being utilised, the plot to the right of the main entrance in Park Road, would hardly deem it credible that there was a decline from the Park Road end to the other extremity of over five feet.

This is the case, however, and with other minor declinities the necessity of levelling the ground will be seen. This is being accomplished by raising one end by two feet two inches and delving out the other to a depth of two feet, eight inches.

When completed, the actual playing green will be a square of forty-seven and a half yards, and will accommodate seven links; whilst in addition four single links will be provided for practice. There will be a small trench some five inches deep all round the ground, to serve the dual aim of draining the ground and catching the bowls ... Seats will be placed round the green for the convenience of spectators.

The first Worthing bowling green in municipally-owned Homefield Park or 'Peoples' Park' (*see* plate 193) was 47½ yards square, whereas the modern green must be not more than 44 yards. There were seven rinks instead of the usual six. Four additional single practice rinks were a helpful feature. The rinks were referred to as 'links' in early Worthing reports: was this an error by local reporters or was it the standard term then in use?

The provision of two bowling greens at the south-east corner of the park came in for some adverse comment, mainly because it was in an area formerly reserved for a children's playground.

193
A rather dismal view of Worthing's first municipal bowling green looking north. This card was used by the first secretary when writing to other clubs to arrange fixtures. Postally-used in March 1909.

Worthing Bowling Club was formed on 17 April 1907. The *Worthing Gazette* contained a full account of the meeting:

Bowls

Formation of a local Club

A Bowling Club for the borough is now an accomplished fact. The formal resolution determining to establish such a welcome addition to local organisations was arrived at at a meeting held at the Nelson Hotel on Wednesday evening [17 April]. It was formally proposed by Councillor Gray seconded by Mr Arthur and assented to by the Worthing Bowling Club. Annual subscription to be 10/6d.

The chairman (H. Barnwell) dwelt upon the desirability of forming a club devoted to the pastime of bowls, suggesting that, if other towns could support such an institution, it was surely possible here. They ought, in his opinion, to be able to form a really good club. In addition to residents, he thought there were visitors who would like to join as temporary members ...

The rules of the new club were agreed at a further meeting held on 30 April 1907. The first officers were chosen: the president was the Mayor, Alderman F.C. Linfield, J.P., with Councillor E.W. Morecroft as Vice-President. Mr. G.V. Bell was the first Captain, with Messrs. H. Barnwell (Vice-President); H.W. Sandell; W.H. Ellsworth (landlord of *The Nelson*); E.H. King and M. Lowther on the committee. Councillor Gray acted as secretary and to him was accredited the formation of the club.

The first match played by the Worthing club was a home game against Littlehampton on 29 May 1907. Worthing won. Although the *Worthing Gazette* report of the formation of the new Worthing Club in April 1907 suggested that this was the first bowling club in the town, this was not necessarily the case. The same local newspaper in July 1906 reported a game between Homefield Park Club and West Worthing Bowling Club. The Homefield Park Club and the recently formed Worthing Bowling Club were officially playing each other by at least September 1907, so they were different clubs with a different membership, as they are today in the 1990s. Even simple local research can be extremely complicated!

The Worthing bowling green in Homefield Park soon attracted favourable comment. This is the report of a match between the Worthing Bowling Club and the Haywards Heath Club in July 1907:

The members of the local Bowling Club received a visit from the representatives of the Haywards Heath Club on Wednesday and the match which was played on the Bowling Green in Homefield Park, ended in favour of the home players ...

During the afternoon the local club entertained their visitors to tea and the latter expressed themselves in eulogistic terms on the pretty situation and the excellent condition of the green ...

Councillor Thomas Gray, secretary of the Worthing Club, sent picture postcards of the local Homefield Park bowling green when writing to other clubs about club matches and fixtures. One of these rare, possibly privately commissioned cards is plate 193. This was posted in March 1909 about a match against the

Windlesham Club at nearby Hove on Friday afternoon, 6 July 1909. The communication cost a halfpenny, plus the small cost of the postcard.

At a match arranged between the municipal club and the Council on Saturday 4 September 1909, it rained all afternoon! It so happened, however, that the mayor had arranged to provide tea for the teams. As the club did not then have a club-room, the outdoor tea had to be abandoned, and the players returned home wet and thirsty. The *Worthing Gazette* reporter commented on this:

> Members of the Club took advantage of the opportunity to impress upon the Mayor and his colleagues the desirability of erecting a small Pavilion at the side of the bowling green. It would certainly prove a great convenience to the Club which now has a membership a little in excess of forty and something may possibly be heard of the suggestion before another season arrives.

Before the month was out the secretary of the Worthing Bowling Club had written to the Council concerning the much-needed pavilion. His letter was reported upon at the General Purposes Committee on 28 September 1909, but was not discussed until the January 1910 meeting:

> The Secretary on behalf of the Committee of the club points out in his letter that it is the invariable custom for a pavilion to be provided on a Bowling Green, for the entertainment of visiting teams and for the storage of bowls, etc. that the income received by the Corporation for the use of the green justifies some expenditure in necessary improvements, of which, in their opinion, the erection of a pavilion is the most pressing.
>
> The club committee suggest—
>
> 1). That the Council should provide such a pavilion which could be obtained for £32.
>
> 2). That, if the initial outlay is a difficulty the club would be willing to find the money, the Council repaying the amount by instalments out of the fees obtained for the use of the ground, or
>
> 3). That the club be allowed to erect a suitable building an undertaking being given to remove it if and when called upon so to do ...

The committee, as might be expected, opted not to expend £32 on the pavilion but to charge the club an annual ground-rent for the privilege of providing their own building—to Council-approved plans and on a designated site:

> Resolved that the Council be recommended to sanction the erection by the Bowling Club Committee for the use of the members of the club and at their cost, of a suitable pavilion of approved design, and on a site to be approved by the Council, in consideration of the payment by the Club to the Council of the sum of £3- 3- 0 per annum by way of ground rent, and subject to the Club giving an undertaking to remove the same on three months previous notice being given by the Council requiring them to do so.

The annual ground rent was reduced to one guinea, but the plans were not approved by the Council until March 1910; towards the end of May the committee was still discussing the wording of the draft agreement between the club and the town. As a *Worthing Gazette* report rightly stated, the proposed pavilion 'will meet a long felt want, and one which for the reputation of the town ought to have been supplied before'.

This attractive pavilion is depicted in plate 192. The inclusion of the new pavilion in the photograph helps to date the card to 1910 or slightly later. To me as a present-day bowler, club member and umpire, it seems remarkable that as late

194
The original café and club-house in Worthing's now internationally renowned Beach House Park. What a fine array of bowlers and what a foundation they laid. Dated *c.*1925.

195
A real-photograph picture postcard of the newly laid out Beach House Park looking south. The play area was then equally divided between tennis and bowls. Now it is entirely given over to bowls and is the 'mecca' of English, if not world, bowls. Postally-used in August 1927.

196
Two glossy real-photograph picture postcards of bowling greens at Worthing. Standard post-1930 cards which are of little interest or value unless you are researching the history of bowls in Worthing or the development of the park.

WORTHING. — Broadwater Village.
Children going home from School. — LL.

197
A charming French-produced Lévy card showing children wandering home from school at Broadwater (Worthing) across what is now a busy main road, *c.*1908.

198
A rare real-photograph fun postcard of children fishing in a roadside pond at Goring (Worthing) with the church in the background. Once again there is a main road here today. Dated *c.*1908.

as 1910 Worthing Club members should be playing in suits, with hats, and in most cases wearing street (heeled) shoes.

Other remarkable aspects of this bowling scene are the complete lack of a ditch and raised bank around the green, for many years an essential requirement laid down in the 'laws' of the game. The green appears to have been marked out on a flat area with white lines (as for tennis) with white-painted timber laid over the lines to contain any wayward bowls.

I cannot in this book describe the later development of bowls in Worthing, how the town became a mecca of the sport or of how the new Beach House Park (plates 195-6) was developed and improved by the town, until in the post-war period it has played host to the world on three occasions. My research was prompted by my real-photograph postcard, which cost a mere 50 pence.

This résumé of the birth of bowls must of necessity stop at the end of the Edwardian era; but hundreds of later cards (e.g. plates 194-6) show the various

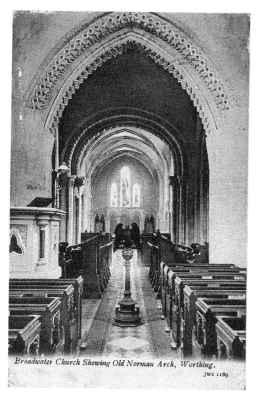

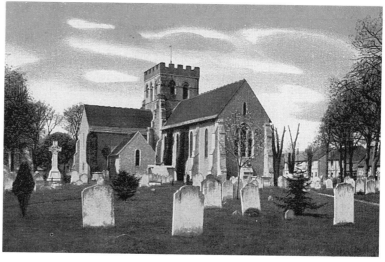

199 *(left and above)*
Two standard mass-produced picture postcards of the ancient Broadwater church. Even this has changed or is changing, so these *c.*1910 views are of interest.

200 *(below and right)*
Two standard well-produced but monochrome views of local churches. Both cards (by J. Davis and Wrench) were printed in Germany. Not the most popular subject today, especially outside their locality. Postally-used in 1906.

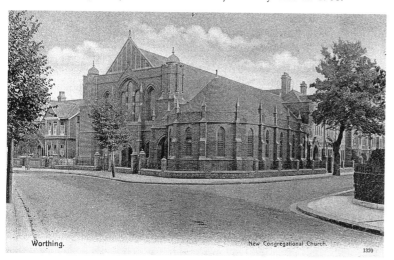

pavilions in Worthing's Beach House Park and how these attractive public gardens have gradually been taken over by bowling greens at the expense of pre-war tennis courts (plate 195). Like so many facets of the town, the history of this park and of the game of bowls can be well illustrated with local picture postcards.

It should be easy and interesting to recreate in picture form the small villages which today have been incorporated in characterless large towns. Here in Worthing we had seven or eight such communities, with their churches, schools, post-offices and other facilities. Each had character and characters, both of which may be illustrated in picture postcards. A French Lévy postcard of schoolchildren at

Broadwater is at plate 197. Another example, a real-photograph card, is also a charmer, but few local inhabitants may today identify its location, within the Worthing boundary, unless they recognise Goring church in the background (plate 198).

Churches may be considered the most static and constant of buildings. My local Norman (or earlier) church may not have changed much in its outward appearance (plate 199) although there are ambitious plans for a new entrance and extensions.

Postcards of this or any other local church (plate 200) can be purchased for the approximate equivalent of a pint of beer, ten cigarettes or a short bus journey—all passing delights. With little difficulty a collection of cards showing exterior and interior views of 'your' churches can be formed. You would be welcomed with open arms by most dealers, for church views are not in general demand today.

Why stop at the purchase of these cards? You could visit each church, research its history, list the vicars, look around the gravestones—what interesting or amusing inscriptions you can spot. You may have passed these churches hundreds of times—why always pass?

You may collect postcards relating to so many aspects of your town and its surrounding district or countryside. Town halls, theatres, streets, shops, parks, transport, schools—the list is almost endless. Edwardian and later—even modern—postcards will supply the impetus, and your local library or museum should be able to supply the raw material for your personal research. You will be surprised at how engrossed you can become in the search for background information. Having researched some special aspect of your town, do send a copy to the library or museum so that all can benefit from your work.

You need not stop there. You could prepare a short talk on your chosen subject. The cards can easily be turned into slides, by you, or a friend or by a professional photographer. Once you have given one or two well-received talks the word will probably spread and you will be invited to give others. You will also find that you will pick up new information from members of the audience.

You could also write a short article for a local paper or magazine. Again, cards or photocopies of them (see page 185) will provide helpful illustrations. In time you may find yourself writing a book on the subject—which is, after all, what I am doing now. However, you can spend years in researching and writing a book at considerable expense, but there is no guarantee that a professional publisher will share your enthusiasm. From his point of view it must be commercially viable. Present-day costs of book production are very great and the risks high. The exercise nonetheless will be rewarding in non-monetary terms. My father had a saying—if you want to learn a subject, write a book about it!

Chapter IX

Collecting, Buying and Selling

An unlikely picture postcard subject but the old removal vehicles are of interest to collectors or social history students. A rare and interesting card, valued at £20 or more.

There are very many ways of collecting postcards, as many ways as there are collectors, for a collection should be personal to you. It is unique. There are, however, some basic divisions. Some folk collect cards purely as an investment. I would not recommend this, or indeed the collecting of any type of object purely as an investment. There are better and perhaps more rewarding reasons to form a collection.

The best of reasons is because you like such objects, you find them interesting, even stimulating. You enjoy the search, the chase, the new 'treasures', which need not be costly! You also enjoy learning more about your pieces, meeting fellow collectors and in general researching the subject and adding to our general fund of knowledge. These are some of the ideals that collecting is all about.

Some folk collect postcards but not because they are postcards! For example, our local museum has just purchased a large collection of local-view postcards. They have been purchased only because they represent the best photographic record of the town, not because they were somebody's collection of postcards. The very many cards in our reference library collection and in the County Record Office are similar. These cards record our locality and as such they are valuable or interesting photographic documents.

Many of my local cards, too, were purchased because of my interest in the changing face of the town. I have, however, expanded my interest to take in cards which record the social history of the town and its inhabitants; the sports and pastimes; the types of entertainments enjoyed; the modes of transport available; the local industries; the hotels and shops. All this and so much more is available to study in picture postcards. Not any old postcard, but carefully selected examples, for any collector must be selective. If you are not, you have merely an impersonal accumulation!

Most collectors today tend to specialise. One really has to define one's interest because there are so many categories of cards available that no one person could hope to collect the entire range. It would be too costly, impossible to house or display and quite daunting in quantity. Stand by any table at a postcard fair, and you will hear that each person will ask for a different subject. Any Worthing? Any Brighton? Any windmills? Any actresses? Any stations? Any piers? Any ferries? Any airships? Any trams? Any cats? Any Lucie Attwells? and so on. We are subject collectors, forming a worthwhile interesting collection. Most of the above-mentioned groups comprise what are loosely called subject cards. Many subjects will run to a far larger collection than would one restricted to one village or small town. Dealers tend to love subject collectors.

Those looking for cards of 'my town' outnumber all others, because topographical cards are the most interesting and collectable and because there are so many different towns and villages and facets for study in the history of any location. This book shows some of the ways that you can collect and research postcards relating to my own home town of Worthing. This seaside resort is not remarkable but the enjoyment you can reap from its postcards is certainly remarkable. This type of collecting can be repeated for each and every location.

Postcards may well form only the vital backbone to the research. The flesh will be added and expanded in the form of further study. Perhaps a small library of related reference books, or maybe your own files, or press or magazine cuttings. Take, for example, a collector of windmill postcards. The cards themselves will show the picture of a long-lost windmill, but such a collector will want to research each specimen. He will probably already know which of the many types of mill was shown. He will now delve into its history, discover the working period, when it was altered, burnt down, rebuilt and finally abandoned or destroyed, the site perhaps having a more financially rewarding use.

Many collectors study in depth the products of one postcard publisher—Raphael Tuck, being a classic case and deservedly so. It will be less costly, however, to research the products of a smaller firm or even the work of one local photographer—as I have done on a modest scale with my elusive E. Edwards & Son (*see* Chapter VII).

You can, of course, collect the cards of any one period—the Edwardian period (1901-10) is very rewarding as it coincides with the Golden Age of the picture postcard. You can collect and research war cards—the Boer War, the First or Second World Wars. You can collect royal subjects, political cards—the suffragette movement, perhaps. All these are obvious choices among British cards. If you want a quick cross-section of postcard subjects, treat yourself to a catalogue or price guide. You will be surprised at the range available.

I must, however, also mention modern postcards, for they are still being produced and used in vast quantities. As I walk along our main shopping streets I am greeted by racks of modern local-view and other glossy, pretty-pretty or comic cards—as my grandfather would have been in 1910 or my father in 1930. The tradition continues. You should include some of these in your collection, for up-to-date cards remind us that all our cards were once modern. Do remember to add a little pencilled note, recording where you purchased the card, the date and the price. These facts and any other relevant information you can record will be of great interest to following generations.

Apart from the thousands of standard type, traditional cards still on sale, there are many other modern cards being issued in relatively small issues by specialist publishers or individuals. These moderns comprise a vast subject outside the scope of this book but useful details of new issues are regularly given in *Picture PostCard Monthly* and the leading publishers or dealers in such examples advertise in the same magazine. Such modern cards are modestly priced and most of interest, although to me they do not have the charm of Edwardian cards. It is all a matter of taste, or varying interest. The postcard field in limitless.

Once you have made your choice, you will give some thought as to how you can store or display your cards to advantage. Methods range from the staple shoebox to quite costly special albums. You certainly need to take care of the cards, handling them as little as possible, protecting them from light and heat, keeping them free of acid-inducing material. Remember all standard cards are paper or thin cardboard, most are colour-printed (colours fade or change) or are photographic and liable to fade. They were, after all, produced to have a short life and to be thrown out after their journey had been completed. Today most collectable cards are well over fifty years old, while early Edwardian cards are some ninety years old. Treat them with great respect.

Some folk spend good money having their cards mounted and framed to hang on the wall, as has happened in the case of the fine Worthing cards shown in plate 201. I would not recommend this for the light, especially sunlight, could well fade the images over a period of years and almost certainly the edges of the card mount will leave a high-tide mark on the card. Further, most postcard images are too small to make much impact in a room.

I have, however, had some of my special local-view cards professionally enlarged and had the enlargement mounted and framed. In the enlargement one may lose a degree of sharpness, but unless you are closely studying the print, it is of no great consequence; it is the overall effect or atmosphere one is trying to capture. *Picture PostCard Monthly* from time to time carries advertisements of specialist postcard enlargers. These may be less expensive than a local photographer. Some modern photocopiers reproduce (and slightly enlarge) postcards most successfully on glossy paper. They will also reproduce in colour. If you wish to

201
Three local-view postcards depicting Worthing pier after the 1913 gale and as it was previously in its glory. They are mounted behind glass for display.

hang picture postcards on your walls as a picture, it might as well be a good photocopy, which can be replaced when it fades. You must keep the original card in a safe dry place, out of sunlight. This advice mainly relates to rare costly cards; it is not worth the trouble with a common 50-pence specimen.

It may seem appropriate to display your collection in an old period album of which very many remain. I do not favour this, if your collection is going to be a living one, and you are going to add to the selection and to rearrange the pages. The old pages will be very fragile by now, the paper may well be stained and grubby, many of the cut corner fixings will be torn, so that your cards fall out. Even if you can find such an album in pristine condition I think you will find the old method of slipping the card into four corner slots is apt to damage the corners, which will affect both the look of the card and its saleability. In time, too, the corner-cuts leave slight depressions on the card, especially if the album has been stored flat with other objects on top, compressing the pages. All albums should be stood upright and not packed closely one to another. Let air circulate.

There are many schools of thought about the different types of postcard album. Personally I favour and use 'Hagner system' albums and loose pages. These albums and their matt-black pages are marketed in England by Hagner International (U.K.) Ltd. of Itchenor in West Sussex and should be available through stamp dealers, for these albums were introduced to house valuable stamps. The philatelist is much more particular about preserving his treasures than the postcard collector. The Hagner company claims that theirs is the only stamp album which guarantees total protection and long-term conservation of stamp collections. The polyester film of the divisions is claimed to be one hundred per cent inactive, with no additives which could cause damage to stamps. Even the glue is stated to be chemically inert. If all this is good enough for rare stamps, it should be safe for our postcards.

The loose pages are available in various styles, mainly to suit stamp collectors, but cards fit well into the pages with two strips. These are available as double-sided pages, so that four cards can be displayed on an open, double page. The advantage of these pages is that the postcard, protected by a transparent flap, can very easily be slipped in or out and the positions changed with no trouble or risk of damage. The only difficulty is that the albums and the leaves are rather expensive, especially if your collection is a large one. Nevertheless it is better to preserve your valuable postcards in a reliable way and to display them in an attractive manner. Whatever you do, do **not** stick the cards down with glue or paste.

I have previously stated that cards should be handled as little as possible, and then by holding them by the edges. Do not put hot and sticky fingers over the face of the card. This is particularly important with glossy-surfaced real-photograph cards. Most dealers protect their cards in little clear plastic envelopes, so that they can be handled by would-be buyers without risk of damage—a wise precaution. Alas most dealers, on selling the card, retain the cover for reuse. You can, however, purchase your own stock of protective envelopes. These certainly should be used if the cards are likely to be handled to any great degree.

A further word of warning. If you write on your cards, perhaps the price (as do the dealers), use a soft pencil on the address side and write very lightly. It might be better to write on a 'Post-It' note and affix this to the card. This type of page has a slightly sticky edge, which enables it to be peeled off at will without any damage to the surface of the paper. Do **not**, however, use the type of sticky label which may have to be soaked off, damaging the card. If in doubt use a soft pencil, but certainly not ink. All this assumes that you wish to preserve the commercial value of the card.

This leads to the difficult subject of values, and of buying and selling postcards. I have quoted the asking price of some cards illustrated in this book. You may well have found it difficult to understand the very reasonable prices. You are not alone. I cannot understand either, neither can most dealers! Any one card is worth different amounts to different people. I have given over £500 for a single card, obviously a very special one to me. Yet that same card would not be worth a pound to a collector of windmill cards, of cats or any other specialist category. Conversely, I am not interested in windmills and would probably let a very rare example escape for a pound or so.

The difficulty of valuing postcards can be evidenced by the different views held about used or non-postally-used cards. Valid points can certainly be made for each class.

Most non-collectors might imagine that an unused mint card must be more desirable or valuable than one that has a message added, and which has been sent through the post. Yet in many cases the postally-used card will be rarer than the mint specimen, if only because very many specimens that are still available were purchased solely to be added to a collector's album. They have the advantage of being in a near-mint condition but they lack other possible attributes.

A postally-used card should bear a stamp and a postmark. The latter, if clear, will at least show the date of posting and therefore the earliest possible date for the publication of that card. The low denomination postage stamp is unlikely to be of value, but the postmark or cancellation might be of interest to a specialist. Christmas Eve cancellations on Christmas cards are of interest, as are first-day issue cancellations on early Official cards or on the issue of new stamp designs.

There is also the possibility that the written message is of interest, especially if it relates to the card. I have purchased many a card more for the added message than for the subject on the view side. Some messages are merely humorous, at least to us now, or relate to the postcard collecting hobby. Several such messages I have quoted at the head and foot of the various chapters. Other observations that add to the interest and value of a card from a social history or local research viewpoint, have been quoted in the text.

Unfortunately many postally-used cards that have not been carefully preserved in an album have become dirty or tatty over the years. Obviously this materially affects the value and in such cases a clean and unused card will be much more desirable.

202
A rare trade privately commissioned real-photograph postcard showing Mr. W. Wade's central motor garage and bicycle shop in Worthing. Printed by The Metaline Company of Tottenham and posted to Mrs. Wade in May 1907.

Catalogues in general are unhelpful in giving guidance on the possible different values for used or non-used cards, except for some early cards. As an extreme case I can cite the value of £400 quoted in the *IPM Catalogue of Picture Postcards and Year Book 1996* for a postally-used first-day of issue (1 October 1870) British Official postcard. An unused specimen of the same basic card is priced at a very modest £5! The reason for this and to a lesser extent some early special issues is that most examples were purchased as mementoes of the occasion or as a possible investment. It was then thought that they were too interesting to be used as message bearers. There is also the point that, being issued before the collecting craze took hold in the early 1900s, few postally-used examples were preserved. Most postally-used picture cards prior to 1897 are especially desirable and more highly valued than mint examples. For post-1900 cards there is not much difference in the value between postally-used and mint cards but if the condition is the same, I would rather add a postally-used example to my collection.

Catalogues or price guides are published to give guidance. Many of us were weaned on John Smith's annual IPM (International Postcard Market) Catalogue and Year Books. This catalogue has changed and been improved over the years. It is published by IPM Publications of Lewes, East Sussex, and contains contributions from specialist researchers.

All catalogues and price guides should, however, be treated with caution. An introduction or foreword should warn you that the prices are averages and that they apply only to cards in a clean and perfect state. The catalogues can be helpful and list the different categories, and the main dealers, postcard clubs and magazines. They also contain many advertisements from suppliers, dealers, auctioneers and so on. They almost certainly indicate which artists are commercially desirable and give some indication of the average price of such work. John Smith, however, makes the overriding statement, 'There is no price control on postcards. The value of any card is in the eye of the beholder'. Remember also the vital difference between a buying and selling price.

I have a shelf full of catalogues but I seldom consult them. My collection is all the better for this. Let me explain. If, for example, a catalogue suggests that the price range £5-10 is correct for your particular subject, you might well throw up your hands in horror and leave a specimen priced at £20 or even at £15. This card might well be a rare or particularly fine and interesting postcard. You could

203
A rare hotel publicity
announcement card giving
interesting details of a now long
defunct establishment.

BLACKMAN'S MANSION HOTEL.

PRELIMINARY NOTICE OF REMOVAL.

BLACKMAN'S TEMPERANCE HOTEL,
CHAPEL ROAD, (Opposite G.P.O.)
WORTHING.

About the end of September, 1906, this Business
will be transferred to **No. 9 & 10 Liverpool
Terrace, Worthing,** and will be known as
Blackman's Mansion Hotel.

This Hotel will contain spacious **Commercial,
Coffee, Writing, Stock, Billiard, Bath,**
and **Sitting Rooms** (Private and General), and
about **25 Bedrooms.** One and half minutes from
G.P.O. and Town Hall.

I shall esteem it a favour if you will make this
known.

J. BLACKMAN, *Proprietor.*

have missed the 'find' of a lifetime, all because you paid too much attention to the catalogue. Recently, at a little auction at the Sussex Postcard Club, a Brighton real-photograph street scene was sold for £105. Ridiculous you may think, but there was an underbidder and I believe the buyer was quite pleased with his purchase. For personal satisfaction and to complete a collection, this card was better value than 20 or 30 ordinary cards which might have totalled more than the price of this one special card.

This £100 plus local-view card and my £500 Art Nouveau specimen received local and national publicity. Such reports of ultra-high prices for any collectable item can be misleading. The public tend to think that any and every old postcard is valuable. This is far from the case. Some are completely valueless or unsaleable. You would be in for a shock if you individually valued the cards in an old family album from a catalogue. You will arrive at a totally unrealistic value (as would also be the case with a stamp collection). The catalogue values are for single examples assuming that there is a willing buyer waiting to purchase. A mixed album will almost certainly contain cards of many types and categories. To sell these cards at or near the catalogue price you would need perhaps 10 semi-specialists. Fifty per cent or more of the cards would probably be of common types that are virtually unsaleable.

The bulk of any non-specialist accumulation will comprise pretty-pretty views or other attractive cards which sold in their millions precisely because they were pretty. A serious present-day collector will only pay several pounds for an unusual card. He or she will look for the out of the ordinary—the rare card of which only one or two specimens may be known: the local-event card or the privately sponsored real-photograph specimen, not a popular beach or High Street scene.

Thus, the sponsored photograph card showing an early view of Mr. W. Wade's General Motor Garage (plate 202) is far more important from a local historian's point of view than a town hall card. This stockist of Humber cycles became the leading retailer of quality British cars in the town, with a massive garage and car park in the centre of the town. The main area remains an open car park whilst the enlarged showroom premises house other retailers. This seemingly dull, rather tatty card recently cost me nearly £40 at auction. I was happy to give this sum, which was obviously lower than my postal bid, because I knew of its importance in recording the early commercial premises of a pioneer Worthing motorist and garage proprietor. No catalogue could guide me in fixing the so-called 'proper price' for this card.

Likewise, most collectors would pass by the dullish advertising card shown in plate 203. It announces the intended removal of Blackman's Temperance Hotel from a main shopping street to a wonderful residential terrace in 1906. Few residents would guess that this terrace once housed a hotel with some 25 bedrooms, a coffee room, writing room, the commercial traveller meeting room, their stock room, a billiard room and seemingly a single bathroom. Such temperance or commercial hotels are now part of social history. This superb Regency-style terrace is happily still preserved and is one of our more beautiful aspects. It is in such good, respectable condition, probably because in recent years the houses have been taken over by professional firms seeking prestige offices in a central position. But what an outcry the private residents must have made in 1906 when they discovered that a hotel would take over two of the houses!

It may be thought that only postcards showing main buildings or important aspects of the town are desirable. In fact the opposite is true. Many seemingly dull scenes can be of great interest to the enquiring local researcher. The rural-looking view shown in plate 204 illustrates this point. It is a nondescript card that might be purchased for a pound or less. Fine large unseen private houses stood behind these walls and trees.

In fact Union Place is in the centre of modern Worthing. Only a small section of the local flint wall now remains, the trees are mostly removed, and it is a wide open road. On the south side it comprises two car parks, the central police station, and the Connaught Theatre. On the north side, one of the old houses serves as the local Conservative Party headquarters. There is also part of Northbrook College of Design and Technology, then the Worthing Adult Education Centre, followed by the letter and parcel sorting offices of the general post office.

This card also enables me to explain that, in most cases, I have taken present-day photographs of the views shown on my Edwardian cards to illustrate the changes that have taken place. This is a very useful and interesting exercise that I would recommend to all collectors of pictorial postcards. Of course, one must add a credit, noting the place and date. The 1915 printed-in-Germany card serves to show how parts of our town—or, of course, any town—have changed over the last sixty years or so.

204 *(top)*
A Chester Vaughan, colour-printed in Germany, local-view card, interesting now for its depiction of a place which has undergone vast change.

205 *(above)*
A modern snap recording the present-day view looking along Union Place—compare with the Edwardian view shown in plate 204.

206 *(top)*
A good real-photograph card showing the still attractive Ambrose Place houses with gardens across the road. A 'Wells' (Harold Camburn) card retailed by J. Keely, stationer of Chapel Road, Worthing.

207 *(above)*
A rare local advertisement card issued by Palmer's, sign-writing specialists who painted local delivery vehicles. A trade commissioned card.

It illustrates how peaceful, even lush, the town was in our grandparents' day. My 1993 snap (plate 205) may seem just as quaint in 80 years' time. This card, however, is of interest to very few collectors; it is probably valueless to anyone outside the town. A dedicated local historian can appreciate its place in the pictorial history of the town.

On the other hand, parts of all towns have been preserved and remain very much as they have been for a century or more. Just across Chapel Road from the old tree-lined Union Place there is Ambrose Place (plate 206), a wonderfully varied continuous terrace of 15 houses with interesting roof lines. The front gardens are across the road, on the left of the photograph. This road happily is very much as it was in 1920, in 1900 or indeed in 1860. Outwardly the main changes are to be seen in the roadway or pavement, which has been sown with parking meters, to control (to some degree) the cars that park on both sides of the road. The railings and balconies remain and have been well kept up by the residents. The owners' gardens have, in many cases, been partly turned into parking lots for their cars. But it is a wonderful road in which to live: very central, with a church at each end. The G.P.O., museum, library, Town Hall, Assembly Hall and theatre are all within a hundred yards or so. A pleasing old view but a rather ordinary card, worth only a pound or two.

The local advertising card shown in plate 207 is, however, of considerable interest. In commercial terms it is far more important than a view card. Early cards depicting motor cars, lorries, buses or trams can be very desirable, especially when the subject is shown in close-up. This particular Worthing card does not, in fact, advertise the Cokeham Manor Farm Dairy and its transport fleet, but rather the professional skill of the sign-writer, for the address side is printed with the message— 'The writing on this Van is the work of PALMERS, 19 ROWLANDS ROAD, WORTHING, Sign Specialists and Grainers, Experts in Marbling and Gilding. Phone 1736'. Copies of these cards would have been used by both the dairy and the sign-writer—but few advertising cards were preserved in postcard albums, hence their quite high value to specialist collectors today.

Ruling prices are dictated by supply and demand. Obviously, a small supply and a large demand result in high prices—at least in relatively modest postcard terms. But demand is of prime importance; a rare, or even unique, card will be over-priced at a pound if a customer cannot be found.

Although this book is chiefly concerned with local views and local studies, three more personal interest cards are included. Plate 208 shows a steam-powered Kemp Town brewery delivery lorry unloading beer barrels outside the *Railway Hotel*, north of Lancing station, just to the east of Worthing—what a splendid sight! I like, too, the cyclist with his trailer attachment—difficult to value, as these interesting studies become rarer and rarer, but I would happily give £25 or so for such a local-study example.

Even better is the photographic card at plate 209, which shows local delivery lads lined up in front of the old Heene Road baths, as part of the traders' section of the Motor and Cycle Carnival held early in September 1908 (other studies of

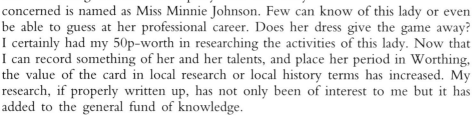

this event are at plates 182-5). What a pity that nobody troubled to pencil on the back their names. The card is unused and was probably owned by one of the persons depicted in this postcard. It would certainly have been sold in very restricted numbers in September 1908. Perhaps only one or two copies still survive and I was very happy to pay the asking price of £25 for this photographic postcard, from a dealer who knew his subject and had access to collectors of such individual local-event material.

In contrast, the unexciting photographic card at plate 210 cost a mere 50p at a postcard fair. The photograph was taken at, and the card published by, the Worthing Portrait Company and the lady concerned is named as Miss Minnie Johnson. Few can know of this lady or even be able to guess at her professional career. Does her dress give the game away? I certainly had my 50p-worth in researching the activities of this lady. Now that I can record something of her and her talents, and place her period in Worthing, the value of the card in local research or local history terms has increased. My research, if properly written up, has not only been of interest to me but it has added to the general fund of knowledge.

You may not have guessed it but the costume Miss Johnson was wearing is a swimming suit! The local *Worthing Gazette* of 19 June 1912 gave a good account of her activities:

A Home in The Sea.
A noted Lady Swimmer
Miss Minnie Johnson's long professional career
How to keep free from illness

As a healthful exercise swimming is unquestionably growing in popularity, and more especially would this appear to be the case with ladies.

We have in our midst at the present time, in the person of Miss Minnie Johnson, a singularly gifted professional exponent of the art of swimming.

210
A seemingly uninteresting photographic card of 'Miss Minnie Johnson'. A privately commissioned card published by the Worthing Portrait Company, *c.*1907-12.

Miss Johnson is now installed at this Municipal Institution The Corporation Baths on her own account, in the capacity of Teacher of swimming ... and the steady growth in the number of pupils affords proof of our statement as to the increased popularity of swimming among ladies.

Minnie Johnson was born in Brighton and learned to swim at the Hove baths when she was five. She was reputedly teaching swimming at the early age of ten. At 15 she was actively engaged in London and provincial Music Hall, at Olympia and Westminster Aquarium. She also taught Queen Alexandra and other members of the royal family.

Although the foregoing information is taken from a 1912 local newspaper, we also learn that Miss Johnson performed on Worthing pier in summer 1907:

Those who remember the Season she spent on the Pier five years ago will readily recall the cleverness of the display which she gave in her crystal tank ... she scattered a number of shells on the floor of the tank and then proceeded to collect them in a basket; she ate and drank, did needlework, wrote her name on a slate and performed somersaults beneath the water and finally remained in an attitude of prayer for a space of ninety seconds, whilst the orchestra played—Sweet Spirit, Hear my Prayer.

Minnie 'performed at almost every Pier on the coast and on the continent. In Germany in particular, she was regarded with particular favour'.

The last card that I purchased as I was preparing the acknowledgement section of this book will serve as my final illustration. A photograph of workmen erecting a telegraph pole may not perhaps be classed as a 'local event' in the accepted sense.

At the monthly meeting of the Sussex Postcard Club at Hove, a dealer from whom I had purchased many other cards said 'Oh, Mr. Godden, I have a very interesting Worthing card put on one side for you'. As it had been put aside I knew it was going to be a costly purchase! (plate 211). It is a good sharp professional photograph for its period, but an unlikely subject for a postcard; it is a wonder that it has survived for nearly ninety years, or that the photograph was taken in the first place.

The card was posted at 9 p.m. on 20 February 1906, addressed to Frank Tuff Esq., 22 St Paul's Church Yard, London. The message adds greatly to the card's interest and unusually fixes the location of the action: 'An 80 ft. telephone pole being erected by John behind Jubilee Buildings, Chapel Road ... Albury'. John was obviously one of the team depicted, perhaps one of the Tuff family that travelled around the country erecting telephone poles under contract. In 1906 it took 10 workmen overseen by two foremen, using hundreds of yards of thick rope and tackle. Perhaps in a few years' time telegraph or telephone poles will be a thing of the past. We will have underground cables or will have done away completely with the need to use wires.

In the meantime this item of local history has been added to my collection, treasured even though it is torn and costly. In this case, the dealer knew he had a customer for such a card and he was able to purchase it from its owner at a good price. In turn, I was pleased to give an unusually high price for a card that I found interesting. In time, too, I will get around to researching the present-day scene.

Dealers and most collectors are looking for scarce cards of desirable types. The market is, however, saturated with dross—mass-produced common standard cards. The dealers are overstocked with such cards. They hawk them around from fair to fair with little or no likelihood of sale, even in a 50p bargain box. They are unlikely to pay out good money to buy duplicates of cards they have been trying unsuccessfully to sell for years!

The dealer is in the market to buy new stock, but it has to be of a type that his customers require. Collectors become more and more particular as their collections grow and already contain the bulk of available postcards. That family album which you (with the help[!] of a catalogue) may have valued at £300 may attract an offer of only £30 from a fair and knowledgeable dealer for the three cards of interest to him. There are good commercial reasons for this. You are not the only person trying to sell such a collection.

Local- (say Worthing-) view or local-event cards sell best in their locality. There will be no demand for even the most interesting Worthing card in Aberdeen or Swansea. Likewise here in Worthing few, if any, collectors are particularly interested in Scottish or Welsh views. The dealer system and the auctioneers help the cards to filter back to the best market, normally the place whence they were first posted. This filtering can be international as well as national. Worthing cards sold here to a French or German visitor in, say, 1905 will most probably have been sent to a friend in their own country and perhaps added to their postcard album. When these cards come on the market now, the tendency is for them to come back to this country for sale at the best price. Likewise many foreign cards in British collections will be returned to their country of origin. Each stage in the filtering or return journey will involve some cost, as each dealer in the chain or the auctioneer will expect a mark-up to cover his working expenses.

As for the pricing of postcards. I obviously cannot turn this general introduction to picture postcards into a catalogue or price guide, nor would this be particularly helpful.

However, most, if not all, established dealers have a very fair working knowledge of the market price of their stock. They will ask a fair price—if only because they are in business to sell their cards. It should follow that if you spot a good clean card that you like or is of interest to you, then (provided you have ample spare funds) you should take the opportunity to make a purchase, without worrying too much about catalogues or price guides. Before long you will be able to rely on your own knowledge of price levels within your own collecting field.

211
A rare real-photograph card of a team of telephone pole erectors at work in central Worthing in February 1906. Several such RP local cards show various tradesmen at work. Not tourist-subject cards but so interesting from a local or social historian's point of view. Postally-used in February 1906, with related message.

You will notice a wide divergence of price, even with cards of a similar type. This will always be so. You cannot form a worthwhile collection by only buying bargains. All too often there turns out to be a good reason why a card seems underpriced; it may have a torn corner, be stained, even a reissue or modern photocopy!

Buying

In former days one could find full albums in local non-specialist auction sales or in second-hand shops and market stalls. Now, however, such sources will very seldom yield worthwhile purchases. Most old albums will almost certainly have been plundered of the better specimens or the whole collection may comprise mundane dross, perhaps especially placed in an old-looking album to catch the unknowledgeable. Occasionally, you may be lucky; the risks are great and it is probably better to buy individual cards that you want from a specialist dealer.

Some full-time dealers trade from an open shop, but they are relatively few, for the profit margin on cards is small and the cost of a shop large. Most dealers, many of whom are part-timers, display their stock at special postcard or 'collectable' fairs which are held from time to time in most large towns. Here they merely rent a trestle table or two to display boxes of cards, usually grouped into named categories. Most cards have the asking price pencilled on the reverse or on the protective envelope.

For a very costly card, you can try modest bargaining, or, if you are purchasing twenty or more cards from one dealer and you are a very regular customer of his, you may be able to shave the total price a little. Remember, however, there is very little profit margin in these low-priced articles, and in most cases you must expect to pay the marked price. Credit cards are not acceptable—cash is the preferred mode of payment. Cheques are only a fair method of payment if the sum involved is large and if you are well known to the seller. Cheques can and do bounce, and these days probably involve bank charges. When buying at busy fairs and postcard markets, you will not be offered a receipt, although one can usually be obtained, on request! Do not carry loose, un-bagged cards in or out of a fair; there is a great security problem and you may land yourself in an embarrassing situation.

Fairs come in all shapes and sizes, ranging from the giants, such as the annual BIPEX (British International Postcard Exhibition) at the Royal Horticultural Halls, to modest evening or Sunday events in church halls. You may not find bargains but you have the choice of many thousands of cards presented by specialist traders who have invested time and money in gathering together a worthwhile stock. Treat them and their cards with respect and replace unwanted cards in the correct place or hand them back to the exhibitor. Have in mind what category of card you are interested in—you cannot expect to examine a dealer's entire stock. Go for your chosen subject—be it windmills, Worthing or worms.

Most of my postcards have been purchased at postcard fairs, mainly because it is a convenient and time-saving method of purchase. The collecting magazines, such as *Picture PostCard Monthly*, list or advertise most of the major fairs. Once you have made the acquaintance of a friendly dealer, he too may give you a list of venues he will be attending. Expect a crowd at the popular meetings, especially around the tables of the leading dealers who are known to carry interesting stocks. Do not expect to find chairs—the general rush may be like a jumble sale!

Other special purchases have been made at auction sales. Most of the leading auction houses hold a few postcard sales each year and several specialist postcard auctioneers hold sales every month or so. These firms advertise in specialist magazines, price guides or reference books. You can subscribe to their illustrated catalogues which, though costly, are indispensable to me, for I choose purely from the printed descriptions or illustrations, placing postal bids for the items I fancy.

In general, this works very well and saves me much time and trouble in not having to travel long distances from the south coast to view the sale. However, if you decide to purchase cards in this way, read very carefully the various 'conditions of sale' and other notices printed in the catalogue. The bill sent with your purchases (providing, of course, that your postal bid was successful) will be inflated by charges for postage and packing, the so-called 'Buyer's Premium', and VAT is added to such extras.

Several local postcard collectors' clubs exist, and are sometimes listed in specialist magazines or reference books such as *The Picture PostCard Annual*. Your local library may have details of such a club in your district. These clubs may well hold occasional sales or auctions of members' cards.

You can advertise for postcards. However, you are entering the market rather late in the day and you might well be offered a dealer's unsaleable lines. A more direct approach is to write an article on your pet postcard subject or interest and to mention that you would like to purchase further examples. You can also give lectures on your hobby and thereby advertise your wants, but you will need to be a reasonable public speaker and have a good range of slides. If you are offered postcards as a result of an article or talk you will have to put a value on the card, possibly lower than the owner may think reasonable!

Buying direct from a knowledgeable dealer is the best method. You can see and handle the card, perhaps discuss it with the seller and form your own judgement on the asking price. Buy because the cards interest you, and treat your collection as an interesting, harmless hobby, and not as a form of investment.

For this reason I have only written about selling in very general terms. This, my first, book on picture postcards is entitled *Collecting Picture Postcards*. I have as yet very little experience of selling cards, hence it is best to leave the subject well alone. However, many of the points made in this last chapter apply equally to selling as to buying—condition and subject being the main points to watch. Certainly, I am unable to value other peoples potscards, but your local professional dealer or auctioneer should be able to assist.

> *'The only postcards which are of interest to collectors at the present time are romantic ones from the First World War, early Valentines and early funnies.'*

From a national newspaper's Sunday supplement of November 1988. Where do they get such information?

Have fun and enjoy your cards

Select Bibliography

The number of books published on various aspects of postcard collecting is now very large. It is huge if we include the hundreds if not thousands of books on different localities illustrated almost exclusively with picture postcards.

I have, for example, 10 well-illustrated local history studies on the Worthing district and this example can be repeated for many towns and villages in the land. Excellent as these works may be, they are not helpful to postcard collectors, as little or no information is given on the prime source of the illustrations—the postcards. We are not told of their history, details of the publishers or the local photographers who took these photographic records. It was this failure to appreciate the background to picture postcards that prompted this book.

Nevertheless, such books are of interest within their locality, as one finds details of the scenes depicted, gleaned from old inhabitants or from research in old records. Such local history studies, with titles such as *Old Muchbinding in Picture Postcards*, should be available in local bookshops or in the local library. They add to interest in the locality and in local-view postcards but they are not books on postcard collecting.

Obviously the library of a specialist collector, who loves to delve into the early history of the postcard or of the collecting hobby, will be very much larger than the relatively small number of general works required by the new or casual collector. The specialist might, for example, have several learned books on printing processes, or on photography. Others may research postal history and include works specialising in postmarks.

However, the general collector or those interested in local-view cards will need very few books. Indeed, he or she can get by without any reference books. I, however, suggest the following titles which will, I feel, give reliable guidance and add to the pleasure to be gained from your collection.

Byatt, Anthony, *Picture Postcards and their Publishers* (Golden Age Postcard Books, 1978)

Carline, Richard, *Pictures in the Post* (Gordon Fraser Gallery Ltd., 1959)

Coysh, A.W., *The Dictionary of Picture Postcards in Britain 1894-1939* (Antique Collectors' Club, 1984)

Dagnall, H., *The Evolution of British Stamped Postcards and Letter Cards* (privately published, Edgware, 1985)

Duval, William and Monahan, Valerie, *Collecting Postcards 1894-1914* (Blandford Press, 1978)

Holt, Tonie and Valmai, *Picture Postcard Artists* (Longman, 1984)

Holt, Tonie and Valmai, *Picture Postcards of the Golden Age, A Collector's Guide* (MacGibbon & Kee Ltd., 1971, revised edition published by the Postcard Publishing Company, 1978)

Klamkin, Marian, *Picture Postcards* (David & Charles, 1974)

Monahan, Valerie, *Collecting Postcards 1914-1930* (Blandford Press, 1980)

Saleh, Nouhad A., *Guide to Artists' Signatures and Monograms on Postcards* (Minerva Press, Florida USA, 1993)

Smith, Jack H., *Postcard Companion. The Collector's Reference* (Wallace-Homestead Book Company, Radnor USA, 1989)

Staff, Frank, *The Picture Postcard and its Origins* (Lutterworth Press, 1979)

Willoughby, Martin, *A History of Postcards* (Studio Editions, 1992)

The specialist collector is referred to H. Dagnall's privately published 1985 book, *The Evolution of British Stamped Postcards & Letter Cards. Their History & Documentation.* Other specialist books have been mentioned in the relevant parts of my main text.

The collector may well consider investing in a postcard catalogue. I have already stated my views on catalogue price guidance, but catalogues include much other information and many advertisements from dealers and auction-houses. They also list the very many postcard subjects and the main postcard artists. Brief comments on the various subjects or categories are given with comments on price trends.

Some past catalogues, such as Stanley Gibbons publications, have included quite detailed specialist studies of different types, but at the time of writing (1996) the collector had only one British catalogue—the *IPM Catalogue of Picture Postcards and Year Book*, compiled by J.H.D. (John) Smith, with specialist contributors. This well-illustrated work is published by IPM Publications of Lewes (Sussex). Copies may be purchased direct from the publishers, or most leading dealers carry stock.

Price guides lead us to auctioneers' catalogues. These can be surprisingly costly and, whilst they only give the basic description of each lot, the price 'estimates' may be of interest. Catalogues are, of course, all but indispensable if you are going to buy at auction.

Auction sales and the auctioneers are advertised in *Picture PostCard Monthly* (with Collect Modern Postcards), published by 'Reflections of a Bygone Age' (Brian and Mary Lund), 15 Debdale Lane, Keyworth, Nottingham NG12 5HT. This publication is strongly recommended to all collectors. The main articles, letters, queries, details of exhibitions, auctions, new publications—as well as the many advertisements—are extremely interesting and represent very good value for the modest annual subscription. We await its monthly arrival with bated breath. Mr. and Mrs. Lund also publish the *Picture Postcard Annual*, which contains several helpful features and listings.

In various places in my text, I have indicated local reference works— dictionaries, local newspapers, etc.—which yield a rich harvest of background information on many of your pictorial cards, if you wish to delve a little deeper below the basic photographic image.

Apart from books on postcards and source material on your local scene, there are also books and magazines angled at the local historian. There are, for example, *A Companion to Local History Research* by John Campbell Kease (Alphabooks, 1989) and *Local Historian's Encyclopedia* by John Richardson (H.P.L., 1993). Your local library may also subscribe to *The Local Historian*, the journal of the British Association for Local History, or the *Local History Magazine*.

In Chapter VIII there are examples of some of the interesting facts that can be unearthed and which will add to your understanding and appreciation of your locality and its past times, its people, their lives and recreations. Such social history source material should be available in your public libraries, reference libraries or museums. Such institutions and their collections have been provided over the years by rate- and tax-payers, and they are staffed by helpful well-informed staff who should welcome your interest in such material—use it well and with care.

Index

Page numbers in **bold** type indicate illustrations